MOUNTAIN BIKING
BRITISH COLUMBIA

The Trail Guide
&
Inspirational Resource Book

For information contact:
Cycling B.C for address of publisher

Mountain Biking British Columbia:
The Trail Guide & Inspirational Resource Book

ISBN 0-9680342-1-7

Cover Design by Mind's Eye Studio, Kelowna B.C.
Typesetting & Layout Design by Brian Armstrong, Vernon B.C.
Cartoon Images by Allester Bradbury, Vernon B.C.

Cover Photographs: Blair Polischuk

Group Shot: Cheakamus Challenge 1995, (dis)organized start
The World's a Gym Photo: Carvin Marvin Penner
Unknown Rollerblader in Pit Meadows
Unknown Young Rider, Bart Simpson and Bean
Ancient Cedars
Author Photograph

Bar Code: by some people in Vancouver

Printed in Canada

MOUNTAIN BIKING
BRITISH COLUMBIA

The Trail Guide
&
Inspirational Resource Book

Table of Contents

Photograph by Blair Polischuk

MOUNTAIN BIKING
BRITISH COLUMBIA
The Trail Guide

Introduction

Photograph by Blair Polischuk

MOUNTAIN BIKING
BRITISH COLUMBIA
The Trail Guide

Please Read This First

Mountain biking is a dangerous sport and riders are solely responsible for their own safety while riding. This book is meant as a tool to help you locate trails. Reading it is not a guarantee that you will not get lost. The trails mapped and described in this book are in a constant state of change. The trail rating system is designed to assist you in choosing a ride, use it! There are many people who assisted me in gathering the information for this book. They are herein referred to as assistants. This includes Cycling B.C.

Users of Mountain Biking British Columbia: The Trail Guide agree to waive any and all claims against the author, publisher and assistants for personal injury, death, property damage (someone else's or your own), getting lost, thirsty, sick, or tired while riding. Many of the trails listed herein are on private property and users of Mountain Biking British Columbia: The Trail Guide do not assume that publication of these trails constitutes permission to ride them. All riders must obey all posted signs, and be 100% responsible for their own actions.

We have done our best to ensure that the information in Mountain Biking British Columbia: The Trail Guide is accurate, nevertheless, we are not responsible for any discrepancies or inexact information.

Reproduction of this book, in whole or part including the maps, is prohibited by copyright law.

Now, go out and ride, but remember, *you're on your own!*

MOUNTAIN BIKING
BRITISH COLUMBIA
The Trail Guide

Trail Rating System

The infinite variety, and changing nature of mountain biking trails makes rating them with precision a difficult task. Despite the lack of objective methods for rating trails, I feel we have done a sufficient job in rating the overall nature of the ride. Riders still must read the description and look at the rating, as all trails have a unique flavor. The trails in this book have separate ratings for physical difficulty and technical difficulty. In this way the rider can distinguish the two most important elements of a trail in a concise manner. Do not take these ratings lightly. If a trail is rated physically difficult you are going to hurt a bit. If its technically difficult, puncture wounds may occur. A host of variables can make a trail even more difficult then its rating. So read on, and choose your trail wisely

Ratings for Physical Difficulty

Easy - A ride that is easy will be flat or with little gain in altitude. Ride should take less than 2 hours.

Moderate - Expect climbs of up to 1000 feet. Often climbs are short, and on terrain rolling. Some fitness is required to complete the ride. Ride times can be 2 hours plus.

Difficult - Expect a multitude of steep climbs and gains in altitude of up to 3500 feet or more. Fitness is required to safely complete the trail. No posers allowed.

Ratings For Technical Difficulty

Easy - Trails that are located on well maintained gravel roads or gravel paths. You could safely take your grandparents on most technically easy trails.

MOUNTAIN BIKING
BRITISH COLUMBIA
The Trail Guide

Moderate - Trails that are technically moderate can vary from rougher logging roads and double tracks, to single tracks that are generally rid able by most mountain bikers.The single tracks are free of hair-raising descents and the plethora of obstacles that require expert level skill. Moderate single tracks are often fast, and more open, making them enjoyable to all riders. Expect some obstacles and loose cond tions, but nothing that a keen novice couldn't ride. Often a moderate trail will have short sections that are difficult, and will be walked by less experienced riders, but it's nothing that is sustained.

Difficult - Trails that are difficult can vary from steep, washed-out double tracks to single tracks full of logs, rocks, roots, exposure, and other trail nasties. The range of difficult trails can be quite pronounced: a flat trail full of logs is much easier then a super steep descent where all riders can expect the odd crash. The var ing levels of single track descents is boggling. But they are all Difficult. Treat this category with respect.

Plus Sign: A plus sign, and a Physical or Technical icon, mean that the trail is rated between the level indicated and the next level.

Odometer: Indicates kilometers (N/A=not/available, not/admittable, never/again?)

Stopwatch: Indicates estimated time required to travel the route. These times will vary with riders' abilities, weather and trail conditions. They are estimates only. (N/A=not/available, not/ about to turn around, not/another flat?)

Photograph by Matt Pinto

MOUNTAIN BIKING
BRITISH COLUMBIA
The Trail Guide

Message from the Author / Publisher

by Darrin Polischuk

Between these pages is more information about mountain biking in British Columbia than has ever been put into print. The amount and style of information will be presented in detailed maps, great descriptions, or both. You will find the trail you're looking for, unless your route finding skills are noteably weak. Usually, once you locate the trailhead, you just follow tire tracks.

Mountain Biking British Columbia unlocks the trails that were once for 'locals only '; the trails that were always there but known only to a small number of local area people. Undoubtedly a few folks will be put off that their local area is now public knowledge. But sharing of trail information with responsible riders, and giving these riders, novice or elite, a great new trail to ride and smile on, is more important then hoarding trails for a so-called worthy few. Our sport is growing up, and as more riders walk away from bike stores with their new cycles it is necessary to tell them where to ride, and what is expected of them. Not to do so is irresponsible.

With the publishing of so much trail information, comes added responsibility for all riders. To be a responsible rider you have to put something back into the trails. See the message from Cycling B.C. for more on this, and don't take it lightly! A portion of the proceeds from every sale of **Mountain Biking British Columbia** are put into a Trail Enhancement Fund. Local clubs will be able to access this money in the future to assist in trail efforts in their own communities.

One of the coolest aspects of mountain biking is the excuse it gives you to travel all over the province and ride different trails. Riding and exploring new terrain is really what our sport is all about. This book unlocks some of the best riding in every major region of the province, often within a short drive or ride from a good cafe and bike shop. **Mountain Biking British Columbia** is not a definitive, wilderness mountain biking book, but rather a guide to where people are riding everyday in their own communities. Use it in good health, be prepared for the unexpected, and most importantly, HAVE FUN!

MOUNTAIN BIKING
BRITISH COLUMBIA
The Trail Guide

The Philosophy and Magic of Mountain Bike Trails

by Darrin Polischuk

The forces of nature, humans, and animals, have done a wonderful job carving trails throughout British Columbia. These special ribbons of earth can reach out and touch our tires as if made by the hand of a benevolent god. Impeccable, perfect, buffed, sweet and tasty, are just some of the words commonly used to describe trails. The trail communicates with the rider via the bike. The trail is the thing . . . the "stuff" of our sport, and the bike is the divining rod through which the communication takes place. Without the incredible variety of trails our sport would not be the magical metaphor for life that it is.

To say that the trails determine our experience is to gloss over what they do for you, to sterilize what is unique and alive about them for everyone who rides. Trails can change with weather and with attitude. If you are "on it" during a ride the trail can feed your ego, and be your unconditionally supportive friend. Let a bit of self doubt trickle in, usually associated with some rain and mud, and the same trail can quickly turn on you like a fickle high school buddy. The same trail that *"Impeccable, perfect, buffed,* propped you up as a super hero a few days *sweet and tasty, are just some* ago can suddenly rep- resent the personal *of the words commonly used* demons that haunt you on your ride, or in *to describe trails."* your life. Like I said, a mountain bike trail, you, and your bike, can dance the tune of life together in any manner you choose. The life you live on a mountain bike trail is the same life you lead when the ride is over. The trail does more than determine our experience, it gives us a reason to ride, and therefore live as we choose. Without it there would be no mountain biking, no Sunday ride with friends, and no race courses on which to challenge our power, speed, and skills.

Mountain biking trails in BC are not a one size fits all proposition. No two trails are the same. An open fast single track in the desert setting of Kamloops is a completely different trail, and riding experience, than a rooted, steep, technical trail on the west coast. As you can see, the term "mountain bike trail" is ambiguous. For example a gravel forest road, or a single track under the forest canopy, are both considered a "mountain bike trail", despite the obvious differences. Consequently, there is a need to be more concise when using the term mountain bike trail. With this in mind, I thought an elementary classification of trails would be useful to decode this book, and to help clarify those directions from friends that inevitably find their way onto a crumpled napkin at Taco Time.

For starters, a gravel road is more of a road than a trail; nevertheless it is the easiest type of trail to ride on, and is often part of a ride involving other types of trails. The gravel road can be a local municipal road, a Forest Service road, or logging road. This type of trail is often called a "fire road". This is an American

MOUNTAIN BIKING
BRITISH COLUMBIA
The Trail Guide

term and distorts the real purpose of these roads both past and present. The Forest Service roads are built for hauling out logs and their surface condition can vary a great deal. An active haul road is practically a gravel highway built in the bush. Time, and the forces of nature, can transform a logging road into a 4wd type of surface in a few short years. Overgrowth and erosion can make an old logging road into an fun challenging double track. Often a good single track will be resurrected from a decades old logging road built to haul out those old growth stumps that haunt much of BC's backcountry.

Zig-zagging throughout the second growth forests of BC are old skidder trails and mining roads. They resemble an old logging road bed but are usually narrower. These types of roads are often rated as four wheel drive access only. Old skidder trails and logging roads have varying surfaces. Some can have smooth surfaces free of technical obstacles, while others may have a surface full of baby head size boulders and all sizes of logs. The variety of surfaces on these trails can make riding easy and fast, or slow, bumpy, and challenging. They're excellent for climbing because the grade will usually fall within the range of a mountain bikers capabilities. Often the best mountain bike loops use these old roads as climbs, and when combined with single track they make for a most excellent adventure. When downhilling on these trails the speed, subtle twists, and turns, are reminiscent of skiing on great snow. This is middle and big ring stuff, where the real speed freaks emerge with a glaze over their eyes, and a grin from ear to ear.

The ultimate mountain biking experience almost always includes a healthy dose of single track. Like all other trails, single tracks have their variations, which can be surprisingly pronounced. The mildest single tracks are often found along old road beds. These single tracks have the consistent grade of a road but with the subtle challenges of a narrower track. Because the trail sits on an old road bed it is usually free of roots, rocks and other trail obstacles. This type of less 'technical' single track is the best place to introduce new riders to the joy of riding a narrow trail.

MOUNTAIN BIKING
BRITISH COLUMBIA
The Trail Guide

Single track is considered the real stuff of our sport. Good single track is to a mountain biker, as powder day to a skier or snowboarder, and a big wind day to a windsurfer. An experienced rider can sense where the single tracks are. Like a good hunting dog, the rider scans the sides of trails always looking for the obscure trail head leading to a secret stash of the good stuff.

The expert level single tracks throughout the province reflect the extreme nature of the B.C.'s geography. Those who frequent these trails are masters of the steep, technical and gnarly. When you choose to ride one of these crazy trails you're continuously confronted with the possibility of crashing. But the challenge of the ride, and the high you get when you clean a difficult section, smothers any fear that could overtake you.

Today, single track riders in B.C. float over trails too difficult to walk down, and mountain bikers in general continue to push themselves through bizarre envelopes where the instinct for self preservation is tossed aside. Many of the single tracks have sec-tions so steep and technical you think it's *"Those who frequent these* impossible to ride down. As you're pon-*trails are masters of the steep,* dering the gravity of it all, someone whistles *technical and gnarly.''* by you, cleaning the section you thought unrideable. On the next outing you push your own limits, and in doing so, evolve with the sport. If this is appealing, then you'll find a comfortable home on the super technical and extreme single tracks of B.C.

Single tracks in B.C are not the sole domain of the super skilled mountain biking gods. Plenty of moderate trails exist, many of which are animal paths. For example, an environmentally irresponsible cow will always take the path of least resistance creating a curvy fast single track that you can trust. These cattle, and wild game trails, are scattered throughout B.C. For the most part they translate into a fast, twisty, and fun ride. The only negative aspect of these trails are the fecal treats that dot the bed, that's right cow poo! So remember, look ahead, and keep your mouth closed when dodging the little methane bombs.

Humans have also intervened onto the natural landscape to create trails. For years hiking groups and recreational land authorities have built trails. Hiking trails are often closed to mountain bikers or have too many dismounting sections which make them less than enjoyable as MTB trails. In the last 10 years mountain bikers have started to build trails specifically for their needs. The trails constructed by mountain bikers, for mountain bikers, are always a fun challenge, and usually an example of some expert level technical riding. Motorcyclists have also built trails throughout the province. The motorbike trail can be an excellent mountain bike downhill, but often they are too loose and rutted to make it a suitable cross country trail. If a single track is loose, fast, and full of bermed corners, chances are it's a popular motorbiking route.

MOUNTAIN BIKING
BRITISH COLUMBIA
The Trail Guide

Mountain biking trails are always evolving. Season by season, subtle changes in the character of the trail is noticed by those who frequent them. In one season a trail can becme extinct, overgrown and plugged with deadfall, if not maintained. On the other hand, popular trails can fall victim to overuse. A highly used single track, poorly built on a steep slope has a limited life span. Over one season, a great, steep shot down can become severely rutted and an unrecognizable remnant of its former self.

I struggle to be a mountain bike racer and often dream of having the talent of those pro riders who lap me in a race. And to rub iodine in my already shattered and fragile athletic ego, these gifted pros usually pass me while talking comfortably! I gasp and choke to say "hello", but usually can only muster enough strength to nod! But the thing is, who really cares? How can you determine who is having more fun, the super competitive athlete, or the person who is discovering the simple joy of hopping over a log? All mountain bikers, from elite racers to beginners, are sharing in one of the world's coolest activities, period! As mountain bikers we are self powered, and do little or no harm to our fragile environment. Riding a modern suspended mountain bike is possibly, dare I say, better then some sex???

> *"How can you determine who is having more fun, the super competitive athlete, or the person who is discovering the simple joy of hopping over a log?"*

While on the trail, anyone who takes time out to reflect on the luxury and leisure of our society must realize that residents and visitors to our little mountain biking heaven called British Columbia have won the lottery of life. If you have a bad day, get stuck in traffic, or can't afford new tires for another few weeks, simply take a step back and reflect on how absurdly fortunate our society is that we can devote so much energy and money into something done purely for fun. Try to explain to the South American peasant who probably picked the coffee bean you are currently drinking that our society devotes so much time, money, and energy to leisure, and you would most likely be called a liar. As we approach the next millennia, leisure pursuits will begin to occupy more of our productive time as fewer people work, and those that do work will probably be more productive. What better way to soak up this new-found time, and divert you from the stressful issues of the world, than biking on a trail with your dog and a few friends.

A former riding partner would capitalize on moments that truly were a diversion from real life and say: "I'm having an I love B.C. day" . . . That simple statement reflects the appreciation that people who live and visit our province have for it, and how mountain biking on a perfect trail can be the best way to express that appreciation.

MOUNTAIN BIKING
BRITISH COLUMBIA
The Trail Guide

To New Mountain Bikers

by Darrin Polischuk

Every year a staggering number of mountain bikes are wheeled off showroom floors. Many of these bikes are headed for nearby trails, while others will be imprisoned in the garage as prop to hold up your golf clubs, or as a foundation for a spider condo. If your bike collects more garage dust then trail mud, I guess mountain biking is not your thing. On the other hand, if you wake up one day camping in the rain at a local race, with dirt and grease under your nails (having spent your last hundred bucks on a new tire and entry fees), then you can proudly call yourself a dirtbag, a rubberhead, or a hard-core mountain biker. Most of us slip comfortably into the middle of these extremes, with our bikes collecting equal amounts of trail mud, and garage dust. As a new mountain biker, you will feel yourself becoming positioned somewhere on this spectrum while your bike's identity is in a state of flux between cool status symbol, clothes drying rack, or your best friend.

As a new mountain biker you will challenge yourself, and quickly discover the limits of your comfort zone. Some new mountain bikers attack the sport without fear of falling or failure, while others take a safer, more cautious approach. "Do I try riding this gnarly-ass steep pitch and maybe make it, or maybe fall? Or do I walk it, knowing that the trail will still be there tommorow?" Either way, you will improve with more time on the trail as the new world of mountain biking unfolds.

Despite the revolution in backcountry transportation that mountain biking is, it is not an easy sport. Sure mountain biking is 'cool'. In the nineties anything remotely 'extreme' is exploited to sell everything from beer to toothpaste. But what these images fail to relate to new riders who are drawn to the sport, is that it can be very demanding. I don't want to scare you, but riding on the trails requires fitness, skills, and the confidence to put yourself at risk from time to time. While learning to ride you will fall, probably bleed a bit, and slowly accumulate the scars of experience. Fortunately, while this is happening you will also get very fit by riding trails that can open your eyes to life as it should be lived. Not a bad trade off.

"Feel the elements on your face, ride to a swimming hole, jump in, and pity the folks who drive their cars to the gym and not the trails for a workout."

As I ride by the local 'fitness center' on a spring day I feel like running in and telling all the robots on the latest aerobic equipment what a blast working out on a trail is. The tenacity required to watch the sweat drip off your nose while going nowhere, and seeing nothing, is more than sufficient to become a great mountain biker. No matter how slick a workout machine is, the 'reality

MOUNTAIN BIKING
BRITISH COLUMBIA
The Trail Guide

workout program' will always be better. Feel the elements on your face, ride to a swimming hole, jump in, and pity the folks who drive their cars to the gym and not the trails for a workout.

As a new mountain biker you will climb up the fitness wall and be astonished how quickly your body adapts to the stresses of riding. Sure it can be painful, but just remember, the fitter you become the longer you can ride to access the truly great trails in our province. Without maintaining a minimum fitness level, mountain bikers no matter how keen will hurt so much on *"Any Chimpanzee can pedal a* climbs that the joyous descents will turn *bike on a smooth surface, but to* into trembling nightmares instead. Fortu- *truly have fun on the trails some* nately, all humans adapt about the same *bike handling skills are needed."* to physical stress; in other words, despite how hopeless you feel as you struggle up the smallest hill, it will get easier. Trust me. Talk to people on the trails and ask them to relay a story of their first few rides, and how terrain they once thought unconquerable became less of a challenge over time. Don't worry about going too fast at first. When climbing, settle into a comfortable rhythm and be glad that the rewarding downhill awaits.

The greatest thing about mountain biking is that it's not purely a fitness sport, but also requires skill. The best trails always have technical obstacles like roots, rocks, stream crossings, tight corners, etc. to make the ride an interesting, fun, challenge. On these technical trails the old cliche ' it's just like riding a bike' does not apply. Any Chimpanzee can pedal a bike on a smooth surface, but to truly have fun on the trails some bike handling skills are needed. Nothing extreme or un-attainable, just a bit of balance, and knowledge of how your machine works. Before heading out on the trail for the first time go to a safe grassy area and goof around on your bike for a while. Practice doing front and rear wheel lifts, tight circles, stalls or 'track stands'. Get to know how your bike responds to braking. Notice how the rear brake has a fraction of the stopping power compared to the front, and that front brake application requires a certain body position and attitude to counter-act the forces that want to throw you forward. I strongly recommend new riders take a 'learn to ride clinic' or attend a 'mountain bike camp' where these basics, and a host of other skills, are taught in a safe, fun setting.

As a new mountain biker, the jump from easy and moderate single track to more difficult trails comes with more experience, skills and fitness. No magical formula needed. Just a desire to ride more, and take a few chances to discover how amazing the mountain bike really is at riding over almost anything the trail throws at you. The learning curve will be filled with bumps and bruises, and eventually the formal MTB rite of passage, 'going over the bars'. Welcome to the world of mountain biking, learn to tread softly, fall graciously, and enjoy the world's greatest sport with the coolest people.

MOUNTAIN BIKING
BRITISH COLUMBIA
The Trail Guide

Hello Mountain Bikers

by C. John Wakefield, Cycling B.C.

Cycling B.C. is a non-profit association that was formed twenty years ago to manage and develop bicycling for recreation and sport in British Columbia. We used to be known as BABC (Bicycling Association of British Columbia) and we operate under the umbrella of the Canadian Cycling Association.

Although we are the governing body of cycling, we are primarily funded by our members. In 1995, our association had over five thousand members from all disciplines of cycling. About two-thirds of our memberships are mountain bikers of which the majority are involved in competition.

Cycling B.C. has been directly involved with mountain biking competition and recreation since the late 1980's when the popularity in mountain biking began to soar. Since that time, Cycling B.C.'s Off-road Recreation and racing committees have been working on many of the issues related to this activity.

Many changes have taken place in the time since Cycling B.C. first started up. Off-Road cyclists within British Columbia have grown in number from one hundred to one million in two decades. The overwhelming majority of you are interested in recreational cycling and Cycling BC is developing initiatives to meet your needs.

"Partial proceeds of this book will go to our Trail Enhancement Fund."

This book is an example of those initiatives. We felt that a quality guide book of mountain biking areas would help make your off-road experience more enjoyable.

Partial proceeds of this book will go to our Trail Enhancement Fund. The local clubs who are active in trail maintenance and advocacy will be able to secure some of these ear-marked funds for enhancing the trails featured in this book. Join in and help out if you see them at work! In order for us to better serve the cycling population, we need your support.

Cycling B.C. is also promoting the 20/20/20 plan first started by the International Mountain Biking Association (IMBA). This plan calls for each mountain biker to spend $20 to become the member of their cycling association (Cycling BC), $20 to join your local club and twenty hours of trail maintenance per year. If you can't afford the money put in the time and visa versa. If you can, do both.

MOUNTAIN BIKING
BRITISH COLUMBIA
The Trail Guide

By working together, individuals like you, associations and user groups can ensure that we will all be able to continue to participate in our favourite activities.

If you would like any information on becoming a Cycling B.C. member, a list of affiliated clubs, volunteer opportunities, or any further information, call the Cycling B.C. office at 737-3034.

Happy Trails,
C. John Wakefield

MOUNTAIN BIKING
BRITISH COLUMBIA
The Trail Guide

Trail Etiquette

Used with permission from Cycling in B.C. '96

Mountain biking is a great way to enjoy the outdoors, and continues to gain in popularity. When you are trail riding, it is important to be aware of and follow certain rules, especially as trails become used by more and more people. The following rules of trail etiquette have evolved over the last decade to take into account the various needs of different types of trail users: hikers, horse riders, and off-road cyclists. For the safety of both you as a rider, and of others on the trail, please respect these rules.

Be Aware

Be aware of other trail users. Always anticipate a horse or hiker around a blind curve and slow down. Prevent the sudden and unexpected encounters made possible by a bike's quick approach; use a bell and friendly greeting to let others know of your presence.

Yield the Trail

Yield to hikers and horse riders. When encountering hikers, slow down to their speed, or stop and pull over. When encountering an equestrian from the front ALWAYS stop. Get off your bike and move to the lower side of the trail to let horses pass, because they are less easily spooked by an object lower than themselves. A clearance of two or three metres is recommended between you and the horse, depending on the terrain. From the rear, follow passing directions given by the horse rider.

In general, cyclists going uphill have the right of way. Yield to other cyclists you encounter.

Ride, Don't Slide

Learn how to minimize damage to trails through proper riding techniques. Don't skid. It's neither a safe or efficient way to ride; it will degrade the trail surface; and may cause the trail to be closed to bikes. Take that turn slowly, or if it's a tight switchback, dismount and walk it. Feather your brakes down steep descents to hone your riding skills and prevent skidding.

MOUNTAIN BIKING
BRITISH COLUMBIA
The Trail Guide

Avoid extremely muddy areas. Wait for trails to dry out in the spring or after rains. Riding wet and muddy trails is hard on your bike and on the trail. Tire ruts become paths for water erosion. If you must negotiate a puddle, however, ride straight through it rather than widening the trail.

Stay on the designated trail. Meadows are easily damaged by fat tires. Carry your bike over fallen trees and obstacles. Don't short-cut switchbacks and corners.

Be Courteous

User conflicts can lead to trail closures. Cyclists are the newest group to use trails — in a dispute, we are the first to go. Respect private property and "No Trespassing" signs. Leave gates as you find them. Do not litter. Carry out what you bring in with you, and if you have extra room, carry out more than your share.

Be Prepared

Carry a spare tube and pump, tools, adequate food, water and clothing, small first aid kit, etc. A short cycle in is a long walk out if something goes wrong with your bike. Check the weather forecast and inquire about trail conditions and closures before you go. Let someone know where you're going and when you'll be back. Most important of all, wear your helmet and cycle safely. A successful trip is one without injuries.

MOUNTAIN BIKING
BRITISH COLUMBIA
The Trail Guide

Bicycle Helmet Facts

Used with permission from Cycling in B.C. '96

In the past five years in B.C., there have been 9,400 bicycle accidents involving motor vehicles. 52 people have died.

In 1993, there were 10 fatalities; 8 of the victims were not wearing a helmet at the time.

For every reported accident, there may be up to 30 others not reported. Only accidents involving motor vehicles are required to be reported.

Head injuries cause 75% of all cycling deaths and account for almost 50% of all acute cases resulting from cycling accidents.

Hospital costs for a patient with a head injury average $1000 a day . . . or between $100,000 and $200,000 a year, if care is extended.

Voluntary usage of helmets is estimated at about 5% nationally.

Studies in the U.S. have shown that helmets will reduce the risk of head injury by 85% and brain injury by 88%.

Helmets will stop injuries, but not accidents.

As of September 3, 1996, it will be mandatory for all cyclists in B.C., whether operating a cycle or riding as a passenger on a cycle, to properly wear a bicycle safety helmet. It will also be an offence for parents or guardians to knowingly permit a person under the age of 16 to ride a cycle without a helmet.

At press time, the Provincial Government had not yet set the fine levels, helmet standards and exemptions to this legislation. Fines will not exceed $100. Municipalities will also be permitted to make bylaws requiring the wearing of bicycle helmets on pathways not covered under the definition of a highway in the Motor Vehicle Act.

YIELD TO

Photograph by Blair Polischuk

MOUNTAIN BIKING
BRITISH COLUMBIA
The Trail Guide

Buying and Fitting a Helmet

Used with permission from Cycling in B.C. '96

Buying a safe bicycle helmet is easy thanks to the work of several standards associations. Look for a bicycle helmet which has been approved by the Canadian Standards Association (CSA), the American National Standards Institute (ANSI), the Snell Memorial Foundation, or the American Society for Testing & Materials (ASTM). Any of these approvals mean that the helmet meets safety standards. Do not buy a helmet which has not been approved.

Bicycle helmets come in a wide variety of styles and price ranges. You should be able to find a helmet for as little as $40 — even one that looks good on! Helmets have come a long way in the last few years; most are now very light and quite stylish.

Do not use other types of helmets while cycling. Hockey helmets, mountaineering helmets, etc. are not designed to protect you from the types of crashes experienced by cyclists, they may impair your vision while riding, and they are much less comfortable in use.

1. Bicycle helmets come in a variety of constructions. Some have an outer shell of hard plastic, others have a thin plastic "micro-shell", still others have a fabric covering instead of a *"Helmets have come a long way* shell. All three types are safe (as long as *in the last few years; most are* they have CSA, ANSI, Snell or *now very light and quite stylish."* ASTM approval). The hard-shell type is heavier and can be less comfortable to wear for long periods. If you choose a fabric-covered helmet, the covering must stay in place over the helmet to protect you. By far the majority of helmets sold today are of the micro-shell type.

2. All bike helmets rely on a liner of hard styrofoam to absorb the shock of an accident. This foam should not give, or feel spongy when you press it. After an accident you should always replace your helmet regardless of its apparent condition. Even minor knocks may undermine the structure of the foam and impair its function in the future. Fine cracks or internal damage to the helmet may be invisible. Replace your helmet every 3-4 years even if you have not had an accident.

3. Typically, helmets come in 2 or 3 sizes: S-M, M-L, etc. A series of foam pads inside the helmet help it to fit the specific size and shape of your head. Your

helmet will come with an assortment of pads of different sizes. Choose the pads that create contact with your head without gaps or squeezing. The helmet shouldn't shift from side to side or front to back on your head except by compressing the pads.

4. The chin strap of your helmet must also be adjusted to fit you. Depending on the design of the helmet, the strap will adjust in several places: at the buckle beneath or beside the chin, below the ears, or at the back of the helmet. You must adjust the overall length of the strap so that it holds the helmet on securely, and you must adjust the relative lengths of the front and rear straps so that the helmet sits levelly on your head. It is especially important that the helmet covers your forehead. If it doesn't, or if you can push the helmet to expose your forehead, then you won't be protected in a crash.

Be patient; fitting a helmet is a process of trial and error. The salesperson you purchase your helmet from will be glad to help you adjust it. Watch them do it because you should know how to keep your helmet properly adjusted too. Adjust it whenever it seems loose, so that it will work properly in case you need it to.

Having trouble getting your children to wear helmets? Remember, you are their best role model. Always wear your helmet when you ride. And after September 3rd, you can tell them, "It's the law!"

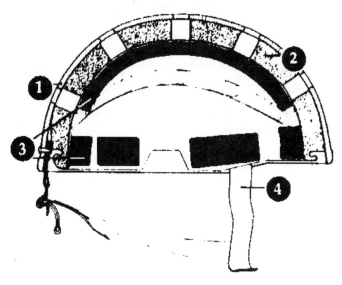

MOUNTAIN BIKING
BRITISH COLUMBIA
The Trail Guide

Mountain Biking 101: Loving it and Learning it!

by Joan Joans, West Coast School of Mountain Biking

The numbers of mountain bikers is rising rapidly and so is the need for skill clinics, clubs, camps, and tours. Mountain biking programs are springing up at community centers, ski areas, and other locations throughout the province. Unfortunately, there is no provincial system for evaluating or accrediting programs. Nor is there a guide book available listing the many opportunities out there for enthusiastic mountain bikers. The burden rests on each individual to find quality programs suiting their needs.

As programs become more popular their overall condition will improve. Experience and reputation ensure that as the good get better, more people will be attracted into their programs. This is one of the great strengths of private enterprise; the weakest are weeded out. Usually they're the ones with the inferior product.

In British Columbia, the provincial cycling association, Cycling B.C., is the best resource for information on programs for all types of cyclists. For years they have actively supported the development of coaches. Individuals interested in coaching are encouraged to take a Level 1 Off-Road Technical course; a program developed by the Canadian Cycling Association, recognized by the National Coaching Certification Program and taught throughout the country. At present there are 35 Coaches in British Columbia. They are qualified to coach athletes and teach clinics. This is the only nationally recognized qualification available to would-be coaches and teachers of mountain biking. Holding a license from Cycling B.C. guarantees a certain quality of education, however, the Level 1 course is no longer available. There are many competent coaches who have not taken this program, and also many people who do not need coaching training to run their mountain biking business: eg. tour guides, trail patrols. It may be beyond the scope of Cycling B.C. to develop courses for these professionals but they are developing standards for all clinics, camps, and tours.

> *". . . you should ask several questions before signing yourself or your children up for a clinic, camp or tour."*

Standards are frequently implemented in other sports but are a new concept to mountain biking. According to John Wakefields, off-road technical director at Cycling B.C., the association has decided to develop standards for off-road education programs. Sometime in the future everyone teaching clinics, camps, and leading tours may be asked to comply with these standards. Doing so could become a prerequisite to receiving insurance.

(Continued on page 30)

Introduction

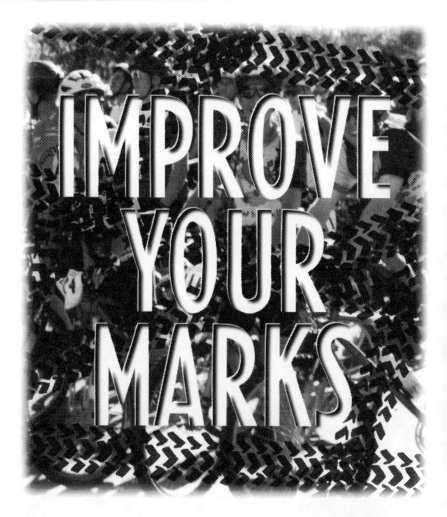

IMPROVE YOUR MARKS

West Coast School of Mountain Biking Inc.

Upgrade your mountain biking skills at the West Coast School of Mountain Biking, located in Belcarra, just 45 minutes from Vancouver.

Learn everything you need to know; beginning to advanced techniques, racing, trials, bike maintenance, trail building, wilderness first aid, instructor certification and more. We offer women's only, coed and youth programs.

For information on our Sunday 3:00 - 9:00 pm clinics, Monday and Wednesday evening clinics, camps and custom programs, call Joan Jones at 931-6066. Enroll now at the WCSMB and quit spinning your wheels.

Mailing Address:
943 Merritt Street
Coquitlam, BC Canada V3J 7K9

Phone (604) 931-6066
Fax (604) 931-7433
Web site: ww.vkool.com/EMP/

MOUNTAIN BIKING
BRITISH COLUMBIA
The Trail Guide

(Continued from page 28)

For now you should ask several questions before signing yourself or your children up for a clinic, camp or tour. Experience, first aid training and leadership skills are needed for any programs to be high quality. Here are a few suggestions:

1. "What formal qualifications do you have? Teaching? Coaching?
2. "What about First Aid skills? and Leadership?"
3. "What is the ratio of instructor to participant?"
4. "How is everyone, (me and you), insured?"
5. "Do you have permission to use the land and/or trails?"
6. "Any references?"
7. "Do you have any previous experience?"
8. "Are there any prerequisites?" e.g. fitness, skill level?

So good luck with your off-road adventures, whatever they may be. Hope to see you out there, on two wheels and knobby tires, riding B.C.'s best dirt. Happy trails!

Photograph courtesy Norco

Introduction

MOUNTAIN BIKING
BRITISH COLUMBIA
The Trail Guide

Origin of the Species ???

by Darrin Polischuk

For some unknown reason the state of California is the main source for many of the world's great trends. Together with surfing and skateboarding, mountain biking is undoubtedly one of the more worthwhile trends to come out of this area, (with the possible exception being America's greatest cultural export, the TV show "Baywatch"). While you may criticize California for giving us such titillating diversions from real life, they have more than redeemed themselves by creating the mountain bike.

You have to wonder where the initial impulse for taking a bike off-road originated? Wherever the source of the spark, it is a certainty that bikes were taken off-road in Asia, or Europe, years before the California boys tried it. The reason I can make this claim without research is because that in these societies bikes are ridden for transportation, not recreation. The chances of someone, somewhere, having had to ride a bike off the main road is sim- *"The sport was destined for* ply too great. So why give total credit to the *success when the right type of* Americans? However, the leisure-orientated *people became involved and* culture of the United States brought a *focused on building good bikes* unique twist to the world wide activity of *and having fun riding."* riding a bike; the idea of doing it off road, and just for fun. If you live for the weekend when you can take off on a ride with your friends, then you'll agree that as mountain bikers we owe a debt of eternal gratitude to those who started the momentum toward the invention of the mountain bike. We can live without "Baywatch", but to live without the mountain bike would be difficult. Consequently, as your buzzing down your favorite trail, or riding a new one, think back to the early days of the sport and be comforted by the thought that the smile on your face is brought to you by a unique group of funhogs who combined the need for some serious fun with uncanny mechanical abilities.

Society desperately needed to be rescued from the disco days of big cars and big hair, and who would have predicted the path to cultural and recreational enlightenment would be paved by a group of herb loving hippies who knew how to fix and design bikes. North American culture gradually welcomed individuals with a more relaxed view toward life, and who demonstrated how much fun could be had by simply riding an old clunker bike off-road. The sight of a cyclist wearing corduroy flairs, work boots, and a motorcycle helmet, bombing down a fire road on a modified beach cruiser with a dog in tow must have seemed strange. Yet it obviously had a very contagious element of fun,

MOUNTAIN BIKING
BRITISH COLUMBIA
The Trail Guide

because from these simple roots mountain biking was born and quickly became one of the worlds fastest growing sports. The early riders didn't use the term "mountain biking" like we do today. In fact, early off-road pioneers Thomas Rithchy and Charlie Kelly tried to put a trademark on the name "mountain bike", but failed in their attempt (Bicycling, March, 1996). Consequently mountain bike won out over "all terrain bike" or "ATB". Somehow it would seem odd to use the expression "all terrain biking" when phoning friends for a Sunday ride.

Pine Mt. and Mt. Tam, in Marin County, California are generally agreed upon to be the sight of the sport's origins. By 1976 the worlds first mountain bike race was held on the east face of Pine Mt. called the "Repack Downhill". It was called the Repack because riders needed to repack their coaster brakes after each run. Gary Fisher held the course record on the Repack Downhill from 1976 to 1984. The first Repack had a field of six riders and two dogs. Compare that to the size of a weekend event today, where 350 riders is an average turnout!

"Fortunately those who became riders were a recreationally thirsty bunch willing to sacrifice some common conveniences to get set up with the latest off-road goodies."

The early bikes were all custom built, and continuously modified to suit the rigors of nearby fire roads. The exact details of mountain biking origins are fuzzy. Joe Breeze credits many of the Marin Gang with getting their ideas from an unknown group called the "Cupertino guys" who showed up at a cyclocross in 1974 (Bicycling, March, 1996). We do know that by the summer of 1977 Joe Breeze delivered his first custom mountain bikes to nine friends, and the sport has never looked back.

By the summer of 1979 custom hand made mountain bikes were commercially available, and by 1981 the first mass produced mountain bikes filled the growing demand. Many of the American industry heavyweights today were part of the early mountain biking milieu in Marin County. People like Otis Guy, Tom Ritchey, Charlie Kelly, Gary Fisher, Joe Breeze, and many others that were present during the sport's early days continue to influence the evolution of bikes and the sport as we know it today.

If this were an American publication I would wax poetic about these mountain biking forefathers and take for granted that up in Canada they were simply followers of yet another American trend. However, it didn't take too much digging around to discover that in British Columbia, as early as 1978, the same mountain biking virus was spreading almost simaultaneously among a group of

Introduction

MOUNTAIN BIKING
BRITISH COLUMBIA
The Trail Guide

bike store owners and their customers in Vancouver. Here, the need for off-road parts to modify older cruisers and road bikes created a demand for stronger rims, hand made Ritchey off-road handle bars, and beefy cantilever brakes. In these early days a hand made Ritchey mountain bike would sell for about $2500, making the sport accessible only to the very committed, or the substantially wealthy. Fortunately those who became riders were a recreationally thirsty bunch willing to sacrifice some common conveniences to get set up with the latest off-road goodies. It took a special type of person to be an off-road keener in the early days, and we owe thanks to those brave souls who endured many a day on sloppy shifting, sketchy braked bikes who helped refine the breed we ride today. The sport was destined for success when the right type of people became involved and focused on building good bikes and having fun riding.

A history of mountain biking in British Columbia cannot be completed without mentioning the input that Rocky Mountain Bicycles had on the growth and development of the sport, and on the bikes. Rocky started out in 1981, and a year later produced Canada's first home grown, production mountain bike. At this time good off-road bikes were difficult to get your hands on, and were often quite expensive. In the early eighties, you were likely riding a Rocky Mountain, or a Specialized Stumpjumper. Ironically, Specialized, an American company, would send some of their products north to B.C. for testing on our demanding Pacific Northwest trails. Our abundance of severe riding terrain made the best testing ground for early bikes, and forced those who were riding often to focus on the continuing evolution of the machine. Some of the names synonymous with the early days of mountain biking in B.C.

MOUNTAIN BIKING
BRITISH COLUMBIA
The Trail Guide

reads like a who's who of the sport in Canada today. Grayson Bain and Larry Ruble (Rocky Mountain), Jacob Heilbron (Kona), Pippen Osbourn and Peter Hamilton (Syncros), Paul Brodie (Brodie), Don Whitticker (BLT lights), and Chris Dekerf, were some of the people who grew out of the fun and creative milieu centered in the early Rocky Mountain days. Today, many of these people are responsible in one way or another for the products and fun you have when riding the trails of B.C.

Around 1980 the Deep Cove crew of Chaz Romalis, Doug Lafavor, and Ashley Walker, were rebuilding beach cruisers after Chaz heard of this new craze from a Californian friend. The need to continually tweak the bikes that were being ridden on nearby Mount Seymour, gave birth to the Deep Cove Bike Shop. During these years the difficulty in finding parts that worked lead to communication between all the bike stores who were experimenting with the off-road machine. Soon the hard riding and good times milieu that developed around the shop became legendary. Talk of the mind altering night rides the Cove boys were doing fostered the image of mountain biking as a true counter culture activity. The Deep Cove mystique owes a great deal of the center of the their early involve- and the killer trails who rip it up on

"Talk of the mind altering night rides the Cove boys were doing fostered the image of mountain biking as a true counter culture activity."

it's reputation as hard-core scene to ment in the sport; and talented riders nearby Mount Seymour. The Hell of the North Bike Race, up the Old Buck Trail and down the infamous Severed Dick Trail, continues to remind everyone of the hard core element of our sport. The Deep Cove good time attitude, and extreme riding history on seriously difficult trails, is very much a part of the origins of mountain biking in B.C. Take a close look at the wrinkles around Chaz's eyes. If only they could tell all the stories . . .

By the mid 1980's, mountain biking was well on it's way to becoming a mainstream activity, and hot beds of riding were popping up simultaneously throughout the province on Vancouver Island, Hornby Island, and throughout the Kootenay and Rocky Mountains. The growth of the sport was steady throughout the late eighties, and in the 1990's the growth curve of the sport shot uphill and has never looked down. British Columbian companies like Rocky Mountain Bicycles, Syncros, Norco, Brodie, Dekerf, Sugoi, Roach Products, and Race Face, have benefitted from the broad appeal that the sport enjoys today. From the Repack Downhill in 1976, to the Atlanta Olympics in 1996, it's been a fast paced twenty years and an example of evolution that

MOUNTAIN BIKING
BRITISH COLUMBIA
The Trail Guide

would have Darwin rolling over in his grave with excitement. If I had access to a time machine, nothing would be more fun than to take a fully suspended downhill weapon, and an ultra light cross country bike, and visit the pioneers of our sport on one of their favorite rides. Just imagine the conversation . . . and the riding!

As the sport continues to mushroom, growing pains are inevitable. The amount of people who now ride in the backcountry far surpasses what was comprehensible a few short years ago. The various land authorities are now struggling to deal with a recreational boom that was, for the most part, unforeseen. The struggle to maintain access to trails, and to involve land authorities in mountain biking issues, will be the most important unwritten history of our sport. All riders need to recognize the efforts, past, present, and future, of those individuals and clubs, that work hard to make our sport thrive. Failure to be involved in finding a way to share the provinces trails with others, and eventually be viewed as legitimate backcountry users, could make our sport's history happy, but short.

Photograph by Blair Polischuk

MOUNTAIN BIKING
BRITISH COLUMBIA
The Trail Guide

Bears

by Darrin Polischuk

While riding in B.C.'s backcountry it is inevitable that an encounter with some wildlife will occur. Media stories of cougar and bear attacks may make it seem commonplace, but riders must realize that any actual incidents with wildlife, (other than humans and animals scaring the hell out of each other), are extremely rare. Nevertheless, the more you ride the greater the chance of encountering a black bear, or more rarely, a grizzly. So read on.

It's bikers that usually sneak up on and scare bears, who are generally just hanging out looking for grubs and berries. A typical bear encounter occurs when the biker is travelling at speed. You may feel most vulnerable when climbing a hill, but the noise of breathing and grunting will warn bears of your approach and they can escape. It is important to remember that bears want to escape, and aren't interested in hunting you for food. Bears are most likely to attack if surprised or scared and have no way to escape the situation.

Most bear encounters are brief, with the human and bear staring bewilderedly at each other for a few seconds before the bear escapes into the woods and the human is left to puzzle out what just happened. However, if you confront a bear that has no escape route, or worse yet is with its cubs, keep your wits about you and the following hints in mind. Bears have poor eyesight, and when they rear up on their hind legs, waving their head back and forth, they are simply looking and smelling in an attempt to identify you. This posture is also used to make the bear look big and intimidating. Both of these behaviors should result in the bear running away.

> *"On the other hand, if you face a bear that has lowered its head, laid back its ears, and is making a "woofing" sound, or snapping its jaws together, you're in a serious situation."*

On the other hand, if you face a bear that has lowered its head, laid back its ears, and is making a "woofing" sound, or snapping its jaws together, you're in a serious situation. These are signs that the bear is in an aggressive pre-attack mode. Your options at this point are somewhat limited. The official advice from Parks Canada is to slowly back away, talking quietly to the bear while looking for a suitable tree to climb. Be aware that Grizzlies are not good at climbing but can still scramble over 4 meters up a tree in a pinch. Black bears

Introduction

on the other hand, are good climbers, and a tree may not offer you safe refuge. Keep your bike between you and the bear as it may be the last line of defence. Even if the bear charges, be aware that they will sometimes "bluff" charging then turning away at the last second and escaping. If charged, don't run away. Back away slowly and hope the bear is bluffing. In the event of an attack you may have to "play dead". People have survived bear attacks by dropping to the ground, curling up into a ball, and covering your face, neck, and abdomen. This may sound difficult, but it's better than trying to duke it out with a 400 kg grizzly.

Try not to get too stressed about this information, and view bears as part of our province's backcountry. Check with local authorities about bear conditions in the fall, and keep in mind that if you are attacked while riding, you'll be among the first.

MOUNTAIN BIKING
BRITISH COLUMBIA
The Trail Guide

Weather, and Some Geography Stuff . . .

by Darrin Polischuk

A h yes, the weather. No other topic is so freely discussed by friends or strangers than the weather. Outdoor recreational enthusiasts like mountain bikers are even more in tune to the fluctuations and seasonal differences in British Columbia's weather patterns than our sedentary friends and neighbors; because the weather feels quite different from the seat of a bike than the couch of your home. Whether you choose to plan your outings around the "forecast", or simply plough through and ignore the weather, you can't do anything in B.C. without experiencing the elements first hand. British Columbia's diverse physical geography is responsible for shaping equally diverse weather outcomes.

British Columbia has an amazing variety in terms of temperature and precipitation fluctuations. In the Interior Plateau a daytime high during the summer can easily reach 40°C, while on the coast, a same day high will be a comfortable 25°C. Precipitation also varies a great deal throughout the province. The west coast has a reputation of raining all the time. While it does rain a great deal on the coast, the majority of the precipitation falls in the winter, and the summers can actually have frequent dry spells. In Vancouver only 10% of the yearly precipitation comes in the form of summertime rain. The trails in these coastal areas usually dry out nicely in the summer, giving mountain bikers welcome relief from the muddy conditions of spring, fall and winter.

> *"The trails around Osoyoos are actually in the northern most tip of the Sonoran Desert!"*

The interior valleys, on the other hand, are some of the provinces driest places. The valleys around Kamloops and the Okanagan receive about 50% of their yearly precipitation in the winter as snow. This makes for dry trails in the spring, and dusty trails in the summer. The trails around Osoyoos are actually in the northern most tip of the Sonoran Desert! It's not uncommon for valley bottoms of the southern interior to have dry riding conditions in the middle of winter, while local ski hills still have plenty of snow. Precipitation throughout the province is spread out very unevenly. WHY?

The uneven distribution of precipitation, and the differences between our almost Mediterranean coast and the much colder and drier interior, can be explained by the province's arrangement of valleys that parallel the coast and something called the 'orographic effect'. Once you understand these two simple things, the seemingly bizarre differences in our topography and weather will be demystified.

38   *Introduction*

MOUNTAIN BIKING
BRITISH COLUMBIA
The Trail Guide

British Columbia sits at a mid latitude, and its weather is constantly effected by the Pacific flows that continually move toward the coast. The Pacific Ocean moderates the temperature in summer and winter. The Vancouver Island and Coast Mountains are the first to intercept these moist Pacific storms. The results are heavy rains on the west facing, or windward slopes of these mountain ranges. As moist weather systems hit the windward slopes they rise, cool, and deposit the majority of their moisture. The tendency for air to lose moisture at greater elevations is known as the "orographic effect". On the east facing, or leeward slopes, the air descends into the valleys, warms, and the effect is a dispersal of cloud and dramatically less precipitation. The result is a sharp contrast in precipitation and vegetation on the leeward slope or "rain shadow" area. Take a drive east from Whistler on the Duffey Lake Road toward Lytton to view the dramatic contrast of a "rain shadow" within the span of a few hundred kilometers.

A similar scenario is out played out in each of the mountain ranges and valleys of B.C. The Vancouver Island Mountains produce a rain shadow for the east facing slopes and the Gulf Islands. This rain shadow is most evident in the Courtenay/Comox area, and on the nearby islands of Hornby, and Denman. The next wall to catch the moisture is the Coast Mountains and the rain shadow it produces is the most dramatic, extending from the Interior Plateau to the Okanagan. The Okanagan Valley is very dry in the valley bottom, but the west facing slopes of the Monashees is another wall that collects the Pacific moisture. The process repeats itself in the Columbia Mountains, the next big depot for large amounts of precipitation. Each of these mountains and valleys also reproduce their own rain shadow effect.

> *"Take a drive east from Whistler on the Duffey Lake Road toward Lytton to view the dramatic contrast of a "rain shadow" within the span of a few hundred kilometers."*

The diversity of B.C.'s topography is visible on a large valley to valley scale, as well as within a more confined area. In a single valley ,or on the same ride, differences can be quite pronounced. Elevation, slope exposure, and prevailing winds play a major role in dictating the differences in terrain you find beneath your knobbies. Remember the "orographic effect?" As you ride up from a valley bottom the amount of precipitation received on a trail increases. As a result, the type of trail and the surroundings correspond to the increase in precipitation. The difference between scrub grasslands in the valley, and the large trees at higher elevations, is the work of this precipitation. At times the differences are so pronounced that each small area is it's own world. This is called a micro-climate. A grove of cedars in an area dominated by other tree species is good evidence of a micro-climate.

MOUNTAIN BIKING
BRITISH COLUMBIA
The Trail Guide

The steepness and exposure of a slope are other factors that can drastically change the ride experience. Simply put, the more northern facing slopes receive less sunshine than their southern facing comrades. The result is a slope that evaporates moisture much slower than a slope that is facing the sun all day. Therefore, it is not uncommon to ride into a thickly forested north facing slope and eventually emerge into an open grassy area that has sunshine late into the afternoon. In the spring, the southern slopes dry up much earlier compared to those that are shielded from the sun. Slopes that are steep will always dry out quicker than a slope that is shallow. Steep slopes that have direct southern exposure will be the driest, while shallow north facing slopes will generally be the wettest. Keep this in mind when riding in the spring, or any season when you want to avoid wet trail conditions.

Nothing earth shattering here, just a small sample of basic geography that relates to the mountain biker. As you ride the trails of B.C., look for examples of the things I have mentioned and let mountain biking assist you in understanding our physical world.

Photograph by Blair Polischuk

MOUNTAIN BIKING
BRITISH COLUMBIA
The Trail Guide

Mountain Biking And The Erosion Myth

by Darrin Polischuk

Over twenty years ago mountain bikes slowly began to creep onto backcountry trails that for years were the domain of hikers, equestrians, and in some instances, motorcycles. This invasion for the most part was unforeseen, and the number of visitors to trails over the years have skyrocketed. Along with an increase in trail use came a corresponding increase in trail damage. It seemed logical then, that the new group (the mountain bikers) must therefore be responsible for trail detereoration. While this is logical, it is by no means correct.

The forces of erosion are impossible to ignore by mountain bikers, or anyone who uses trails. The landscape you see everyday has been created by erosion. About 10,000 years ago the mountains emerged from a blanket of ice. The slowly melting glaciers are largely responsible for carving out the mountains we play in today. The forces of erosion continue to change the landscape surrounding us. As water flows down the mountain it also carries rocks and soil. During periods of heavy rain the power of erosion is most evident; roads can be washed out, and landscapes severely altered.

Erosion is most evident to mountain bikers because the trails are altered by the presence of bikes, horses, and hikers. The only scientific study done on the physical impact of user groups was carried out by Seney (1990) at Montana State University. This study showed that mountain bikes did not produce any trail damage that was significant. It went on to state that it is diffi- cult to distinguish the impact from a moun- tain bike over that of a hiker in terms of water runoff, sedi- ment runoff, or soil compaction. In fact, it was concluded that horses produce signif- icantly more runoff than other groups be- *"the notion that mountain bikes create more damage than other user groups is a result of our sport's popularity, not the fact that mountain biking in and of itself is detrimental to trails."* cause they dug up the trail. The study also remarked that construction of the trail is a very important factor. In other words, a well placed and constructed trail stood up to use. Steep trails suffered the most damage by all users.

The myth, therefore, of mountain bikers being the scourge of the trails is unfounded. This is not to say that mountain bikers float over trails leaving no trace. Excessive braking on steep trails, trail widening, and the cutting of shorter routes, are the main reasons bikes deteriorate the trails. The impact of moun- tain bikes, however, can be limited with common sense riding techniques, and properly built and maintained trails. There are clearly more mountain bikers on

MOUNTAIN BIKING
BRITISH COLUMBIA
The Trail Guide

some trails than any other user group and the impressions we create are very evident. Use equals abuse, this can't be helped. But, the notion that mountain bikes create more damage than other user groups is a result of our sport's popularity, not the fact that mountain biking in and of itself is detrimental to trails. If there was a massive surge in the popularity of hiking, in a world where mountain biking had been around for decades, claims of trail abuse would likely be directed toward this user group as well.

It is important that all users recognize that they disturb trails in different ways. No one group is more righteous than another. Once this fact has been well established, then the goals of maintaining access to land can proceed with a unified, multi-purposed voice.

Photograph by Darrin Polischuk

MOUNTAIN BIKING
BRITISH COLUMBIA
The Trail Guide

Management of Mountain Bicycling

by Michael J. Milne (B.Sc., M.Es.)
Professor of Geography at Okanagan University College

As residents and visiting mountain bicyclists in British Columbia we must realize that we are onto something special. We have more opportunities to take part in our recreational pass-time than most people on the face of the planet. The reason for this wealth of opportunity stems from the objectives of the management agencies responsible for crown land, as well as our urban, provincial and national parks. Along with these opportunities comes an element of responsibility. After all, these lands belong to the people of Canada. In a nutshell, our responsibilities relate to the preservation of access to recreational lands for our generation, and those to come. As you may have already deduced, the onus of this responsibility lies with everyone who uses, or even thinks about using, British Columbia as their playground. While this may sound a bit heavy, surveys have shown that mountain bicyclists are generally well educated, interested, and willing to learn new ways to preserve their sport.

We all have our tragic stories, conjured up around the campfire, of great rides that were once accessible but are now closed for one reason or another. Well, those stories are becoming more the norm than the exception in the North American mountain bicycle scene. Land management agencies most often cite environmental and social impacts as justification for closing our favourite single-tracks. This is where the system, at least in our eyes, breaks down. The most obvious solution to the problem of reduced accessibility, and loss of opportunity for those up and coming generations, is not to give the management agencies any reason to act. This means that we have to know what kind of damage we are capable of, and we have to know how to mitigate what has already occured.

> *"As you may have already deduced, the onus of this responsibility lies with everyone who uses, or even thinks about using, British Columbia as their playground."*

Social impacts are those that involve other trail users (hikers, horseback riders, motorcyclists, other mountain bicyclists), and in some way diminish the quality of the experiences that people are having on the trails. Current outdoor recreation research has shown that mountain bicyclists tend to offend other users because of the speed at which they travel, and the surprising quickness with which they make their almost silent approach. In some cases, as with horseback riders, this sudden appearance can spook the animal and have potentially fatal results for all parties involved. The easiest way to reduce social impacts and conflicts with other trail users is to look ahead, speak up and warn of your approach, slow down, and greet everyone in a friendly manner. After all, we mountain bicyclists are the "new kids on the block" and we are being closely scrutinized for proper conduct. As the saying goes, "it only takes one bad apple . . .", so spread the word and treat others with respect.

MOUNTAIN BIKING
BRITISH COLUMBIA
The Trail Guide

Impact on the environment is the other main reason for trail closures, but this too can be easily mitigated with sound judgement, and utilization of the geographic knowledge you gained earlier in the book. Most environmental impacts stem from increased erosion caused by riding in wet and muddy conditions. Additional impact to the trails is caused by excessive skidding, instead of maintaining traction, on steep descents. It is at this point that most riders fall back on the old "well you know, it's not us that do the most damage out there, it's those damn . . ." Finger-pointing never *"Finger-pointing never achieves* achieves any pro-gressive results. The *any progressive results."* majority of trails in British Columbia are managed under a multiple-use designation and will remain that way. This means that all users are part of the same group and should have a common goal. Every form of trail user has an impact, whether it's on soils, vegetation or wildlife, but finger-pointing only creates hard feelings that eventually lead to segregation and an overall reduction of outdoor opportunities. All we have to do is look south of the border to see widespread closures caused by social and environmental impacts.

Back to managing those soil impacts, well quite simply, attempt to ride on dry trails as much as possible and be sure to stay on existing routes. As you learned earlier, dry trails are usually those with southern exposures, coarser soil types, and are generally more exposed to prevailing wind conditions. Seek these types of trails out after rain and save the dark, twisting, single-tracks until dryer days. As for staying on existing trails . . . this one should be obvious. New routes cut through the forest or down exposed hill slopes scar the landscape, and give land managers even more reason to close whole areas to mountain bicycling.

The second type of environmental impact involves wildlife. Just the presence of any type of trail user in backcountry areas is enough to drive large carnivores, moose, elk and deer away. Trail users should always try not to spook wildlife, and of course, never chase any. It may take only one encounter between running deer and a mountain bicyclist to deplete that particular deer's precious fat reserves which it will need to survive the upcoming win- *"The best thing to do is stay alert,* ter. Documented cases do exist where *and remain on existing trails."* grizzly and black bears have attacked mountain bicyclists who simply got too close, or did not bother to make a wide enough loop around the animal they confronted. There is only so much we can do to remain distanced from wildlife. After all, it's hard to predict what might lay around the next corner. The best thing to do is stay alert, and remain on existing trails.

Many of us mountain bicyclists would love to head out and build our dream trail. That perfect combination of double-track climb and challenging single-track descent. We must remember, however, that British Columbia is already criss-crossed with countless roads and trails, both in use and abandoned. We must also remember that the recent Forest Practices Code restricts any trail or

(Continued on page 46)

MOUNTAIN BIKING
BRITISH COLUMBIA
The Trail Guide

MOUNTAIN BIKING
BRITISH COLUMBIA
The Trail Guide

(Continued from page 44)

recreational facility construction without written approval of the forest district. Routine clearing of existing routes is of course all right, and greatly appreciated by both land managers and trail users alike. The construction of new trails and facilities, however, directly conflicts with attempts to limit soil and vegetation disturbance, and limit impacts on wildlife. If you or your local mountain bicycle club has aspirations for trail construction, then pursue the proper channels of approval and contact your local forest district for direction. If and when possible stick to established routes, even old abonded logging, mining and exploration routes can easily be cleared for some mountain bicycle travel. Remember, each time we head out cross-country we are impacting the land and wildlife. This only gives land managers a reason to restrict the outdoor activities that we all enjoy.

> *"If you or your local mountain bicycle club has aspirations for trail construction, then pursue the proper channels of approval"*

The remaining conflict or impact worth considering relates to cattle. Cows and mountain bicyclists simply do not get along. Again, this gives rise to "finger-pointing" and hard feelings among trail users and ranchers in British Columbia. We must remember that cattle grazing is legally allowed over much of British Columbia's crown lands through multiple-use management strategies. Even though cattle can add a "certain spice" to our favourite trail we must remember that a rancher is a taxpayer as well, and that the cattle business provides a valuable contribution to the British Columbia economy. We as mountain bicyclists cannot afford to chase or stampede cattle herds. Every ounce of meat on those cows represents profit to the cattle rancher. If we lean those cattle out by chasing them over the countryside we are directly affecting a rancher's well-being.

The moral of the story is that we are not alone on the trails, and will never be. We must act responsibly and in the best interests of all trail users in order to preserve the vast range of opportunities for outdoor recreation use that draws visitors from around the globe to British Columbia. It is always better to reminisce about the great rides that exist, than lament about those

> *"The moral of the story is that we are not alone on the trails, and will never be."*

which no longer do. Access to trails for all can be preserved through proper management and common sense. Let's avoid creating "the good old days of open spaces and killer single-track."

Introduction

MOUNTAIN BIKING
BRITISH COLUMBIA
The Trail Guide

Gone Riding

by Darrin Polischuk

Everything is all crazy, restless, stressful . . . then you ride

You eat, sleep, drink coffee, sit on the toilet . . . then you ride

You sign on, tinker with your bike, get nervous . . . then you ride hard

People bug you, cars bug you, your mate bugs you . . . then you ride

What are you doing with your life? Parents called . . . then you ride long

A bad mail day, bills to pay, your wheel may be toast . . . you ride anyway

Your helmet smells, your dog smells, you have to do laundry, you smell . . . you ride anyway

if charles bukowski can be a poet so can you . . .

I gotta go for a ride

MOUNTAIN BIKING
BRITISH COLUMBIA
The Trail Guide

Night Riding

by Darrin Polischuk

Someone, somewhere, for some unknown reason, invented day light savings time, and insodoing deprived many a hard working soul of the simple pleasures of riding a bike after a long day's work. Not everyone wishes to extend the day. For instance, nocturnal animals like bats, cats, and owls do their best work in the dark. But for mountain bikers vision is important, and if you don't live near the arctic circle, chances are that on a warm spring evening you'll want to ride your bike after the sun begins its predictable journey to the other side of the earth.

For years cyclists were forced to end the evening ride when darkness descended. Today, the crazy and resourceful folks in the bicycle industry have made it possible to ride comfortably under the stars. Rechargeable batteries and powerful lights provide plenty of illumination on the trail. The night ride has since taken on an identity of its own.

The evening group ride is a ritual repeated throughout the province by plenty of trail-hungry hounds who refuse to let sunlight get in the way of their favorite form of cultural expression. For a night ride to be fun and safe it is best to travel in a small group, about 5 riders being the perfect number and 10 being too many if any consistent forward progress is one of the ride objectives.

Night riding can hone your reaction time and force you to consult a higher Zen-like power to assist you in navigating. Knowing a trail will help you to negotiate it at daytime-like speeds. Ride on unfamiliar turf, however, and your speed is dictated by your trust in the trail, field of vision, and Jedi-like abilities. At night, the dullest of single tracks can become a video game impersonation of what virtual mountain biking may be like for the poor souls who will inhabit what is left of the earth in a hundred years. The point is simple; mountain biking at night makes you feel like you are 12 years old again cruising the neighborhood after dark. When you were 12 the purpose of riding at night was blurred into a collage of: looking for and avoiding trouble, looking for and avoiding girls/boys, and looking for and eating food. Now that you're older life hasn't changed much except that you've just become more subtle about doing the same things. When we ride at night,

> *"At night, the dullest of single tracks can become a video game impersonation of what virtual mountain biking may be like for the poor souls who will inhabit what is left of the earth in a hundred years."*

MOUNTAIN BIKING
BRITISH COLUMBIA
The Trail Guide

the ride itself is just an excuse to get out with riding soul brothers and sisters and do what must be done: namely ride, talk, and be human. Nothing new here, but doing it at night is just plain cool.

The temperature can drop quite drastically with the sun, so bring warm clothes, gloves and booties if it's an early spring ride. Hands and especially toes can be victimized by the cold nights, which brings me to my last point on night riding: conversation.

On a night ride, talk is always one of the best parts of the evening. For unknown reasons people communicate easier, with more openness and less hesitation, when in _____ the dark. Think about it: candle *"The conversation quickly took a de-* light dinners, pil-low talk, and camp *viant turn when one rider mentioned* fire stories, are all evidence that as a *what he'd seen surfing the internet,* species we are more willing to talk *which lead to a discussion about the* when the lights are low. I guess eye *off beat film 'Bitter Moon'."* contact scares some folks. So it's logical _____ that group night ride conversation should flow in a pure stream of consciousness uninterrupted by anything associated with reality or light.

I recall an early spring ride where, somewhere between getting lost and riding through the snow, conversation was interrupted by the group's admission that we all had frozen toes. This reminded me of a story where an Irish road cyclist named Paul Kimmage, while riding in the Tour of Italy, had to pee on his frozen hands to warm them enough to make braking down a mountain pass possible. No one was contemplating this desperate act, but suddenly each rider took turns talking about anything related.

Conversation flowed freely about the healing properties of urea, how surfers soak their feet in urine to help heal cuts after walking on the coral reef, and how the various Indian Nations that lived on the prairies used urine as a mosquito repellent. The conversation quickly took a deviant turn when one rider mentioned what he'd seen surfing the internet, which lead to a discussion about the off beat film 'Bitter Moon'. Before we descended to the inevitable level of "guess what I cruised on the internet" one rider desperately tried to change the conversation back to bike parts, specifically the new V braking system.

Suddenly one of the more restrained riders, and a newcomer to the weekly night riding ritual, mentioned that he'd once secretly tried to get the squeak out of his brakes by peeing on them, but was afraid to tell anyone. We all listened attentively . . .

Introduction

MOUNTAIN BIKING
BRITISH COLUMBIA
The Trail Guide

The Seasons

by Darrin Polischuk

Every year the seasons generate an explosive pallete of colors that spatter over the mountains and valleys of B.C. The sharp images, and made-in-heaven views, form the backdrops for our rides. In the spring, trails slowly emerge from beneath the snow unveiling their one true purpose; a home for mountain bikes. The greenness of spring leads into the long days of summer and warm evening rides. In the fall, all the stunning colors can make a ride more visual than physical. For those who ride in the winter, the green under the coastal forest canopy sharply contrasts with the white of nearby peaks. Colors are in a constant state of flux, and as the seasons change, so do the trails and our experiences on them.

Spring

Spring is definitely the season that provokes the most excitement for many mountain bikers. Everything about the freshness of the air and the feeling of the bike after a winter layoff is special. If you could capture the energy that most mountain bikers have in the spring, I'm sure you could light the city of Vancouver for a month.   Living in the north, or the interior, means that alternative winter activities like cross country skiing, snow boarding, snowshoeing, ice hockey, or downhill skiing have occupied the cold winter months. These are noble pursuits, and if we lived in a land of perpetual winter many of us would survive and have fun doing so. But when spring arrives at the west coast, and then a bit later to the interior valley bottoms, a mountain biker's cravings are satisfied once more and the world regains a state of harmony and balance.

In the spring, super-keeners chase the snow line up from the valley bottoms. Trails that seemed routine in the fall come alive in the warm spring sun. It's as if your senses were in hibernation during the winter. You always knew what the trails looked like, felt like, and smelled like, but somehow in spring you rediscover the simple joys of riding for the first time. So your butt hurts a bit more in the spring, and maybe the trails are a little muddy and slick, but who cares . . . you're finally RIDING AGAIN!! If you think this is just the ranting of some over-caffinated super-keen rider, you're right. Nevertheless, there are times when we all succumb to the seduction of the couch. But seriously, if you are not at least a bit stoked to ride in the spring then you best give this book to someone who will put it to good use.

Introduction

MOUNTAIN BIKING
BRITISH COLUMBIA
The Trail Guide

A possible remedy for spring time flaccidity is to go out and buy some cycling stuff for yourself, or your machine. It doesn't have to be anything expensive, just something new. I am not espousing rampant and unnecessary consumerism here. It's just a simple suggestion for those who need a kick start off the couch. Coffee works for me, but some may need the enticement of a new toy to get it in gear. Acquiring new cycling stuff after all those lonely, contemplative moments on the throne over the winter, (just you, your thoughts and a mountain bike mag full of enticing ads for products that supposedly propel us beyond our genetic limitation), can be just the elixir with which to toast the season.

Often something as inexpensive as a new water bottle is all that's needed to get you out on the trails. Personally, I think its something about the smell of new cycling stuff that makes me want to ride. Those research and development guys are secretly leading us into the bike shops because we're all unconscious slaves to our olfactory glands. (Watch for scratch and sniff adds for new bike stuff in your favorite mag soon!)
If your funds are as low as your motivation, just browse a bike shop and smell some new gloves or a tire, it may work! If the shop employee catches you in the act of rubbing your nose on some new merchandise, explain your purpose. I'm sure they'll be very understanding and point you toward the best stuff in the shop. Once you are back on the trails it's easy to re-aquaint yourself with the obvious visceral joys of mountain biking.

Spring means muddy trails, not just wet and a bit muddy, but down right get stuck, tide commercial, complete overhaul, new cables, bike-weighing-50-pounds kind of muddy. There is no better time to demonstrate how politically correct a rider you are than in the spring. Those who choose to ride on soft muddy trails can build up an entire season worth of bad trail karma points on one ride! The enlightened rider, while being closer to the bike gods, also realizes that in the spring, trails with rocky firm surfaces are the place to be. So, to avoid chastisement and a season of bad karma induced flat tires and ugly crashes, ride on trails that will not get thrashed by you or your buddies.

One small hint; you are no longer the only person riding, and in the spring a busy weekend on some wet, fragile trails can create damage that is visible for years, so use common sense and remember to ride through the puddle and not around it to keep the single track from becoming too wide. Remember to slow down and take some time out to soak in the re-awakening world around you and enjoy the freshness of spring mountain biking. Regarding the fitness and training aspect of spring riding, be sure to take it easy in the spring and allow your body to adapt to the new stresses of riding. A spring full of long, slower

MOUNTAIN BIKING
BRITISH COLUMBIA
The Trail Guide

rides will ensure a summer of fast rides and continued enthusiasm. Slower riding in the spring will give you the fitness to do the epic rides in summer and fall.

Summer

The snow has melted on all but the highest trails, mud is now a rarity rather than a constant companion, and the after work ride is no longer a game of beat the sunset. This is summer mountain biking in British Columbia. You feel so light when you go on your first warm weather ride with only shorts and a top that you feel naked. Combine a ride with a quick swim in a warm lake or river and you'll realize that a mountain bike may be your best summer friend. Friends are critical, and make life wonderful, but if one had to choose between a summer alone with a bike or a summer with people and no bike, it could be a disturbingly difficult decision. Your trusty two wheeled friend can deliver you a variety of experiences that other activities and toys can't match. Rain or shine, your mountain bike, the good people you ride with, and a favorite trail, add up to unbeatable summer fun. I could ramble on forever about the virtues of summertime riding but it's more fun to experience than read about. Somehow, none of my words will ever capture the essence of how perfect summertime mountain biking is.

In the summer be aware that the stark fist of removal lurks behind every trail. The possibilities of sunstroke and dehydration are your constant companions and should be treated with great respect. I don't want to sound like your mother here, but insufficient liquids and too much sun can turn a perfect ride into a death march through an imaginary desert. Trust me on this one, take a minimum of two large water bottles on any ride in the summer that will be near two hours in total duration. Also, if you can avoid the midday heat and ride early in the morning or in the evening then do so. Adhering to these simple principles should keep a summer ride from becoming a epic disaster of dehydration and sunstroke. Then again, you may be looking for an easy and legal way to have an hallucinatory mountain biking vision quest . . . If so, disregard the above warning.

Summertime riding also means that your favorite trail will most likely have others on it. Be aware that you are not the only person who enjoys the trail experience. We're all sharing a resource (the trails), and therefore the lessons of sharing and cooperation learned in kindergarten must not be forgotten on a busy trail, mid summer, Anywhere, B.C. Simply put, in the summer many people are out walking on trails with little knowledge of our presence. If the day's ride is in an area that swells in population over the summer be doubly aware of the rules of the trail, and please don't scare any nice hiker folk. A brief review of the rules of the trail should be sufficient to remind everyone of the basic manners required to be a responsible rider.

Make summer the time to ride as much as possible. The agreeable weather and long days remove most obstacles from riding. As far as I know we only live once, therefore we owe it to ourselves to live every day like it may be our last. It follows logically then, that if you are reading this book, a daily dose of mountain biking is how you are planning to spend your summer; living life to the fullest, and maybe a little closer to the edge then many people feel comfortable with. Go out and ride something that scares the hell out of you and put a bit of buzz into the remainder of the summer season.

Autumn

Autumn arrives in British Columbia and provides a welcome relief from the heat and crowds of summer. Personally, the fall is my favorite season to ride. I'm finally fit enough follow most people, and the trails at all elevations are in consistently great shape. Generally the weather is at its most friendly in the fall, and epic rides in the alpine are possible with the fewest worries. However, the best aspect of autumn riding is watching mother nature "do her thing" to the leaves. In fall, the colors are so intense that the view and the trail compete for your attention. Bring your camera and plan a long full day ride where you can drink in the view and celebrate fall riding in style. You owe it to yourself to gather the riding posse for one last kick at the can before the snow closes trails.

In the fall, evening rides become shorter, and those not aware of daily sunset times can get caught on the trail wishing they'd brought their light set. A quick warning for those who are not experienced. A single track in thick trees becomes dark much sooner than the open areas. This may sound obvious, but anyone who rides blind in the dark at least once will be wary of suggestions to spin off "one more loop" when it's far too late in the day.

One of the most inspiring aspects of autumn riding is the thought that the ride you're on may be the last one of the season. You look at the few remaining leaves clinging to the trees and suddenly realize that you're stealing a day from winter, who's waiting just around the corner. The scarcity of good late autumn riding days make them very special, and something to be cherished and talked about until spring arrives.

MOUNTAIN BIKING
BRITISH COLUMBIA
The Trail Guide

Photograph by Blair Polischuk

Introduction

MOUNTAIN BIKING
BRITISH COLUMBIA
The Trail Guide

Photograph by Karen Silversides

Introduction

MOUNTAIN BIKING
BRITISH COLUMBIA
The Trail Guide

Winter

At first thought, the concept of riding in the winter seems a touch absurd and maybe even a bit dangerous. For the most part I agree, but given the right location and weather, winter riding can sure beat the line ups and attitude associated with mountain biking's distant alpine cousins. And apart from a few necessary clothing items, it's free! Winter riding can involve snow as a trail surface, or if you live in B.C.'s banana belt, more likely a severe kind of extra greasy winter mud.

Winter riding in the mud is basically the same as any other time of year except that it's probably colder. Riding in snow, on the other hand, is an entirely new proposition. Given the right temperatures and snow conditions, rides can be a lot of fun and positive traction is possible. Many tire manufacturers make studded tires and chains to enhance traction in the slickest winter conditions. However, if the thaw/freeze cycle sets up the snow with an icy glaze, best stick to the road. Riding in the snow is a very good way to hone your bike handling skills. The basic logic being, if you can handle a slow speed two wheel ice slide, when traction arrives in the spring your bike will feel like it's glued to the trail.

To make the most of winter mountain biking look after your hands and feet, dress in layers, avoid cotton undergarments, (and if your lucky enough) time your rides around the frequent rain showers and the deep freeze that usually visit our province in January. With these simple hints a short winter ride can be good fun with plenty of laughs. And it sure beats sitting on an indoor bike watching the sweat drip off your nose.

The mountain biking season is never far away anywhere in B.C. Usually around February my bike starts to demand a bit more attention than the periodic "hello" with a quick squeeze of the brakes. That kind of quickie doesn't cut it when the real thing is just around the corner. A bike needs to get out of the basement once in a while and see the sun, feel the cold air on it's tubes, and your slightly softer butt squish on its saddle. It needs to hear your giggles echoing through the trees on your favorite trail.

Balancing life's needs with those of your bike takes talent. But those who pay attention to their bikes over the winter are rewarded when their trusty steed displays a renewed affection for its owner at the outset of another solstice. By late February and early March the valley bottoms and coastal regions throughout B.C. are rideable and spring season has begun . . .

Introduction

MOUNTAIN BIKING
BRITISH COLUMBIA
The Trail Guide

On Mountain Biking, Competition, and Variety

by Darrin Polischuk

On Mountain Biking, Competition, and Variety

So you think mountain biking is simply the act of riding your bike on a trail? Well, your basically right. But as the sport evolves so does the variety of riding we like to do on our bikes. It is inevitable: if you put a bunch of humans collectively moving through space on some sort of vehicle, they will eventually become competitive. After all, competition is a natural human impulse. If it wasn't for this *"Can you imagine a 100 m dash where* seemingly genetic compulsion to *the runners all hold hands till the finish?"* try and always be half a wheel ahead of the pack, our evolution as a species, and the subsequent evolution of all sports and equipment would be stunted. Can you imagine a 100 m dash where the runners all hold hands till the finish? Or how about mountain bikers not really caring that one rider has a bike 5 pounds lighter and can now outclimb everyone. Remove the need to compete from the human mindset and notions like these become feasible.

The duality in human behaviour, ranging from highly cooperative to deadly competitive, is apparent throughout history. Compare any violent society from the past with the cooperative hunter gatherer societies and it becomes obvious that we humans share contradictory impulses to cooperate and compete. Mountain biking is only one of the many ways to express our humaness, and in

"The duality in human behaviour, ranging from highly cooperative to deadly competitive, is apparent throughout history."

so expressing, reveals a behavioural duality that is often acted out on the trail. The cooperative feeling is most apparent on group rides where a diverse gathering of mountain bikers share tools, food, and help out slower riders. On these ultimate feel good rides, each participant is equally concerned with the joy and experience of others as much as themselves. It is especially nice to find yourself on a ride dominated by the cooperative impulse when the route is long, and the possibility of a mishap high. Group rides with the primary focus on having a good time can rekindle your faith in the goodness of human nature.

However, if cooperation and not competition were the dominant human impulse, the world would resemble something more pleasant and less troubling than what we see and read about daily. Perhaps people wouldn't be starving in our city streets, and those who are benefitting the most from our societal structure would willingly share their wealth and resources with others. Do you really want to give your ride partner that last chunk of power bar? Or would you rather watch him slowly bonk while you happily ride away with a full belly? Tough choice for the ultra competitive. An easy choice for the cooperative.

It's interesting that as soon as one rider outdoes another on some steep climb or scary descent an internal debate begins. *Should I let the other rider drop me (in essence win), or compete for the lead.* For many, the uncontrollable desire to see a competitor buried by your wave of athletic superiority takes control. Call it competitive, or "dumb ass follow your buddy" impulse. We can't deny it. It's standard equipment on most humans. The need to compete, whether it is with yourself and a tricky section of trail, your weekend ride partners, or a bunch of hard core racers, is all equally a part of what makes mountain biking such an awesome sport. To deny your need to compete is to deny your ancestry.

For many in our society, simply getting back into the woods and beating their chest around a campfire is sufficient to re-aquaint themselves with what it is to be human. Other men and women of all ages need to spoon a healthy dose of giggly mountain biking fun into the mixture, to satisfy the personal needs that everyday life fails to deliver. Whether you compete with others, yourself, or the challenges of rugged terrain, mountain biking can fill your soul in a satisfying manner that doesn't involve trampling on other people, society, or the environment.

Today, those who participate in the sport are becoming obsessed with competition and racing. Mountain bike competition is a very popular recreational activity for riders of all ages and abilities. Weekend races have grown from their humble beginnings into big time events. Those who view the obsession with mountain biking as a purely competitive expression are missing the point of how awesome it is just to ride and explore in the backcountry. Whatever your views, no one is likely to deny that racing a mountain bike is extremely challenging. The feeling you get from competing with others, and the race course, is a process of self discovery. If you don't believe it try a race. If you don't go through a complete spectrum of feelings and emotions before, during, and after a race, you should check to see if you still have a pulse.

If you are the type of person that digs in so hard on race day that walking afterwards is a challenge, chances are that you're a competitive person off the bike as well. On the other hand, if you find talking to other racers as fun as the race itself, then competing may not be the most important reason you ride a bike. Most people are equipped with a mixture of both traits. Going to a race, or on a long epic ride with good company, gives the mountain biker an outlet

MOUNTAIN BIKING
BRITISH COLUMBIA
The Trail Guide

for all of these experiences. Whether it's a big cross country race, or a five hour epic in the alpine, riding becomes an avenue to express many of our essential human qualities.

I'd be a liar if I didn't mention the simple fact that riding with others can actually be a deterent to having fun. Riding partners who whine too much, are always late, and never have any food or tools can make riding alone a pure joy. Riding can be a great outlet for anti-social tendancies. However, riding alone can be dangerous if your common sense is left at home. Nevertheless, I've been on too many rides where my power bars and spare tubes instantly velcroed to someone elses mouth, or onto their bike. It makes riding solo with my dog seems like a stress free dream. Talk to me after a incident-riddled group ride and I'll say dogs are my personal favorite riding partners.

I often think the mountain bike was invented solely to rescue dogs from lame evening walks on a leash and get them ripping freely through the backcountry like they are meant to do. The mountain bike, a good trail, and your best four legged friend are a perfect combination. In many ways dogs are more fun to ride with than humans. They never complain, don't get flats, never slow down, safely drink nasty sludge water, and love to mix it up for the lead on a single track. And best of all they're never late, and are willing to listen to all of the w h i n i n g that re-sulted in you riding solo in the first place.

> *"The mountain bike, a good trail, and your best four legged friend are a perfect combination."*

Dogs who mountain bike have a loyalty to their masters that is the stuff of Disney movies. Riding with your pooch brings you back to an animal-like state; where human and dog are a team on a mission, the dog leading the way swiftly through the woods with a mysterious sense of purpose. And hey, what dog would chew a hole in the chamois of your biking shorts after a fast run in the woods?

Nevertheless, humans are social animals. No matter how great ripping up a trail with your dog is, or how smart he/she may be, they can't talk to you. So riding with others is neccessary to have more fun and keep you from going crazy. There are a few riders you'll love to compete with, and others that will be more social than competitive. With some riding partners the social aspect of the ride makes you forget about the need to compete. What I look for is a balance between the social ride and the competitive ride. Quite honestly, I view this difference as a healthy example of diversity within the sport. There is both a need to ride, and a need to compete. Whatever your opinion and views on riding, almost anyone can challenge themselves like never before by riding with friends or at a race. Either way, the aprés-ride glow, and tales of struggling with life and death on the trail can fill the gap until the next ride or race. At best, a new mountain biker is born whose otherwise soul-less life fills with new friends, new challenges, and a new toy at which to throw scarce disposable income. At worst, well, if you're at least riding and healthy, how bad can it be . . .

Competition

The types of racing and competing today are quite varied. The most popular form of mountain bike racing is the cross country race. It is a mass start event that can have upwards of 100 riders competing in the same category. The course usually consists of a good combination of climbing and descending on terrain that provides a safe and chal- lenging circuit for riders to navigate. The race often is made up of several course laps depend-

> *"At best, a new mountain biker is born whose otherwise soul-less life fills with new friends, new challenges, and a new toy at which to throw scarce disposable income."*

ing on the specific category. A cross country race takes somewhere between 1-3 hours to complete. Categories are divided according to age, gender, and experience/ability. A combination of fitness and bike skills are needed to be successful in cross country.

The downhill race is gaining in popularity and is responsible for many of the recent changes in equipment. Downhillers race against the clock, leaving the start on set intervals similar to alpine ski racing. Downhillers ride on fully suspended bikes and wear safety gear similar to motorcycle racers. The downhill is a very gnarly event and the best riders combine bike handling skills with a touch of daring craziness.

The dual slalom takes its cues from the alpine skiing event but is similar to the downhill. In the Dual slalom, riders negotiate the course in a head to head format. Riders opt for bikes and equipment that emphasize maneuverability, quick acceleration, and traction. The dual slalom is always a crowd pleaser and a fun way to test your bike turning skills.

Observed trials riders are capable of amazing feats of strength and balance doing on a bike what appears to be impossible. To a good trials rider, hopping up on a picnic table is like climbing on a bar stool for the rest of us. The observed trials event is possibly the truest test of bike skills and balance. Riders must negotiate an obstacle course involving natural and human-made hazards. Each time a rider dabs, or puts a foot down, a deduction is made from the riders score. The rider with the highest score wins.

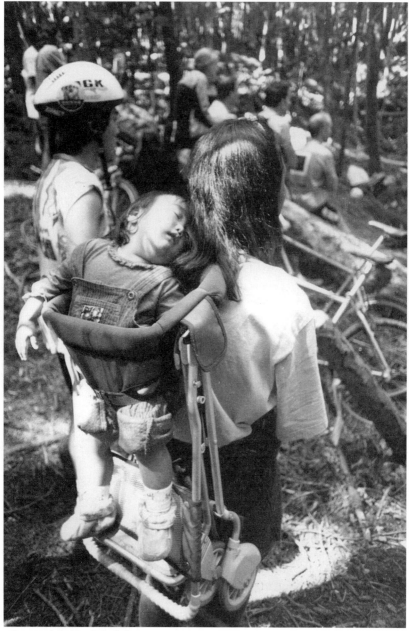

Photograph by Blair Polischuk

MOUNTAIN BIKING
BRITISH COLUMBIA
The Trail Guide

Getting Off . . . The Pavement

by Darrin Polischuk

From old, chipped pavement on country roads to fresh new blacktop, highways are spreading out over the countryside to make our hurried lives easier. But what is the real purpose of pavement? It is a twisted symbol of progress to pave our world. Governments boast of new freeways, additional lanes, and resurfaced bridges as an investment in our collective economic future. Pavement does increase the speed and comfort with which we zoom all over the place, going faster then ever, in faster cars, getting more speeding tickets. But what is the real purpose of this black stuff so worshipped by politicians and car enthusiasts? Sure it is part of the state's "infrastructure", and the movement of goods and people is done more efficiently. But what is the REAL purpose of the black stuff? The real purpose of pavement is to transport people away from the urban world onto the old roads and trails that lead to the places where we can feel human again. When the pavement ends the trails begin, and they lead us into the lakes, rivers, and valleys of B.C.

Introduction

MOUNTAIN BIKING
BRITISH COLUMBIA
The Trail Guide

Some people will argue that the pavement is a recreational resource in itself. Road cyclists, skateboarders, rollerbladers, and street hockey players worship the smooth stuff like a mountain biker worships dirt. Because without pavement their sports are dead. The pavement sports are fun things to do, but something is always missing when you hang out on pavement too long. I was

never sure what it was until I compared sitting down for a while on pavement to the same experience on dirt. When I sat for prolonged periods of time on pavement, I was always on edge waiting for something to happen, usually something bad. One time, somebody gave me money just for sitting . . must have looked a little dirty. That same day I sat down on a trail. I was totally relaxed, didn't have urban terror-type thoughts, and managed to solve most of my problems (and a few of the world's as well). The soothing environment of sounds, smells, and sights, made me realize why we really ride bikes; just to get off the pavement.

Next time you are out on a ride, pick a spot, maybe one with a view, or by a river, and stop for a while. Relax, breathe in deeply, talk, and use all your senses to soak up the world around you. Pick up a plant book, or a rock book, and learn more about the world that buzzes by us. As you sit and toss a few stones into the water you will come to realize that pavement is not progress, but simply a means to get us more quickly to the places we really cherish.

MOUNTAIN BIKING
BRITISH COLUMBIA
The Trail Guide

Thank You

by Darrin Polischuk

You must be wondering how so much mountain biking trail information has been gathered and slammed into these pages for your riding and reading enjoyment. Trail information is out there for all to gather. Simply call up the folks who know, go riding, and try to make sense out of the ride afterwards. Things like a topographical map, a cycle computer, and waterproof paper and pencil help. As does a photographic memory for trails. This is how it all happened. Over the course of a summer I was able to ride all over the province. B.C. is a vast area, and I soon realized that one person cannot ride all the trails in a year. So I called on the keen mountain bikers in communities around the province to send me some of their best trails to be published.

"So I called on the keen mountain bikers in communities around the province to send me some of their best trails to be published."

Everyone I asked complied. I basically took the information and worked it into a format you can use. Often the words are not mine alone but a cooperative effort of those who supplied the trail info and my editing. It is these folks, who toured me around and answered my pesky faxes asking for trail information, who are the actual story behind this book. Consequently, I need to thank a bunch of very cool people, many of whom I ride with, and many others I know simply through phone and fax encounters.

Steve Caulker and David Sudbury gave me a crash course on the Victoria mountain biking scene. Despite being the most tardy of my tour guides, Steve and David had an enthusiastic and visionary approach to mountain biking in Victoria and some of the best bagels I have ever eaten. Look for some good things to happen in the Sooke area as these guys work to ensure mountain bikers will have a place to ride in Victoria after cement and mini-vans take over what is left of the local terrain. Wayne Clayton also needs to be thanked. He provided information on the as yet un-named Hartland area mountain biking park. It is through the tireless efforts of people like Wayne and other SIMBS members that Victoria will remain the hotbed of mountain biking that it currently is.

Thanks to Tom Ward and Sean Ruszyka who pointed me in the right direction in the Burnt Bridge area. The Nanaimo area was gracefully shown to me by Andrew Tuck, owner of Bastion Cycles. Andrew truly believes in the need for everyone to ride a bike, whether to work, or on the trail. His work with The Guardians Of The Abyss Trail Society will ensure that Nanaimo will have a gnarl-ass ride for future generations to bleed on. All the best to your young

MOUNTAIN BIKING
BRITISH COLUMBIA
The Trail Guide

family and good luck on the publishing of your Nanaimo area bike guide. In Parksville Derek Koel and Kebble Sheaff are the trail gurus who have worked hard to create a mountain bike park and a thriving local scene. Thanks for the maps and info and watch out for those RVs while commuting out to the trails! Further up-Island lies the ferry link to Hornby. Tig, Fro, and the crew of trail grommets live the good life. Thanks for showing me the trails and putting on the funkiest of all events. Comox / Courtney has some of the best mountain biking folks in the province. Thanks to James and Les at Blacks Cycle, and watch out for that little trials grommet who schooled me on the hyper-technical trails along the Puntledge River! The Island's final thanks goes to Dan Clement at The Urban Lemming for all the work in getting the message out that Campbell River has plenty of rippin' trails.

Powell River trail information is brought to you via the regional forest service with a bit of help from the boys at Taws Cycle. The riding areas around Sechelt and Gibsons are lush and plentiful. Thanks to Dean Wolansky and your folks for the hospitality and shellfish feast. While exploring Roberts Creek, Glen Illingworth popped out of nowhere with the charm of a perfect tour guide. His knowledge of the local single track, and his infectious enthusiasm for riding is what the sport is all about. The maps of this area are a collection of the Sunshine Coast's local knowledge gathered and organized by Steven Senechal. The sharing of all the local secrets will bring smiles to riders for years.

The Sea to Sky Corridor is such an immense riding area that it was tough to select rides to highlight. Fortunately, Peter Colapinto, who owns The Whistler Bike Company, was able to select the choice rides from the towns of Squamish, Whistler, and Pemberton. Peter possibly has more local trail knowledge in his brain then any other rider in the valley. I'm sure many locals have ridden more trails than Peter, but he is able to remember them. Thanks Peter!

The Lower Mainland was my home for years of mountain biking, bruised knees, and University. Despite countless days on the North Shore I am still amazed at the exploits of the local single track riders. Thanks to Chaz Romalis from The Deep Cove Bike Shop for pointing me toward some of Seymour's more hidden trails. Another North Shore guru is Ross Kirkwood who was glad to show me the way to his trails. Like a proud owner of a prized possession, Ross mapped many of the trails on Fromme, Grouse Mountain, and Cypress. Much of the good solid trails on the North Shore were built with the care and expertise of Ross and a host of other cool riders. If you have been riding any of these trails and have yet to lift a finger to help out, shame on you! Thanks to Julius Wohlgemuth for always being keen to explore, having a wide selection of Power Bars, and not being faster than me!

MOUNTAIN BIKING
BRITISH COLUMBIA
The Trail Guide

Tomas Vrba is, or should be, a mountain biking legend. His idea of a ride is off the scale in terms of length and difficulty. I was warned not to go riding with Thomas, and when he suggested a 4 am. start time, to drive into nowhere and go exploring a 90 km route, I knew this guy was on his own planet. Thanks to Thomas for help with the Eagle Ridge and Burke Mountain maps.

The place that started my mountain biking obsession is Burnaby Mountain. David Eades and the members of the Burnaby Mountain Biking Club provided me with the trail map. Club members have kept many of the popular routes in great shape and they now ride better than they did 7 years ago (or maybe I finally improved my skills enough to ride those trails properly). I hope the confusing land access questions get resolved and the area is open to all trail users forever.

My ride partners for Eagle Ridge were Joan Joans and Laurie Schmidt. 'Shmidtbomb' demonstrates how to balance life and the bike better then anyone I know. Sure he is a slow rider, but he has more fun then a lot of people because of the scarcity of good riding time. I will always ride with Schmidt; he is never late, and is the only rider I know who thinks I am fast, Thanks Laurie. Joan Joans is by far the coolest mountain biking mama on this planet. After riding with her I will no longer think women can't ride the technical stuff. Joan rips down the rough, gnarl-factor with the best of the boys. Thanks for the ride in your Coquitlam backyard and keep spreading the word, you're a true missionary. Take a camp from this girl and learn how to ride with style.

Some of the crew from Crankin' Carvin' got me lost on Burke, but despite spending the night, and gnawing on my own leg for food, I managed to survive. The Blue Mountain exploring days were wet and my trusty foul weather ride partner (see tire vest / skateboard park pictures) 'Carvin' Marvin Penner was the only one to answer the call for another ride. You rip buddy! Marvin also accompanied me on the most of the Mission area rides and I think it rained every day we rode together all year. Thanks to Bruce Wenting for stopping to talk long enough to hear about my asking for trail info in Mission. Dave Darby, a local school teacher in the Mission area, dialed me up for a few of the rides near his home. We owe a thanks to Dave and others for the Bear Mountain Loop in Mission.

Most of the Okanagan rides were previously mapped in my Okanagan Mountain Biking Trail Guide. Thanks to Rod Heater for digging in and mapping the Kelowna area with more accuracy than I could ever hope for. I think Rod gets younger every time I see him. It must be the spanky red convertible! Exploring

MOUNTAIN BIKING
BRITISH COLUMBIA
The Trail Guide

the Salmon Arm rides was done by using a copy of the local Kamloops / Shuswap Mountain Bike Guide. The enigmatic mountain man Chris DeYong made the days fun as only he can, " ahh man I left my front wheel in the parking lot at home". Despite the comedy of errors, our endo contest down Rubberhead will never be forgotten. I think he won!

Matt Pinto brought me from sea level up to the 6000 ft. mark for the Keystone Basin Trail near Revelstoke, demonstrating the positive and negative effects of altitude. He lives at Silver Star while I just got back from Vancouver Island. It was one of the best rides of the year, and a below average pizza never tasted so good. Despite some cajoling, Matt also helped out with the mapping of Grand Forks, Christina Lake and Castlegar. I think it was Charles Bukowski who said, "the only interesting people in the world are the crazy ones", and this archetypal Grand Forks boy demonstrates this every time he rides or skis. Be sure to check out Matt's Silver Star Mountain Bike Camps, and learn the Zen approach to mountain biking from a guy who floats over the trails like only a few know how.

In Golden, a thanks to Ian Millroy for being so thorough with the maps and descriptions of the West Bench trails and for allowing my dog 'Bean' to coil one on his shop floor. The omni-talented Rich Marshall filled me in on a ride near Field B.C. Thanks for the info and the good snowboarding in 95; the board swap stoked me up for the rest of the year, thanks! In Panorama, Nancy Copping assisted me with the trail info I needed. As I went to ride up The Paradise Mine Trail about 3 ft. of snow in early November halted my progress. The memories of the beautiful valley remain despite the early snow and lack of open trails. The Cranbrook area was provided to us from David Clague and the Kootenay Freewheelers. Fernie infor-

"It was one of the best rides of the year, and a below average pizza never tasted so good."

mation was provided From Ralph Simpson at The Ski Base. If you get lost in Fernie blame him! Williams Lake info came from Mark Savard and Jason Poddison at Red Shreds. Thanks for letting everyone know that the trails and people all over B.C. share the same stoke about riding. The Prince George folks seem like the most organized club in the province. Along with the crucial ride information I also received a club handbook. Thanks for showing the way on how big a club can get. Sounds like a fun place to be during the cycling season. But what do you do in January? The Smithers area provided me with plenty of amazing sounding rides. You can't deny the beauty of the north, so why not head up into the heart of B.C. instead of going south this summer, and check into some serious wilderness riding. Special thanks to Doug Herchmer and Glenn Farenholtz for showing interest in the project.

MOUNTAIN BIKING
BRITISH COLUMBIA
The Trail Guide

Mapping of the Nelson was done with the gracious assistance of Bjorn Enga of Radical Multi Media and Marketing, publishers of The West Kootenay Mountain Bike Guide, The Kamloops Shuswap Mountain Bike Guide and a new Sea to Sky Country Bike Guide. In Rossland I was able to hook up with Paul Aubry. Paul runs Chicos Bike Shack and is so stoked about the riding in his home town I think he is vibrating while I talk to him on the phone. Thanks to Paul for helping me out with such short notice. Thanks to B.C. Tel for sending me fat phone bills each month. John Wakefield, Cycling B.C., and the B.C. Off Road Council. who helped get the ball rolling on this project. Without their help I would have been hunted down by the phone cops for not paying my bills. Thanks to the people at Olympia Cycle and Ski in Vernon for not laughing at me while I fumble with my bike, and for answering all my 'dumb guy' computer questions. Also all the shop owners who helped me keep together my ailing bike in one piece through a gruelling year, you are all saviours. Thanks to Cycletech for finally getting me new forks after I blew my 5th Judy cartridge. Thanks to the guys at Mountain and Beach Bikes for hammering on my stupid aftermarket ultra fancy wheel. It is also nice to see you are putting lamination to it's proper use! Powerbar supplied a bit of fuel for the job. I like the mocha flavor, while the bean dog digs banana.

Technical support from my editor and personal saviour Brian Armstrong made this book possible. He took on the daunting challenge of making sense out of all this jumbled information and I think it worked. He is also responsible for elevating my writing skills beyond the eighth grade level. Thanks to David Silversides and the whole family for their support and the crucial field supplies. Blair and Cathy, thanks for the sushi and great photos. Thanks to Allester Bradbury for listening to my cartoon concepts and bringing them to life. The maps were drawn by Liz and Dean of Extreme Mountain Biking People. They transformed my scribbles into a workable map. Their efforts are worthy of a pat on the back next time you see these people at a local event.

I thank my little dog 'Bean' for ripping up the trail everyday and not getting a flat. And finally I have to thank those companies that advertised in this book. Each of these companies realized that trail information is what people want. Their support of this book means they support recreational mountain biking. Keep this in mind next time you go to the bike store! The people involved in mountain biking in British Columbia are the best, and you all made this large cooperative project a reality. If I forgot anyone, and I know I did, I thank you too.

MOUNTAIN BIKING
BRITISH COLUMBIA
The Trail Guide

The EMP Society

Mission: To promote active, healthy lifestyles through mountain biking and to preserve, restore, and develop areas to ride mountain bikes.

EMP was incorporated as a non profit society early in 1992 by Dean McKay and Liz Earle to inject some positive promotion for mountain biking into the B.C. media and to help change the minds of anti mountain bike recreationalists. Then, mountain biking was still a fad with negative repercussions to trails and other trail users. The only places one was legally allowed to ride around Vancouver was Pacific Spirit Park, the Old Buck Trail on Mount Seymour, and the BLT road in Cypress Park. At the same time, off-road events were gaining popularity and the number of riders throughout the city was burgeoning. A crisis was immanent between land managers and off-road riders. EMP was formed to meet this challenge and be the voice for mountain bikers in the Lower Mainland.

Since 1992, EMP and it's core of volunteers have developed a Lower Mainland series of mountain biking events, and in the process helped open up Hemlock resort, Vanner Park, Cypress Park, Grouse Mountain[still in progress] , Everett Crowley Park, and Belcarra to bikes. EMP has taken on the task of meeting land managers, joining advisory committees, writing letters, and actually putting shovels to the trails to get access for mountain bikers in the Lower Mainland. They also run a series of fun school age events that are getting province wide support. Having started educational clinics for mountain biking in 1994, an affiliated company, The West Coast School of Mountain Biking, will carry on the successful operation started by EMP. If it's mountain biking oriented around Vancouver EMP. is involved or supportive!

A volunteer driven [obsessed?] organization, EMP has grown to 1100 members through general membership and participation in EMP events. Staffed by volunteer Liz Earle and headed by President Dean McKay, we now have a board of directors of five people, with a growing list of volunteers to assist us in all our endeavors. Though funding is in short supply, we accomplish a great deal for all mountain bikers through determination, partnerships, and an obvious love of the sport.

Plans for 1997 include some regular tours of some of the best trails in this book. Although no details are available yet, mountain bike parks in Coquitlam and North Vancouver are in the works, as is the ongoing recruitment of corporate sponsors to keep putting the newsletters out. For membership info call EMP at [604] 327-2547 in Vancouver.

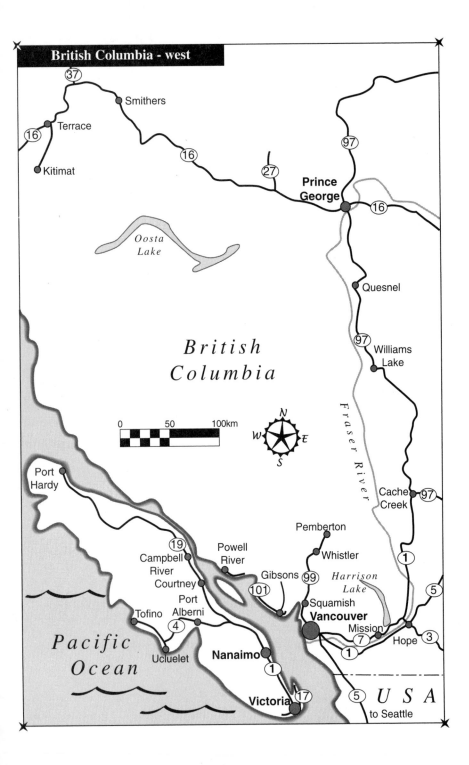

British Columbia - east

MOUNTAIN BIKING
BRITISH COLUMBIA
The Trail Guide

Vancouver Island British Columbia

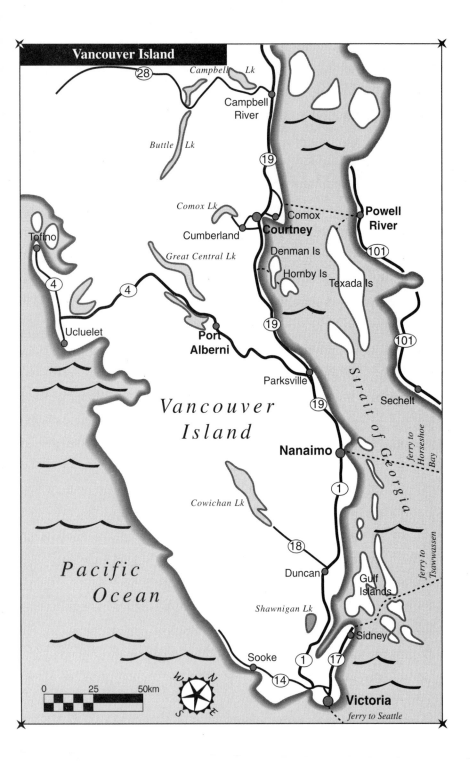

Vancouver Island

MOUNTAIN BIKING
BRITISH COLUMBIA
The Trail Guide

Victoria

Victoria

Millstream Highlands

The Highlands are located about 2 km off Highway #1 up Millstream Rd. Park on the roadside under the powerlines, and go around the gate on your left into this single track area. The Highlands offer a smorgasbord of mountain biking with double track climbs that tease you with single tracks, which all seem to reconnect back to a double track climb. The labyrinth of single tracks really defies mapping. Following a map in this area would detract from the ride experience as there are simply too many trails to explore. While there are trails that lead you away from the main powerline road, the majority of single tracks loop back where you can push the restart button and go again.

Novice and intermediate riders will want to ride to the top where the trails are generally smoother and faster. To access the top, trails riders will want to ride up the main powerline road and veer left at the 'dirt mound'. The climb gets a little steeper here, and riders will want to veer left after crossing the powerline, and get onto the maze of top trails. Give yourself about 30 minutes to climb to the top. Exploring these moderate graded climbs will bring you to a view point on top of Skirt Mountain. If you find yourself on a descent away from the powerline, be aware that you will be climbing out before you get carried away. Most of the trails dropping southeast have climbs that connect with the powerline road.

The single tracks on the lower slopes are generally more difficult because of their northern exposure. These moist, more rooted trails, are quite technical with plenty of sidehills, tough obstacles, and steeper pitches. These trails provide a contrast with the open fast single tracks on the top. Weekly fun looney races have been held on the lower slopes of the Highlands. The suburbs are spreading out into this area soon, so ride these trails before they become the paved home of the mini-van people.

Millstream Highlands (Map p.76)

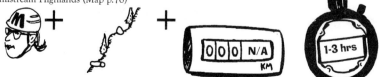

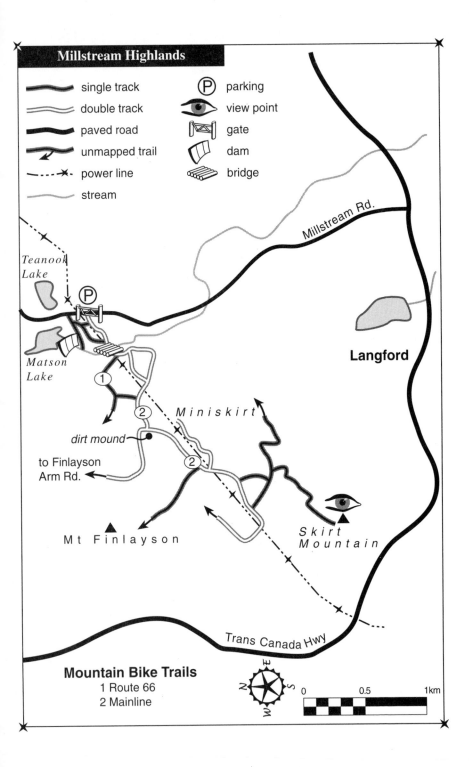

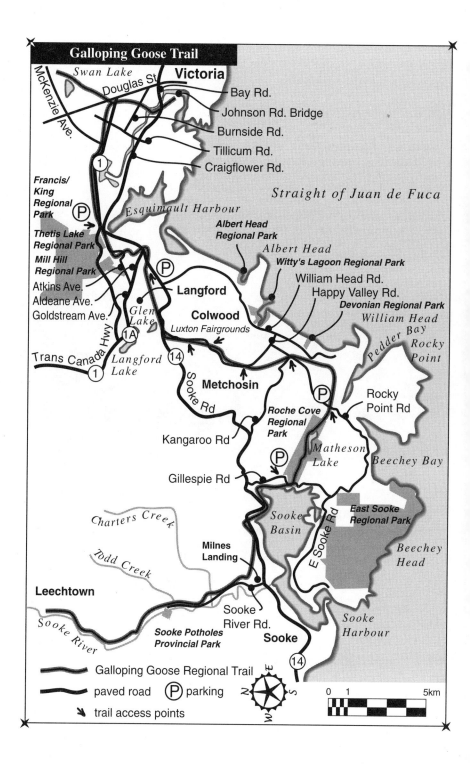

Galloping Goose Trail

Swan Lake

Douglas St

Victoria

Bay Rd.

Johnson Rd. Bridge

Burnside Rd.

Tillicum Rd.

Craigflower Rd.

McKenzie Ave.

Straight of Juan de Fuca

Francis/ King Regional Park

Esquimault Harbour

Albert Head Regional Park

Thetis Lake Regional Park

Mill Hill Regional Park

Albert Head

Witty's Lagoon Regional Park

Atkins Ave.

William Head Rd.

Aldeane Ave.

Happy Valley Rd.

Goldstream Ave.

Glen Lake

Langford

Colwood

Luxton Fairgrounds

Devonian Regional Park

William Head Bay

Rocky Point

Langford Lake

Trans Canada Hwy

Metchosin

Sooke Rd

Pedder Bay

Rocky Point Rd

Roche Cove Regional Park

Matheson Lake

Beechey Bay

Kangaroo Rd

Gillespie Rd

Charters Creek

Sooke Basin

E Sooke Rd

East Sooke Regional Park

Beechey Head

Todd Creek

Milnes Landing

Leechtown

Sooke River Rd.

Sooke

Sooke River

Sooke Potholes Provincial Park

Sooke Harbour

Galloping Goose Regional Trail

paved road (P) parking

trail access points

0   1   5km

MOUNTAIN BIKING
BRITISH COLUMBIA
The Trail Guide

Victoria

Galloping Goose

The Galloping Goose is a multi-use trail that was erected in 1989, giving Victoria 60 km of friendly gravel paths to ride or hike on. The easy rail grade of the Goose is not what I consider mountain biking to be; but the length, history, and beauty of this trail makes it worthy to mention and map in a mountain biking book. Furthermore, all mountain bikers will enjoy riding it.

The Galloping Goose Railway owes its existence to the pursuit and extraction of Gold and Timber. The railway was built to connect the resource-rich Leechtown area with _____ Sooke and Victoria. The name came from *". . . all mountain bikers will enjoy riding it."* the image of a wobbly gas-powered rail car loaded with trees heading down to _____ Sooke. Today, the 'rails to trails' project, affectionately referred to as the Goose, takes people away from the buzz of the city into countryside that is in spots only meters away from the concrete of Greater Victoria. Do the whole ride, or explore sections as time permits.

Galloping Goose (Map p.77)

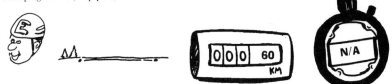

Victoria

Burnt Bridge

The remnants of the 'Burnt Bridge' no longer remain. In its place, a new bomb proof concrete and steel bridge (in a muted 'Judy' yellow) greets riders to the trails around the Koksilah River. The gate itself is a pain to get through but once you squeeze around this obstacle some of the best single track in B.C. is only a bit of sweat, *"The Burnt Bridge Race Classic* and a few thousand crank revolutions *Loop is the best sample of the* away. The Burnt Bridge Race Classic *rides in this area."* Loop is the best sample of the rides in this area. Up the road to Eagle Heights is an- other area that is filthy with trails too numerous and confusing to map. Just get up there and explore. To get to the Burnt Bridge area from Victoria go north on Highway #1 (Malahat Dr.) and turn left at Shawnigan Lake Rd (south end). Next, turn left at West Shawnigan Lake Rd. and left again on Renfrew Rd. Continue onto the gravel road and park at the 3 way intersection near the bridge.

(Continued on page 80)

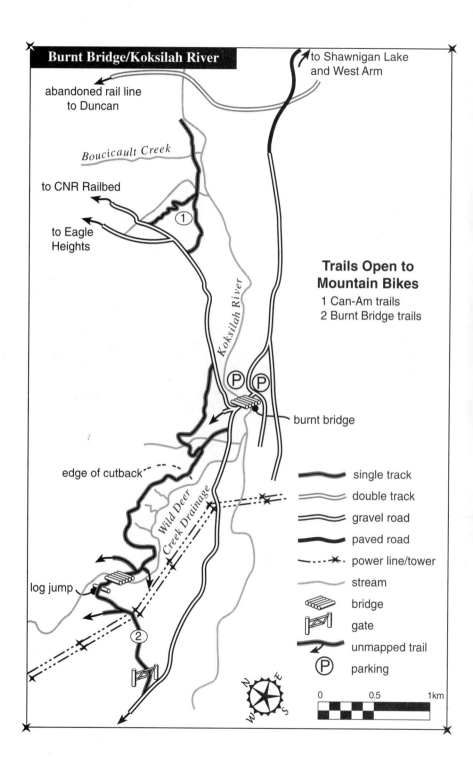

Burnt Bridge/Koksilah River

to Shawnigan Lake
and West Arm

abandoned rail line
to Duncan

Boucicault Creek

to CNR Railbed

to Eagle
Heights

①

Koksilah River

**Trails Open to
Mountain Bikes**
1 Can-Am trails
2 Burnt Bridge trails

Ⓟ Ⓟ

burnt bridge

edge of cutback

*Wild Deer
Creek Drainage*

log jump

②

	single track
	double track
	gravel road
	paved road
·····✳	power line/tower
	stream
	bridge
	gate
	unmapped trail
Ⓟ	parking

N E S W

0   0.5   1km

MOUNTAIN BIKING
BRITISH COLUMBIA
The Trail Guide

(Continued from page 78)

To access the Race Loop follow the wide road to your left after crossing the river. You'll go over a small bridge and ride under the powerlines before turning right about 4 km from the start. As you ride under the powerlines again, veer left and then take an immediate right onto a trail that narrows. Soon you will be screaming down ———————————————— and over a log jump onto a dismount at a *"Soon you will be screaming down* log bridge. Go right after the bridge and *and over a log jump onto a dis-* remember to veer left as you climb to *mount at a log bridge."* the top ridge of a cut-block. Follow ———————————————— this rim trail around the Wild Deer Creek drainage until a steep descent shoots you into the forest and onto nectar single track. Next, you reach a Y intersection. Both trails go back to the main road near the bridge. The left fork gives you more single track as it goes through a intermittent creek and back to the road. Simply, a perfect mountain biking loop.

Burnt Bridge (Map p.79)

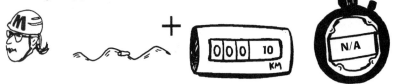

Victoria

Can-Am Trails

These trails are located below the main forest service road and skirt near the Koksilah River. Go right after the burnt bridge and veer right at the first fork, about 2.5 km from the start. Follow along this double track until you see the single track on the left. This trail plummets down. Go left at the intersection and down to a nice lookout of the Koksilah River. Return back on the same trail and take the left fork back to the main road.

Can-Am Trails (Map p.79)

MOUNTAIN BIKING
BRITISH COLUMBIA
The Trail Guide

Victoria

Hartland Surplus Lands / Mount Work Park

It may sound a bit like purgatory, but in reality it's a bit of mountain biking heaven. The 500 hectares of the Hartland Surplus Lands are located adjacent to the Capitol Regional District (C.R.D.) Landfill. A Dante inspired-vision of a smelly hell leaps to mind. But don't let the location next to a landfill keep you from riding this truly great single track area. This waste management facility is one of North America's most progressive, and has much less impact on the senses than you would expect. In the early 1990's the land was slated for de- *"A Dante inspired-vision of a* velopment of a larger garbage disposal facility. *smelly hell leaps to mind."* However, because of a progressive waste man- agement plan less land was needed, resulting in a 'surplus'. For mountain bikers it means that the many years of discussions and meetings held about mountain biking on these lands were successful. The result is a park designated as multi-use, with mountain biking as the primary activity. The actual name of the new mountain biking park is pending, any suggestions? As we went to print, the South Island Mountain Bike Society was in the beginning stages of taking responsibility for the park with a view to managing and maintaining the facility. Consider this a small victory for the legitimization of mountain biking in the C.R.D., and an example other communities can follow.

A 70 car parking lot, washroom facilities, and a bicycle wash down facility is now open. As you approach the parking area the landfill is in sight, but the active areas are currently hidden. It's only 20 minutes from Victoria, so the area makes for a nice short ride if you don't mind the climb up to the park. To access the park from the ferries, take the Royal Oak turn off, turn right on West Saanich Rd. and follow it along to the Hartland Ave. turnoff. To access the park *"It's only 20 minutes from Vic-* from up island, take the Helmecken turn off *toria, so the area makes for a* left to West Saanich Rd. where you go left, *nice short ride if you don't* then left again onto Hartland Ave. From *mind the climb up to the park."* downtown Victoria take Highway 17 to Royal Oak and then go right on West Saanich and left on Hartland, or take Quadra St. all the way to Hartland Ave. From the parking area you head directly into hours of single track, double track, and gravel road terrain. The most direct way in is along the gravel road right-of-way, which gives you a great chance to warm up if you go straight. A right turn has you gaining elevation quickly, and puts you into classic west coast mountain biking. The trails in this area are generally hard packed and in good condition because of the area's good drainage throughout the year.

(Continued on page 83)

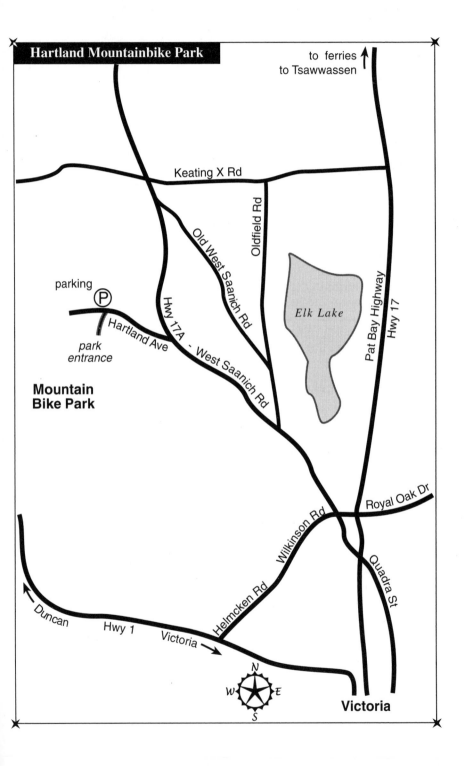

MOUNTAIN BIKING
BRITISH COLUMBIA
The Trail Guide

(Continued from page 81)

Trails range in technical difficulty from level, well packed trails suitable for less experienced cyclists, to radical drops, roots, rocks, and delightful "life-flashing-before-your-eyes" descents. The area does not have any hour long grinds, but many steep short climbs with names like 'puke hill' will challenge all climbers. The area was logged at one time, but is now covered with a thick second growth and numerous groves of magical, orange skinned Arbutus trees. There are a number of great views in the park, and on a clear day the snow capped peaks of the Olympic Mountains are visible.

The mountain bike park would not have matured into what you see today without the efforts of the South Island Mountain Bike Society, members of the community, and C.R.D. Parks. Because this area is in such close proximity to Victoria, whether you want a four hour hammerfest, or a family outing, , it has it all. Plan a return visit, because after you've ridden these marvelous trails, once is never enough.

Nanaimo

Introduction

Nanaimo is located on the protected eastern shores of Vancouver Island and proudly boasts the "mildest and sunniest climate in Canada". The city can also boast about it's mountain biking, as riders from all over the province come to try their hand on the Ultimate Abyss Trail and other rides, all within a short ride or drive from the city. Be sure and check out Andrew Tuck's, 100 Mountain Bike Trails from Nanaimo to Parksville for a comprehensive look at the middle Vancouver Island trails.

Nanaimo
The Ultimate Abyss

The Ultimate Abyss is the most famous trail on Vancouver Island. It was named in 1989 by a couple of local hikers after it's most distinguishing feature, a large crack in one of the hillsides. Unfortunately the Abyss is a victim of it's own popularity. Because the trail is technically very difficult, riders too often

(Continued on page 85)

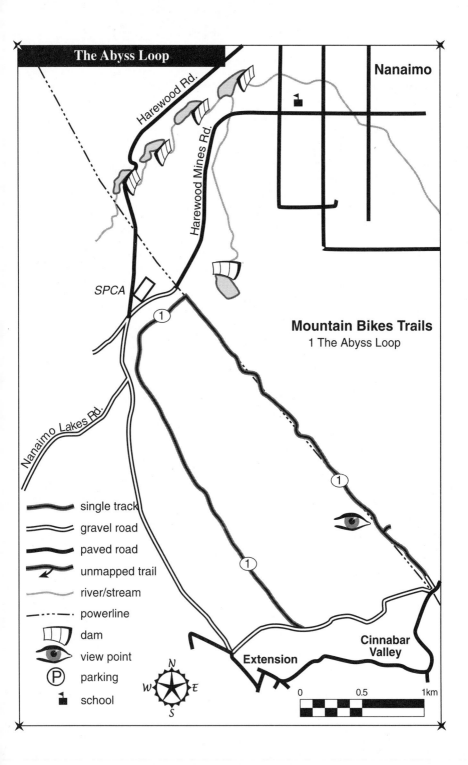

The Abyss Loop

Nanaimo

Harewood Rd.

Harewood Mines Rd.

SPCA

Nanaimo Lakes Rd.

Mountain Bikes Trails
1 The Abyss Loop

single track
gravel road
paved road
unmapped trail
river/stream
powerline
dam
view point
P parking
school

N
W — E
S

Extension

Cinnabar
Valley

0   0.5   1km

MOUNTAIN BIKING
BRITISH COLUMBIA
The Trail Guide

(Continued from page 83)

opt for an easier line resulting in widening of the trail in it's most gnarly sections. Please ride the correct line, or walk. Expect the basic menu of extra gnarly, up and down terrain on this ride. As yet the trail has not been cleaned. If you do it, drop by Bastion Cycle in Nanaimo and let Andrew Tuck know because he promised a beer to the first person to flash this very technical ride. Andrew has been ————————————————— involved on the formation of the *"Expect the basic menu of extra gnarly,* Guardians of the Abyss Trail Soci- *up and down terrain on this ride."* ety [GOATS] to enhance one of ————————————————— the islands more scarier rides. If you ride this trail contact GOATS and put somthing back into the trail to maintain your Trail Karma Point Balance Factor. This trail will give you a small scare, a big grin and plenty of riding tales.

To access the trail by car, begin at the intersection of Seventh St. and Howard Ave in Nanaimo. Drive up Harewood Mines Rd. past the overpass and park on the shoulder of the road under the powerlines. Mount up and ride southwest under the powelines for about 200 meters and take the trail to the right for another 200 meters. You should now be beside power pole #24 - 2, the entrance to the Abyss!

While riding the Abyss ignore the many side trails. Be aware that a side trail has been made at the 2.9 km mark just past the cabin. Ignore this diversion to the left and go straight. ————————————————— When you have done the final smooth de- *"When you have done the final* scent you will be at a waterline access road. *smooth descent you will be at a* Turn left (east) on this road and you will *waterline access road."* soon get to Extension Rd., Follow it north ————————————————— to the highway. From the highway north, turn left at the Southgate Mall. You are now on Sears Rd., which becomes Junction Ave., which turns into Twelfth St., and eventually Seventh St., and back to the start.

The Ultimate Abyss (Map p.84)

MOUNTAIN BIKING
BRITISH COLUMBIA
The Trail Guide

Nanaimo

Westwood Lake Loop

This is a great family type of ride on an easy groomed trail surface around Westwood lake. The trail is either flat or slightly rolling on bark mulch or dirt surfaces. The trails and bridges are in good condition and signs will point you around the lake. Keep your ears and eyes on alert for the beavers who inhabit this human-enhanced, urban lake. This is the best lake in the city to visit; don't forget your swimming suit and some snacks for after the ride.

This is a Regional District of Nanaimo maintained area with picnic facilities and washrooms. To access the trail, drive up Jingle Pot Rd. onto Westwood Rd.

Westwood Lake Loop (Map p.87)

Nanaimo

Westwood Ridge / Rocky Road / 3 Creeks Trail

This combination of trails makes for a great medium distance ride and gives the rider just the right mixture of all the stuff that makes mountain biking the amazing sport that it is. Expect some tough technical climbing and a few dismounts on the way up, but the long fast descent makes up for the tougher than usual climb.

Start this combination ride at the northwest tip of Westwood Lake. When the trail starts to go around the tip of the lake back toward Nanaimo you go right, ending up under the powerlines. Recently, hiking groups have put up signs with different trail names at the beginning of the technical climbing. Once the trail becomes more forgiving you will pass an old cabin site while riding *"Expect some tough technical climbing and a few dismounts on the way up . . ."* an old creek bed. Once past this area avoid your first major right and left. Continue to climb until you are along a fenceline. This is the National Department of Defence Land and shooting range, so obviously avoid it. At the sight of a shack go right and up Rocky

(Continued on page 88)

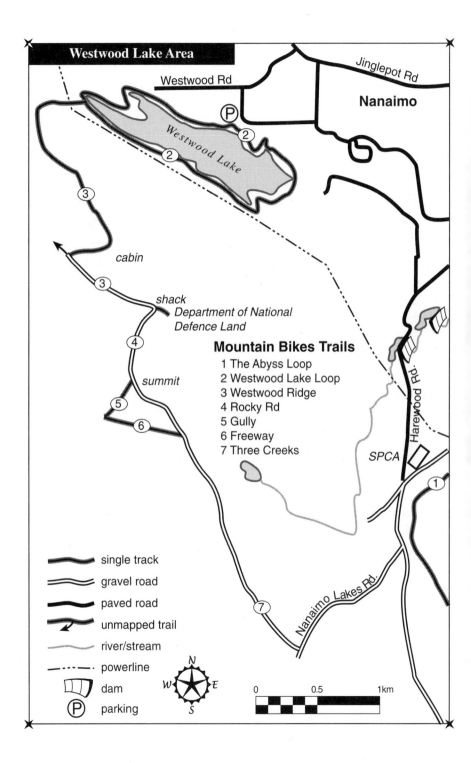

Westwood Lake Area

Jinglepot Rd

Westwood Rd

Nanaimo

P

②

Westwood Lake

②

③

cabin

③

shack
Department of National
Defence Land

④

Mountain Bikes Trails
1 The Abyss Loop
2 Westwood Lake Loop
3 Westwood Ridge
4 Rocky Rd
5 Gully
6 Freeway
7 Three Creeks

summit

⑤

⑥

SPCA

Harewood Rd.

①

single track
gravel road
paved road
unmapped trail
river/stream
powerline
dam
P parking

⑦

Nanaimo Lakes Rd.

N
W E
S

0   0.5   1km

MOUNTAIN BIKING
BRITISH COLUMBIA
The Trail Guide

(Continued from page 86)

Road. Continue past all possible lefts and rights. Once you crest the climb you are on the 3 Creeks Trail. This 3.5 km descent has some fast, well established lines through creeks that range in depth from dry in the summer to hub level wet in the spring and winter. Nanaimo Lakes Rd. to the powerlines will bring you back to Westwood Lake.

Westwood Ridge / Rocky Road / 3 Creeks Trail (Map p.87)

Parksville

The Trails	
The A.M.C. Top Bridge Mountain Bike Park	88
The Hammerfest Race Course	92

Introduction

The little seaside community of Parksville is home to a well established crew of mountain bikers who have worked to create a mountain bike park, and host Vancouver Islands biggest race of the 1996 season. Most people associate Parksville with retired people and tourists walking on the beaches. What many don't know is that the riding surrounding Parksville is typical island cool. Older logging roads link up single tracks that range from groomed and fast, to rocky, rooted, and difficult. While in town, drop into Arrowsmith Mtn. Cycle, which can be found by turning onto Shelly Rd, which turns into Stanford. The shop is located at 423 E. Stanford. Phone 248-5575.

Parksville

The A.M.C. Top Bridge Mountain Bike Park

The Arrowsmith Mountain Bike Club have done a tremendous job of creating an area designated for mountain biking. The Parksville area has many great rides outside the park, but many of them are confusing and usually require a guide to ensure a positive experience. The A.M.C. Top Bridge M.T.B. Park, on the other hand, offers up some great single track in an area that is easy to navigate (although going in circles is a distinct possibility). Before the A.M.C

(Continued on page 90)

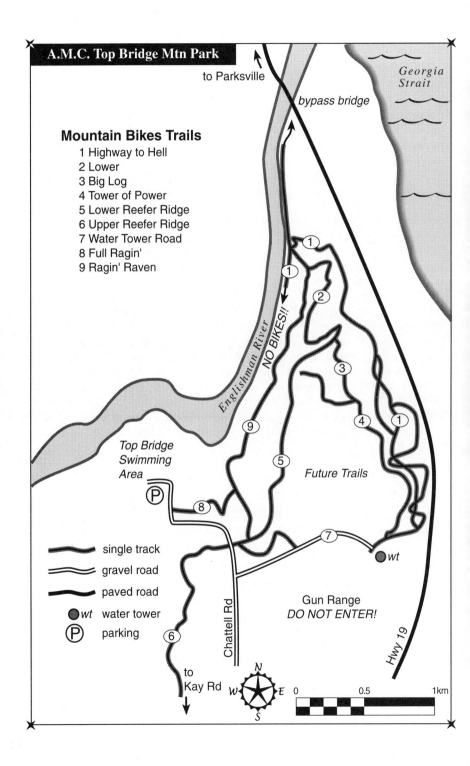

A.M.C. Top Bridge Mtn Park

to Parksville

Georgia Strait

bypass bridge

Mountain Bikes Trails
1 Highway to Hell
2 Lower
3 Big Log
4 Tower of Power
5 Lower Reefer Ridge
6 Upper Reefer Ridge
7 Water Tower Road
8 Full Ragin'
9 Ragin' Raven

Englishman River

NO BIKES!!

Top Bridge
Swimming
Area

Ⓟ

Future Trails

●wt

Gun Range
DO NOT ENTER!

single track
gravel road
paved road
●wt water tower
Ⓟ parking

Chattell Rd

Hwy 19

to Kay Rd

N
W E
S

0   0.5   1km

MOUNTAIN BIKING
BRITISH COLUMBIA
The Trail Guide

(Continued from page 88)

crew was given permission to develop the area, the only trails were Upper and Lower Reefer Ridge. Years of riding has smoothed out these trails, but fun rideable obstacles like rock faces, roots, logs and some loose, sketchy sections, keep these originals ————————————————— on everyone's 'must ride' list. Since re-   *"Since receiving official permission*   ceiving official per- mission to build   *to build trails, the area and scene*   trails, the area and scene has flourished   *has flourished with new rides, and*   with new rides, and even more keen rid-   *even more keen riders."*   ers. To access the park head to the ————————————————— south (Nanaimo bound) weigh scales and Kay Rd., then turn onto Chattell Rd., and follow it past the gun range to the park. All of the on and off ramps may be confusing, but a bit of common sense will see you through this concrete mess.

All of the trails are rideable in both directions except Full Ragin' and B -Trail. Keep this in mind when full-throttling down a hill. Most trails are narrow, and are bordered by trees, cliffs, and salal bush, but are all considered safe from killer-type exposure near cliffs. The area is bordered by private property, and many of the trails continue, but cannot be included on the map. Also, a gun range is located near the park, nuff said . . . The locals recommend jumping off the nose into the Englishman River to cool off after a hot day on the trails. Make sure you take the time out to checkout the First Nations rock carvings on the rock at the river. Just a little reminder about who originally owned the land beneath our tires.

The first trail built was the Ragin' Ravin which follows the ridge high above the Englishman River. Built in 1995, the trail is a nice rough contrast to the buffed up Reefer Trails, and gives those craving a more technical ride their needed fix. Check out the short, ————————————————— groomed switchbacks of Full Ragin'. The re-   *"Keep this in mind when*   claimed Tower of Power is all downhill to   *full-throttling down a hill."*   the river and is a popu- lar ride in both directions. The trail has nice sweeping turns on a smooth surface begging you to do a big mother broadslide turn at full speed. Put on some old work boots and flannel and go for your best Gary Fisher circa 1979 impersonation.

The Highway To Hell starts at the water tower and is mostly downhill, but does have a few short climbs. This trail was built in 1996 and will improve with time and traffic. There is a fun, double-bermed section that begs you to challenge riding partners to a head to head contest of stupidity and bike handling. As you ride along the cliff, the sight of the poor, soul-less masses sitting in their cars makes the day of riding even sweeter, because you're on a righteous trail riding, and they're on the road to nowhere down below. As you near the river be sure and avoid the Hell Trail. If you succumb to the temptation, you will soon discover the origins of the name, after the countless hiking sections turn the ride into something less than heavenly. Instead take Lower Reefer, then Ragin ' Raven, or the Tower Of Power back into the park.

Finally, the B-Trail, or Berm Trail, is a fast, short, but extremely fun descent. Look for a host of new trails in this portion of the park in 1996 and beyond. Be prepared to drop into a full blown dual slalom area complete with gates. The A.M.C. plans on hosting some fun evening races in the summer, so put on the bear trap pedals and go crazy!

The trail ratings apply to the entire park. Most trails are not physically super difficult because of the contained nature of the riding in the park, and the fact that many of the trails can be ridden in under an hour. Then again, if you ride in the park for 4 hours then it can be physically very difficult. Technically the most difficult trials are: Ragin' Raven, Full Ragin', B-Trail, and Highway To Hell. The remaining trails are all more moderate in their technical difficulty.

Photograph by Blair Polischuk

MOUNTAIN BIKING
BRITISH COLUMBIA
The Trail Guide

Parksville

The Hammerfest Race Course

The Hammerfest Race Course is located at Englishman River Falls Provincial Park near Parksville. The course can be found by taking the Alberni Highway inland, and following the signs toward the park. There are washrooms and campsites nearby with hot showers and flush toilets. All of these amenities make an aprés ride picnic a must. The riding takes place on MacMillan Bloedel land so the next time you curse the giant forest companies for their mandate, try to mitigate your nasty thoughts with memories of the great riding and the permission you had to ride on their property.

The course starts with a short climb onto the Burnt Ridge single track. Once you negotiate Big and Little Rock climbs, the course goes back to the main gravel road climb. Next, you jump onto Pete's Power Line Express, a steep climb that brings you to the first summit 4.2 km into the course. A left into Fern Gully awakens you from the view back to some exciting downhill. The Enchanted Forest leads you across the main road into the short and twisty Rotten Trail. Climbing up the power lines you are

"There are washrooms and campsites nearby with hot showers and flush toilets. All of these amenities make an aprés ride picnic a must."

actually on the downhill course. Continue to grunt upward on the last climb of the loop, which rises a leg-searing 140 meters in 1.3 km. Finally, the climbing ends, and some fresh single track called Extreme Dream escorts you down the mountain in fine island style. The single track hooks up with the faster main road of the downhill course. A left onto a new gravel road completes the loop.

The Hammerfest Race Course (Map p.93)

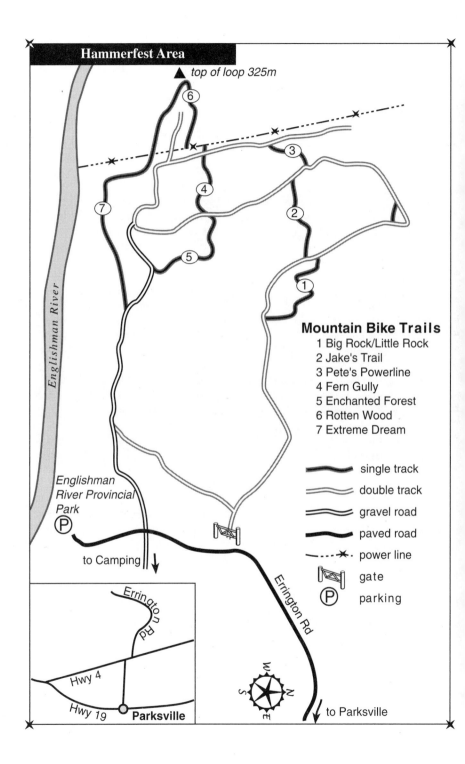

Hammerfest Area

▲ top of loop 325m

6

7

4

3

2

5

1

Mountain Bike Trails
1 Big Rock/Little Rock
2 Jake's Trail
3 Pete's Powerline
4 Fern Gully
5 Enchanted Forest
6 Rotten Wood
7 Extreme Dream

single track

double track

gravel road

paved road

power line

gate

Ⓟ parking

Englishman River

Englishman
River Provincial
Park

Ⓟ

to Camping

Errington Rd

Errington Rd

Hwy 4

Hwy 19 **Parksville**

to Parksville

MOUNTAIN BIKING
BRITISH COLUMBIA
The Trail Guide

Hornby Island

Introduction

The sound of screeching of brakes and laughing mountain bikers have been echoing down the slopes of Mt. Geoffry since the early eighties. Here, a small group of locals and summertime visitors have woven a bit of trail heaven into a relatively small area. In my opinion, the single track on Hornby is perfect. It is fast but still has the ———————————— technical challenges that keeps things fun *"In my opinion, the single* without the rider hav-ing to think about the *track on Hornby is perfect."* need for disability in-surance. The view ———————————— from the bluffs over-looking Denman Island and the Vancouver Island Mountains matches the single track for pure, made in B.C. perfection. It is possibly the nicest viewpoint I experienced while researching this book.

The riding on Hornby occurs on a combination of crown land, regional park land, and private property. This area has been logged twice and is littered with the remnants of logging which forms the backbone of the trail network. To date, the trails mapped are all open to mountain biking, but riders should be very respectful of the wishes of island residents because you are only a visitor to this little Shangri-La.

Hornby Island is also the home of B.C.'s coolest bike race weekend known as Bikefest. This event usually occurs on a July or August weekend, and combines a cross country race, downhill, trials competition, dual slalom, and a little evening social with ———————————— live music under the stars. The Bikefest *"The Bikefest captures the essence* captures the essence of the sport better *of the sport better than any other* than any other event, with the emphasis *event, with the emphasis placed* placed on having a fun weekend. *on having a fun weekend."* Hornby is also the home to TEAM ———————————— ORB, the province's best collection of trials riders. Visiting Hornby somehow gets you keen to practise the moves perfected by these zen, balance masters. The combination of great riding, partying, and camping amid a sea of fellow rubberheads while hanging out on the grooviest of the Gulf Islands makes for a very special summertime experience. Tell only your coolest friends about this one!

(Continued on page 96)

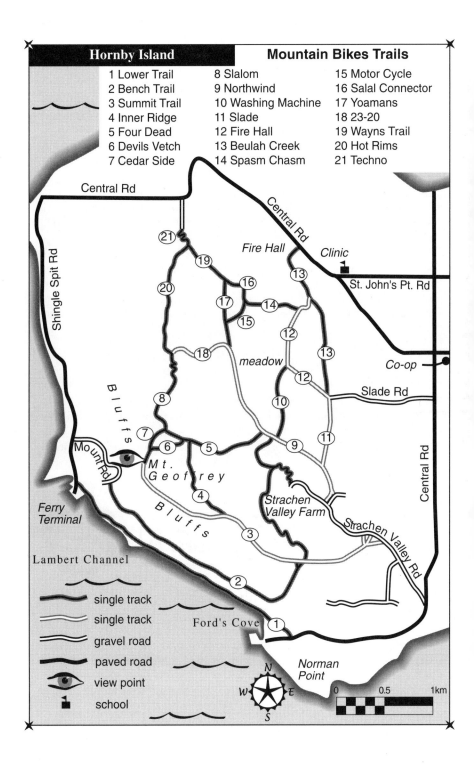

MOUNTAIN BIKING
BRITISH COLUMBIA
The Trail Guide

The main riding can be accessed from the Fire Hall, Slade Rd. Mount Rd, or Strachen Rd. The 2.9 km climb up the Summit Trail to the peak of Mt Geoffry, and the Northwind Trail are the key arteries to unlock the area's trails. Once you can recognize these two old double tracks, the key to exploring this area is in your hands. A good taste of mountain biking Hornby style can be had by climbing up the Summit Trail and taking the Devils Kitchen, or 4 Dead Aliens. Once onto Northwind, be sure and check out the trail which combines Test Tube, and Chris n' Brad's which leads directly to the famous bermed corners of No Horses. The map is much better to use than a detailed description, because the area is littered with trails, and following my directions would detract from the riding and exploring experience. Nevertheless, descriptions of two of the easier trails located on the steep bluffs of Hornby Island are provided.

> *"A good taste of mountain biking Hornby style can be had by climbing up the Summit Trail and taking the Devils Kitchen, or 4 Dead Aliens."*

Hornby Island

The Spit Trail

The Spit Trail connects Fords Cove with the ferry terminal. The trail can be ridden in either direction and is the fastest way across the island. The trail head is located on your right when you come off the ferry, or on your right while approaching Fords Cove off the paved road. The trail is essentially a beginner type of ride but has some tricky sections to keep you on your toes.

The Spit Trail (Map p.95)

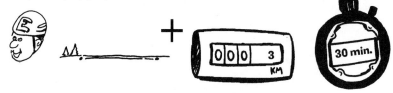

Hornby Island

The Bench Trail

The Bench Trail is an out and back trail that can be ridden in either direction. The easiest access for new comers to Hornby is off of Mount Rd, which is close to the ferry terminal. From the parking area at the trail head, a smooth single track awaits with views that seem to get better the further you ride. At one point the trail splits and rejoins about 500 meters later. Mountain bikers who

MOUNTAIN BIKING
BRITISH COLUMBIA
The Trail Guide

take the right fork MUST DISMOUNT as the trail is very exposed and dangerous, the views are better when you're off your bike anyway. There are other exposed sections of trail where riders who are unsure of their skills should dismount (to ensure continued good riding another day). The Bench Trail is a smooth well worn hiking trail that can be very busy during the summer so be on your best behavior; and don't ruin someone else's day by riding too fast or out of control.

From the Mount Rd starting point the trail will bring you to a three way intersection. At this point you can double back, or take the wider trail on your left which will inter- _____ sect with the Summit Trail. If you go straight *"Anyone caught poaching this* the trail will end up turning into Euston *trail will be publicly flogged by* Rd , then Marlyeboise and onto Strachen *all island residents on a busy* Valley Rd. The more obscure single track on *Saturday at the Co-op."* your left, back at the main intersection, is _____ the Ridge Run which is definitely closed to mountain bikers. Anyone caught poaching this trail will be publicly flogged by all island residents on a busy Saturday at the Co-op.

The Bench Trail (Map p.95)

one way

both ways

Vancouver Island British Columbia

MOUNTAIN BIKING
BRITISH COLUMBIA
The Trail Guide

Comox / Courtney

Introduction

The Courtney / Comox area is blessed with outstanding mountain biking for all levels of riders in a setting that combines the best that B.C. has to offer. Views of glaciers, ocean, lakes and rivers form the backdrop for most of the rides. The geography of the area goes from sea to sky on a shallow eastern facing slope. The Puntlage River and Comox Lake are frequent landmarks, as are old logging and coal mining roads that litter the area. There is also some good challenging single track and 'The Monster Mile Downhill' to be tackled up on Mount Washington. This venue hosts local mountain bike races, and as with most race courses, riders are treated to a nice combination of double track climbing and sweet single track descents. And for those with little or no desire to climb on a bike, the ski hill will operate the chairlift to ease the access to those long downhills. Check with the ski hill about hours of operation and costs. Be sure to drop by Blacks Cycle for all your needs, because these cool folks helped out with the mapping and descriptions of the trails.

Comox / Courtney

Seal Bay Nature Park

Seal Bay Nature Park is a 168 hectare forested area within a short drive or ride from Comox / Courtney. The trails are maintained under the supervision of the Comox-Strathcona Natural History Society. The Comox Indian Band called the area Xwee Xwhy Luq, which means "place of serenity and beauty". This area is a nature park and should be treated as such by mountain bikers. In other words, the trails are really meant for peaceful walks and not ripping fast mountain bike rides. So just take it easy and enjoy the flat single tracks. This is

(Continued on page 100)

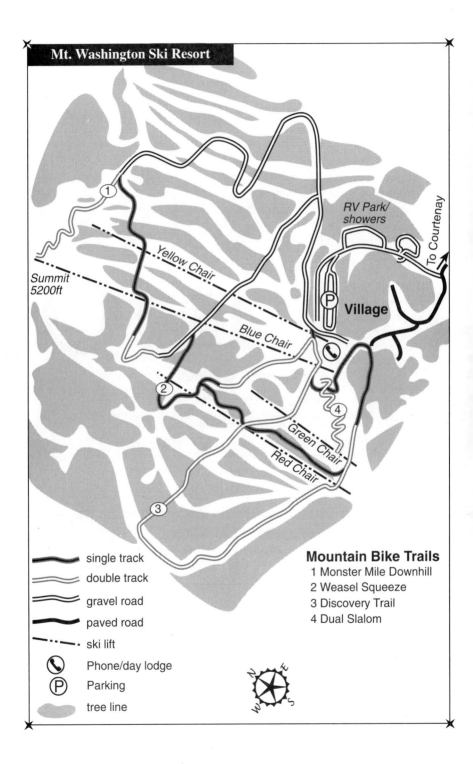

Mt. Washington Ski Resort

RV Park/ showers

To Courtenay

Yellow Chair

Summit 5200ft

Blue Chair

Village

Green Chair

Red Chair

single track
double track
gravel road
paved road
ski lift
Phone/day lodge
Parking
tree line

Mountain Bike Trails
1 Monster Mile Downhill
2 Weasel Squeeze
3 Discovery Trail
4 Dual Slalom

MOUNTAIN BIKING
BRITISH COLUMBIA
The Trail Guide

(Continued from page 98)

one of the best places I have ever ridden where a new mountain biker can enjoy single tracks, and progress in skill level and confidence in a beautiful, non-threatening environment.

To access the trails go left on Anderton Rd. off Comox Rd. Follow Anderton to Huband, right on Waveland, and left on Bates Rd. The trail head area has signs, parking, and toilets nearby. There are NO bikes allowed on the trails east of Bates Rd., so if you want to go down to the ocean walk your bikes, or lock them up and go on a short hike, it's worth it.

Seal Bay Nature Park (Map p.101)

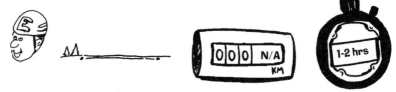

Comox / Courtney

B21 / Boston Main

B21 is a washed out logging road that winds down from Forbidden Plateau to Comox Lake Main. This is a rough ride with plenty of loose rock, and nasty challenges. A few shots at this ride, and the new forks you've been eyeing will become more critical than next month's rent. A good long ride is the climb up Forbidden Plateau logging road and down B21.

B21 / Boston Main (Map p.103)

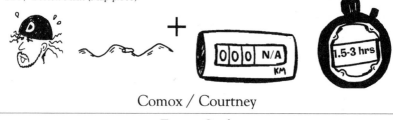

Comox / Courtney

Tomato Creek

Riders can expect 2 steep logging road climbs to the start of the trail along Comox Lake Main. Once on the trail, there are steep single track climbs of approximately 15 minutes. Expect to encounter slick rock faces and climbs with a technical, single track downhill.

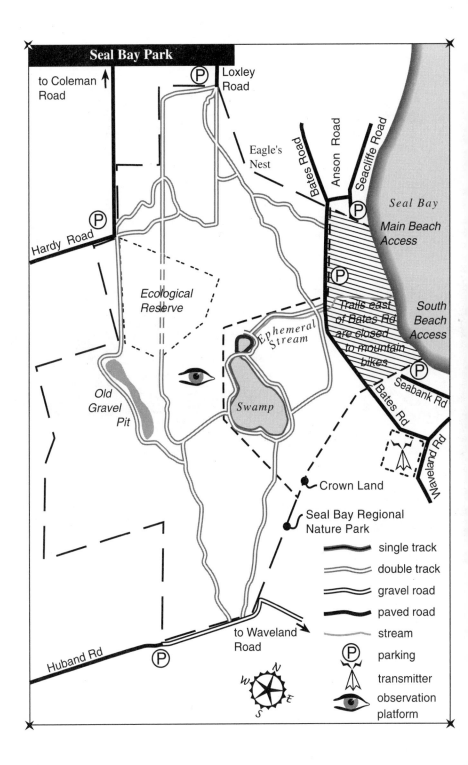

Seal Bay Park

to Coleman Road

Loxley Road

Eagle's Nest

Bates Road

Anson Road

Seacliffe Road

Seal Bay

Main Beach Access

Hardy Road

Ecological Reserve

Ephemeral Stream

Trails east of Bates Rd are closed to mountain bikes

South Beach Access

Old Gravel Pit

Swamp

Seabank Rd

Bates Rd

Waveland Rd

Crown Land

Seal Bay Regional Nature Park

Huband Rd

to Waveland Road

	single track
	double track
	gravel road
	paved road
	stream
ⓟ	parking
	transmitter
	observation platform

N W E S

MOUNTAIN BIKING
BRITISH COLUMBIA
The Trail Guide

Tomato Creek (Map p.103)

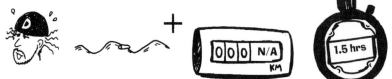

Comox / Courtney

Salamander

The trail begins at the Hydro Dam Park. There are 2 trail heads beside each other. Take the left hand trail, or the one with the outhouse. The other trail is Bears Bait. Salamander is one of the easier and shorter trails in this area, and a great place to bring new riders.

Salamander (Map p.103)

Comox / Courtney

Bears Bait

This trail can be accessed at two points; the Hydro Dam Park, or the Fish Hatchery. The trail follows Puntlage River and offers a little bit of everything in the recipe book of good riding. There is technical single track with logs o' plenty, and rolling terrain.

Bears Bait (Map p.103)

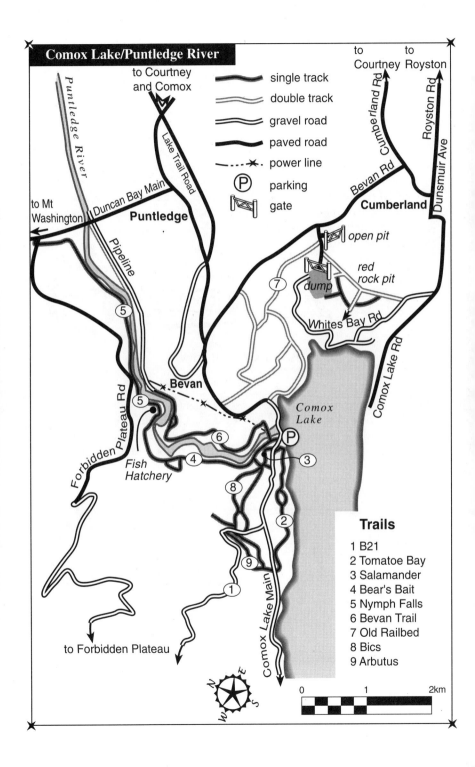

MOUNTAIN BIKING
BRITISH COLUMBIA
The Trail Guide

Comox / Courtney

Nymph Falls

The trail head is located along Duncan Bay Main at the yellow gate, on the left side of the road, just before the crossroads of Forbidden Plateau Rd. and Duncan Bay Main. This is a very technical single track that scoots along to a popular swimming hole. The trail continues until the fish hatchery where you can hook up with Bears Bait. Although the trail does not have any climbs, its overly-technical assault on your body makes the riding more tiring than you would expect from such a flat trail.

Nymph Falls (Map p.103)

Comox / Courtney

Bevan Trail

This is a point to point trail that is accessible from two points. One entrance is located on Comox Lake Main just before the Dam Park where the yellow gate is. The trail head is on the right side of the road before the bridge that crosses the edge of the lake. The other trailhead is located off Beaven Rd. and follows the river on the other side from Bears Bait. This trail is tight single track with logs and other technical challenges.

Bevan Trail (Map p.103)

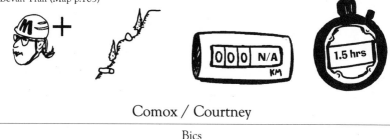

Comox / Courtney

Bics

Bics is located off of B21 and drops the rider from sub-alpine scrub to lower elevation rain forest on a short challenging trail. You can access this trail from the top or bottom of B21. There are some rock face drop-offs and other coastal trail delights.

MOUNTAIN BIKING
BRITISH COLUMBIA
The Trail Guide

Bics (Map p.103)

Comox / Courtney

Arbutus

This trail lies adjacent to Bics and is more difficult than its next door neighbor. This is a bit of a psycho downhill and should scare the crap out of most of you. Expect the basic menu of scary stuff like steep chutes and drop-offs that remind you of gravity's power. Although the trail is not very long, it is very intense.

Arbutus (Map p.103)

Comox / Courtney

The Dump

The Dump probably has more nicknames then any other area in B.C. because it is located on the doorstep of the Pigeon Lake Landfill. You can literally follow your nose on one trail to get a view and smell of the dump site. If you've ever needed motivation to get recycling, then a quick ride on the Sensory Assault Trail will get you to think twice the next time you throw anything in the garbage.

The Dump only has a few trails that actually smell bad, and depending on the winds, most of the trails smell like a forest. Riders can expect *"The Dump only has a few trails that actually smell bad . . ."* consistent single track that rolls and plays within the confines of a relatively small area. This is great moderate single track where riders of all abilities can express themselves.

To access the trails from Comox, drive north on the Island Highway towards Courtney Rd. which turns into Cliff Ave. Turn Left on 17th St. and follow through to the last intersection at the top and turn right on Willemar. Immediately turn left on Cumberland Rd. and follow for about 7 to 8 km until a right at the Esso gas station. Follow the signs to Pigeon Lake Landfill and turn

MOUNTAIN BIKING
BRITISH COLUMBIA
The Trail Guide

left. Just before the entrance to the dump you pass a large open area. About 100 meters ahead on your right is the entrance to the trails. They start out on a old coal railbed that is now a black wide trail. As you go further the trail narrows. About 150 meters farther a trail goes in on the right. If you miss this *"They start out on a old* entrance you will start to ride on old rail ties. Turn *coal railbed that is now a* around and enter the single track here. Take the *black wide trail."* next left and begin to explore. Veer right to- ward the dump, or left onto more trails. This area is bordered by Whites Bay Rd., the dump, and the railbed, so getting really lost shouldn't be a concern. All of the single tracks circle back, or take you to these bordering roads.

The Dump (Map p.103)

Campbell River

The Trails	
Pumphouse	106
Skidmarks	110
Snowden Trails	110
Old Rail Grades	110

Introduction

It sure is comforting to know that almost any place in our province has great mountain biking, and Campbell River is certainly no exception. Bring your bike with you and combine some great riding with the area's world class fishing.

Campbell River

Pumphouse

The Pumphouse trails are a 10 minute ride from town. This is a small riding area where riders can freely explore at will without any fear of getting too lost. These trails are not overly difficult and roll through rock bluffs and forest. Please stay on existing trails.

Pumphouse (Map p.109)

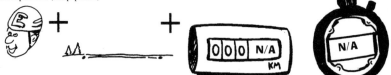

Photograph by Darrin Polischuk

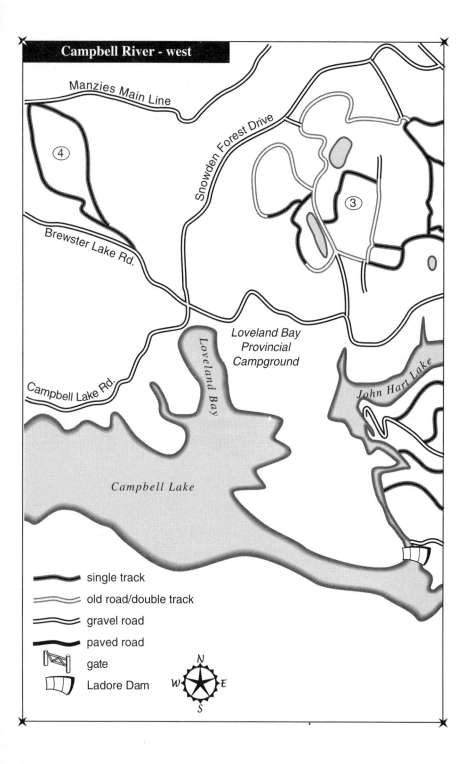

Campbell River - west

Manzies Main Line

④

Snowden Forest Drive

③

Brewster Lake Rd.

Loveland Bay
Provincial
Campground

Loveland Bay

John Hart Lake

Campbell Lake Rd.

Campbell Lake

single track
old road/double track
gravel road
paved road
gate
Ladore Dam

N
W · E
S

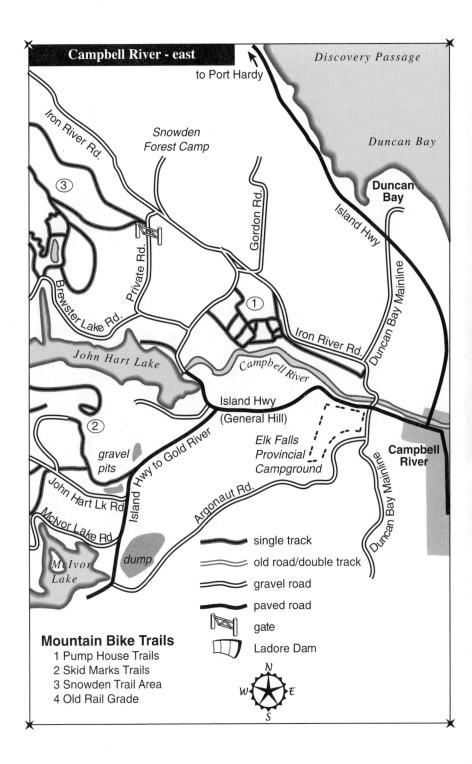

Campbell River - east

Discovery Passage

to Port Hardy

Iron River Rd.

Snowden Forest Camp

Gordon Rd.

③

Brewster Lake Rd.

Private Rd.

Duncan Bay

Duncan Bay

Island Hwy

①

Iron River Rd.

John Hart Lake

Campbell River

Duncan Bay Mainline

Island Hwy
(General Hill)

②

gravel pits

Island Hwy to Gold River

Elk Falls Provincial Campground

Campbell River

John Hart Lk Rd

McIvor Lake Rd

Argonaut Rd.

Duncan Bay Mainline

McIvor Lake

dump

single track

old road/double track

gravel road

paved road

gate

Ladore Dam

Mountain Bike Trails
1 Pump House Trails
2 Skid Marks Trails
3 Snowden Trail Area
4 Old Rail Grade

N
W   E
S

MOUNTAIN BIKING
BRITISH COLUMBIA
The Trail Guide

Campbell River

Skidmarks

The name of this area probable relates to the tire tracks left on the ground, and the stains in your underwear. Riders can expect a 30 minute climb from town into this newly developed area. This is expert level riding on a single track downhill.

Skidmarks (Map p.109)

 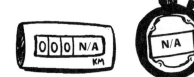

Campbell River

Snowden Trails

The Snowden Trails are a 30 minute ride from town. This is the area in Campbell River that is filthy with trails. At last count there are approximately 50 km of trails that connect moderate single track with old rail grades, and old roads. Riders can expect the full spectrum of moderate mountain biking without any major climbs. The Snowden Trails are part of the Demonstration Forest and maps of just this area are available from the forest service office or at The Urban Lemming bike shop. New trails are constantly being added so inquire at the shop for any updates to this area.

Snowden Trails (Map p.109)

Campbell River

Old Rail Grades

The area that surrounds you was logged by rail years ago. The old rail grades and trestles remain and mountain bikers can enjoy exploring the easy, flat terrain.

Old Rail Grades (Map p.109)

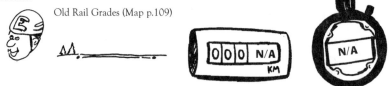

MOUNTAIN BIKING
BRITISH COLUMBIA
The Trail Guide

South West British Columbia

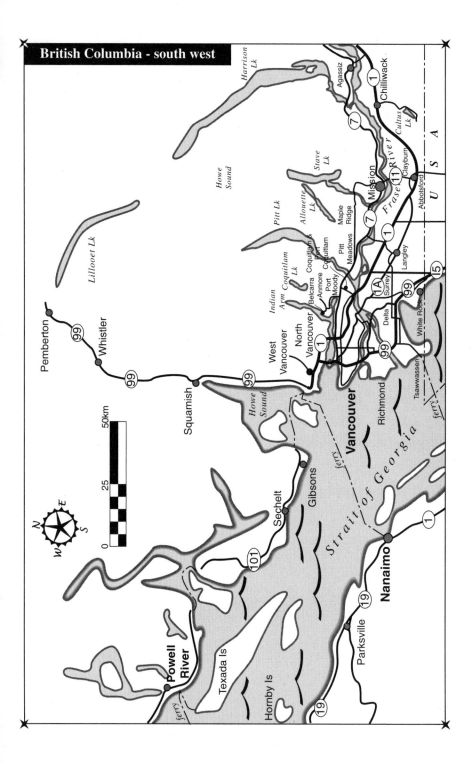

British Columbia - south west

Photograph by Blair Polischuk

MOUNTAIN BIKING
BRITISH COLUMBIA
The Trail Guide

Cypress Mountain / West Vancouver

Introduction

The steep lower slopes of Cypress Mountain has had mountain bikers giggling on its technical trails for over a decade. Throughout these years mountain biking has grown exponentially, yet to my knowledge the District Of West Vancouver does not recognize mountain biking in any of its current bylaws. However, several prominent trails have been built and maintained. They stand as a testament; that well built trails which see some regular maintenance can survive and thrive in wet, heavily used environments.

Except for the BLT Trail, mountain Biking in Hollyburn Provincial Park is illegal. Riders caught poaching trails in the park can expect fines and bike confiscations. Pick up a park brochure to find out the exact park boundaries. The trails on the map provided are outside the park boundary except for a 100 foot ribbon on either side if Cypress Bowl Road.

The property of the trails mapped fall under the jurisdiction of the British Properties Home Owners Association. There has been some work towards official recognition of some mountain biking routes, but nothing official to date. All riders can do is ride as always, stay off B.C. Parks land, and obey posted signs. Until the District of West Vancouver clarifies its position on mountain biking I cannot say what exact trails are open or closed to mountain bikers. *"If you didn't already know about these trails you would have heard about them elsewhere."* The map only points out where the most traveled routes exist and all riders must assume responsibility for their own actions. If you didn't already know about these trails you would have heard about them elsewhere. So read on and be responsible.

Cypress Mountain / West Vancouver

No Stairs Allowed / Panorama / My Friend The Stupid Grouse

If you consider the work of trail builders a divine act, then the actions of Ross Kirkwood and helpers on creating this loop is definitely God-like. This combination ride is the best of Cypress for riders who enjoy a technical challenge, but like a trail on a slope where a battle between gravity and braking power is not

MOUNTAIN BIKING
BRITISH COLUMBIA
The Trail Guide

the dominant theme. This loop requires plenty of skill but will not disable you if mistakes are made.

Just up from the 21st exit by Highway #1 is the trail head of No Stairs Allowed. This technical climb has switchbacks that are near perfection for riding, tight enough to make you slow down and think, open enough to speed away from your less skilled buddies. After climbing, remember that this is the finishing blast on the way down. The No Stairs Allowed trail winds through some houses onto a flat ridge section and upward past a bombed out new development onto the Panorama ————————————————————— climb. This is a slippery climb with apple-sized *"After climbing, remember that this is the finishing blast on the way down."* double track plenty of rocks to bounce you around. It's a bit of a grunt, but so are most fun things in life. As you near the top of Panorama you will sense an opening and view the human-made scree slope of the lookout switchback. On your right is the entrance to this tight, technical little wonder known as My Friend The Grouse.

The first few turns are some of the most difficult on the trail so don't get discouraged if you mess up here. Just dust yourself off, click in, and let it ride. If you plan at all on 'cleaning' this trail looking ahead is important. You are shot out at the Panorama climb where you can repeat or retrace your steps back to No Stairs Allowed and the pavement.

No Stairs Allowed / Panorama / My Friend The Stupid Grouse (Map p.117)

for one loop

Cypress Mountain / West Vancouver

BLT / Sex Boy / Fern Trail

Bacon, lettuce and tomato? Then sex among some ferns? Sounds like an interesting time! The BLT (Boulders, Logs and Trees) is the only open mountain biking trail in Cypress Park. This granddaddy of old roads climbs way, way up to the ski hill parking lot. Since the Cypress Crumbler event in 1995 a few more roads and a short single track have also opened at the top, but nothing else. The real purpose of the BLT is to get riders up to the Fern Trail and to Sex Boy, and a good excuse to eat some fries with ketchup.

(Continued on page 118)

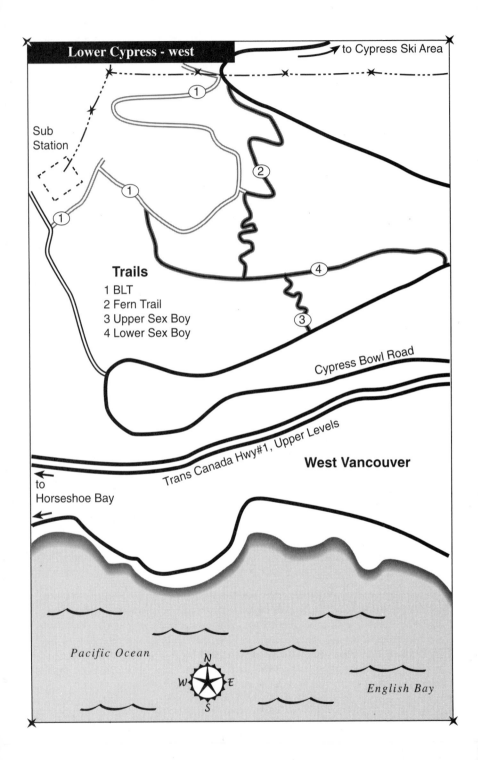

Lower Cypress - west

to Cypress Ski Area

Sub Station

Trails
1 BLT
2 Fern Trail
3 Upper Sex Boy
4 Lower Sex Boy

Cypress Bowl Road

Trans Canada Hwy#1, Upper Levels

West Vancouver

to
Horseshoe Bay

Pacific Ocean

English Bay

N
W E
S

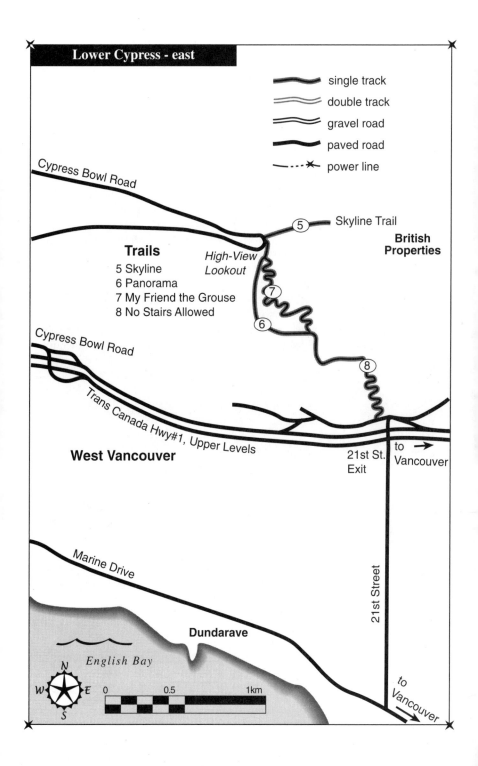

MOUNTAIN BIKING
BRITISH COLUMBIA
The Trail Guide

(Continued from page 115)

To access the BLT drive up Cypress Bowl Road and look for an area to park on your left, part way around the first bend. This old road climbs up to the BLT if you go left at the sub station. The BLT veers away from the powerline cut into the trees where you have to snoop around for the trail head for **Fern Trail** on your right. Enroute the climbing is a bit challenging, but for those who endure, a trip through some ferns on a trail that feels like a animated Disney movie awaits. **Fern Trail** crosses a creek, and traverses the slope, press Bowl Road drops you onto Cypress Bowl Road about 500 meters from the first look out point. The Zenlike ride-by-feel experience of **Fern**

> *"Enroute the climbing is a bit challenging, but for those who endure, a trip through some ferns on a trail that feels like a animated Disney movie awaits."*

Trail can be abruptly halted if you choose to drop into **Sex Boy**. The right turn onto this ultra steep plunge is marked. If you are reading about this trail for the first time chances are you will need a few years of steep riding time under your saddle to really enjoy it. I figure if you walk over 30 % of any gnarly downhill, fun will not be the main adjective used to describe your ride. On a wet day this trail can push the ride-to-walk ratio of all but a handful of single track masters.

There is more of the steep stuff the further you ride up the BLT. Sex Boy is serious stuff and I am not going to serve this up for you on a titanium platter. For those who really want to ride it will be found, and for those who give up to easily, chances are it's a good thing. Ask a local, go out and buy some **Roach** brand body armor, and rip this stuff up.

Fern Trail (Map p.116)

depending on options

Sex Boy (Map p.116)

MOUNTAIN BIKING
BRITISH COLUMBIA
The Trail Guide

The North Shore Grouse Mountain Trails

The North Shore Grouse Mountain Trails

Introduction

The Grouse Mountain / Mount Fromme trail network is legendary among local riders in the Lower Mainland. For years riders have grunted up Mountain Highway and continued upward on the gravel road until the trail of their choice releases them from gravity into single track, fun zones. Those with the legs and patience to get to the top are rewarded with a nectar-like single track to the bottom. Anyone who spends a few days on the trails will probably come away with some scrapes, and a mountain biking tale to parallel most fishing stories. Tales of the super, steep, rooted, single tracks and hairy crashes, continue to feed the legend.

The trails on Grouse did not magically appear one day, but were, and continue to be, the work of some amazingly dedicated folk who realize that to ride on sweet trails means you have to build and maintain them. Much of the trail work is the ———————————————————— result of the efforts of Ross   *"Volunteer some time on Grouse and re-*   Kirkwood, and the   E.M.P.   *balance your trail karma for the season."*   crew, along with countless ———————————————————— volunteers. If you have ridden on Grouse, and never helped out on a trail day, then your high "Trail Karma Point Factor" will come home to haunt you one day in the form of a flat tire or nasty crash. Volunteer some time on Grouse and rebalance your trail karma for the season.

Ross Kirkwood's 7th Secret became the first real mountain bike trail on the mountain, and from this, several others evolved built. Today the Griffen Trail will become the first officially recognized mountain bike trail on Grouse. Named after Marcia Wood's little boy Griffen, the trail is the recipient of a small "Go For Green" grant that will be used to upgrade the trail and erect signs. The official recognition of the Griffen Trail does not give riders the green light to the entire Grouse trail network. To date, riding on the trails

MOUNTAIN BIKING
BRITISH COLUMBIA
The Trail Guide

that deposit you on the **Baden Powell** are of questionable legality. These trails are very steep, and continued wet season use will turn many of the trails into rocky hell rides more suitable for a kayak then a bike. Think about this the next time you're scraping your way down one of these trails with the brakes in full lock mode. There are plenty of trails that are now open to mountain bikers on Grouse. Though many of these trails have been mapped here, there are also many more that have not. Ask around, and do your small part for the good of the trails in this area by riding on open trails. Contact E.M.P about helping out on a trail day.

The North Shore Grouse Mountain Trails

The Full Grouse Mountain Experience

Start the ride with the long climb up the gravel **Mountain Highway,** which used to be the old toll road up to the Grouse Mountain ski hill. About 35 minutes of steady climbing from the gate will get you to the top. This road accesses all the trails in the area. Continue to climb and note the number of major switchbacks you pass. The actual "**Kirkwoods 7th Secret**" starts just before the 7th switchback. If the hard climbing gets in the way of counting to 7 switchbacks, you'll probably hit the top when you're getting tired, and when you pass a main left fork. This trail was built in 1990, has been buffed up considerably since the early days, and is now faster and less sketchy. Thanks Ross! The 7th turns into **The Leopard Trail** after the last turn at the big ridge. This trail takes you down to the 5th switchback.

From the 5th switchback **Crinkum Crankum** ('twisty turny" in Old English), will take you further down the mountain. Be sure to turn right close to the entrance to this section. If you don't, the less than buffed up **Kirkford Trail** will link you up at the 3rd switchback. **The Cedar Trail** is an old logging road that is the first break from gravity on this downhill, go right. Depending on how far down you want to ride on a trail, you can choose between the **Roadside Attraction,** which will deposit you on the main road, or you can ride further down the **Griffen Trail** ending your ride on McNair Dr. If you complete this ride give yourself a pat on the back. Go out and tell some friends, and let the legend of Grouse Mountain live.

The Full Grouse Mountain Experience (Map p.121)

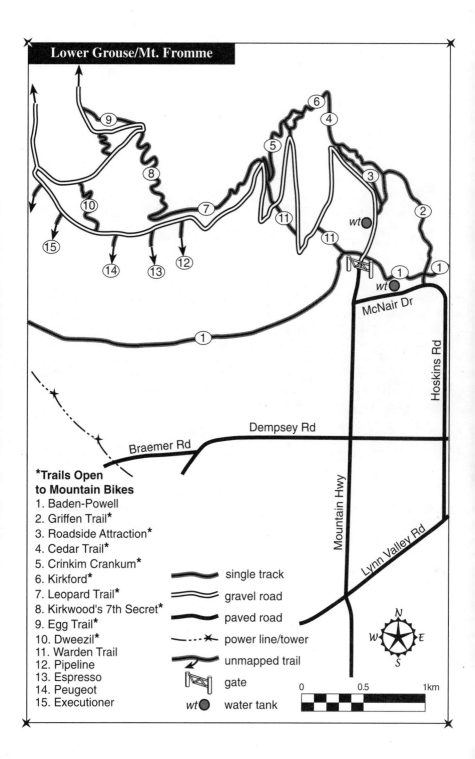

Lower Grouse/Mt. Fromme

*Trails Open to Mountain Bikes
1. Baden-Powell
2. Griffen Trail*
3. Roadside Attraction*
4. Cedar Trail*
5. Crinkim Crankum*
6. Kirkford*
7. Leopard Trail*
8. Kirkwood's 7th Secret*
9. Egg Trail*
10. Dweezil*
11. Warden Trail
12. Pipeline
13. Espresso
14. Peugeot
15. Executioner

single track
gravel road
paved road
power line/tower
unmapped trail
gate
wt water tank

McNair Dr
Hoskins Rd
Dempsey Rd
Braemer Rd
Mountain Hwy
Lynn Valley Rd

0   0.5   1km

N
W   E
S

MOUNTAIN BIKING
BRITISH COLUMBIA
The Trail Guide

The North Shore Grouse Mountain Trails

Mount Seymour Trails

The Oxford Concise Dictionary defines 'gnarly' as "covered with protuberances, twisted, rugged". I realize that protuberances is not is not a commonly used mountain biking adjective, however, gnarly is. And the word is often and accurately associated with the trails on Mount Seymour. The riding on Seymour is similar to the rest of the North Shore; difficult in a unique way. Few areas offer the steep, rooted and uncategorical type of single tracks as does Mount Seymour. The mys- tique of the north shore single track *"The mystique of the north shore* riders is legendary. If you don't believe *single track riders is legendary."* it, ride down a trail like Dale's and note the tire marks next to your footprints. Mountain bikers have been riding here since the early eighties and the area's first race, the 'Seymour Gear Grinder', was held in 1984. The tradition continues with an annual race held on a course that climbs up the Old Buck logging road and down the infamous **Severed Dick** trail among others. Since the early days many new routes have been built and rediscovered on the slopes of Mount Seymour by mountain bikers. Riding within the boundaries of Mount Seymour Provincial Park is limited to the **Old Buck Trail** and the power line access road. However, the park boundaries do not encom-pass most of the good riding in the area.

The North Shore Grouse Mountain Trails

Seymour's Easier Routes

Despite the hard core reputation of the area there are some moderate and easy routes to be enjoyed. For new mountain bikers who want a safe riding experience I would recommend riding the **Riverside Trail**. This trail is accessed at the end of Riverside Dr. Park your car and ride the out and back trail along the Seymour River. Give yourself about 1 hour to get to the twin bridges and back. For those *"For new mountain bikers who want a safe riding experience* who want a *I would recommend riding the Riverside Trail."* longer ride, climb up on the **Twin Bridges Trail** to the Seymour Demonstration Forest Headquar-ters. This long Climb and the **Riverside Trail** are all on a gravel road type surface. Riders can also start an easy route near the cemetery on Lillooet Rd. From here you can ride on the gravel road to the headquarters, where you can either walk into Rice Lake, or ride down the **Twin Bridges Trail** and along the Riverside Trail. All of this riding is technically easy, and a great safe outing for the family. Check out the closed paved road to the watershed on weekends.

MOUNTAIN BIKING
BRITISH COLUMBIA
The Trail Guide

Other easy riding on old gravel roads and gentle double track is found on the lower slopes of the mountain. These trails are accessed off Mount Seymour Parkway, just west of Plymouth Dr., at the end of Tompkins Cres. or off Northlands Dr. The new golf course sadly cuts into some of the terrain, but a new connector trail will get you around the course out to Mount Seymour Rd. Explore these lower routes and gain some skills and confidence before heading up Old Buck toward the more difficult terrain. Apart from a few creek crossings the lower trails are all suitable for novice riders.

The North Shore Grouse Mountain Trails

Mount Seymour's Magic

To access the good stuff you have to endure the climb up Old Buck Logging Road. This road, which is actually a double, and in some places a single track, is a 2.3 km climb to the junction with the Baden Powell Trail. Old Buck was the original road that accessed the alpine. The road was used until the 1950's when the larger road was punched through. The Mushroom was the Information board and terminus of the only link to the top of Mount Seymour.

From the intersection with the Baden Powell Trail go left. The B.P. trail, which has been upgraded on this section, gives you access to the ultra difficult Pandora's Trail on your left. The trail head to this gem is hidden, and if you can't find it you don't deserve to ride it. If you are not a skilled technical rider this trail will be dangerous and frustrating. Continue further along to the entrance of Severed Dick. This trail is the original downhill in the area and still can serve up a nervy ride to the bottom. Continue on to the power line and back into the forest straight ahead. On your left is an ob-scure downhill called Dale's that is possibly the steepest mountain bike trail in the province.

"On your left is an obscure downhill called Dale's that is possibly the steepest mountain bike trail in the province."

Dale's dumps you out on the power line road where a steep climb brings you back to the start. If you continue along to the Mushroom, veer left just below the actual site, toward the entrance to Atomic Dustbin. This trail head is signed. The ride down is fun, a bit rough, and much easier than most of the long downhills in the area. The trail spits you out under the power lines where you can take the switchbacks to the Riverside Trail, or go left up through the creek and onto a trail that will bring you to the Bridal Path if you go left.

If you continue to climb up past the Mushroom and veer left, you will pop out on the main paved road. If you skirt along the edge you can take a trail to the

(Continued on page 126)

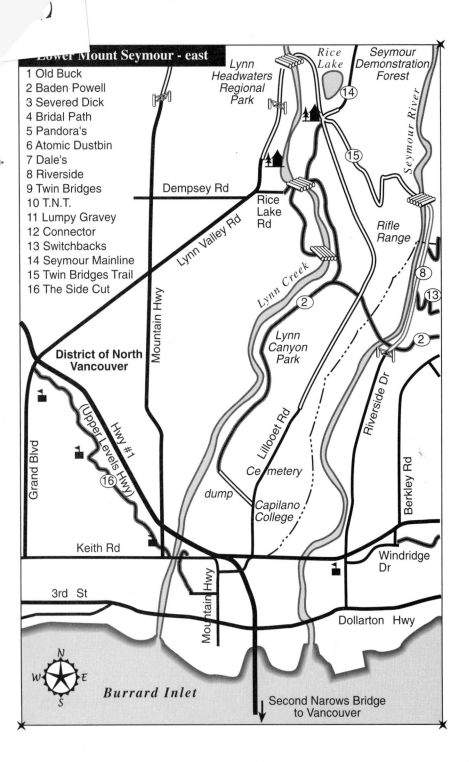

Lower Mount Seymour - east

1 Old Buck
2 Baden Powell
3 Severed Dick
4 Bridal Path
5 Pandora's
6 Atomic Dustbin
7 Dale's
8 Riverside
9 Twin Bridges
10 T.N.T.
11 Lumpy Gravey
12 Connector
13 Switchbacks
14 Seymour Mainline
15 Twin Bridges Trail
16 The Side Cut

District of North Vancouver

Lynn Headwaters Regional Park

Rice Lake

Seymour Demonstration Forest

Seymour River

Dempsey Rd

Rice Lake Rd

Rifle Range

Lynn Valley Rd

Lynn Creek

Mountain Hwy

Lynn Canyon Park

Riverside Dr

Grand Blvd

Hwy #1 (Upper Levels Hwy)

Lillooet Rd

Cemetery

dump

Capilano College

Berkley Rd

Keith Rd

Windridge Dr

3rd St

Mountain Hwy

Dollarton Hwy

N
W E
S

Burrard Inlet

Second Narrows Bridge to Vancouver

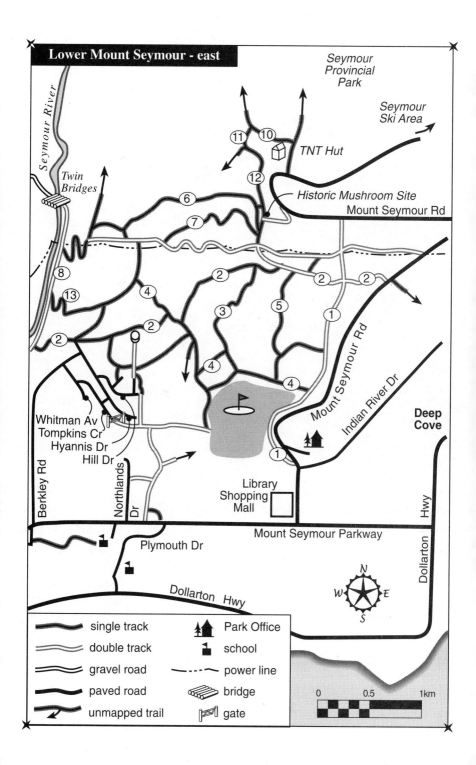

(Continued from page 123)

T.N.T. shack. From this marker a series of steep difficult trails will bring you to the **Connector**. Be sure and stay left at the intersections, as I have not mapped the trails which descend off of **T.N.T.** or **Lumpy Gravey**. The connector is a trail which will bring you to the top of **Atomic Dustbin**. Enroute you will hike through a few creek crossings.

If the long climb up **Old Buck** is not in the cards for the day you can go left onto the new **Bridal Path** part way up **Old Buck**. This trail forms the backbone of the trail network below the power lines. Ride the **Bridal Path** a few times and get familiar with the various trail heads. The **Bridal Path** gradually becomes more technical as you ride westward away from the golf course and is rideable in both directions. This popular and busy trail does not have any long climbs, just plenty of short testy ones.

Coquitlam / Eagle Ridge Trails

I can still remember the days when I would ride my mountain bike past the now defunct Westwood Race Track up an old double track and explore. Every ride was an adventure and the terrain seemed limitless. I thought I was the only mountain biker in the area, sharing the trails with the motorcycles. There were other riders in the late 80's and early 90's, but none so keen and devoted to building great trails and riding them than Tomas Vrba. We owe most of these great trails to the work of Tomas and his helpers.

Having heard of mega-development on Westwood Plateau, I started to explore the area for this book and was amazed at the scale of growth in this once prime mountain biking spot. All of the old access points, and so many great trails, have been bulldozed and replaced with golf courses and monster homes. *Money talks*. Development has not stopped on this ridge. Mapping the existing trails and describing an access that will be secure for more than a year is a challenge.

"Every ride was an adventure and the terrain seemed limitless."

For riders who want to ride up from the Lougheed / Barnet Highway, a fun technical climb called **Dan's Backyard Trail** will bring you close to the good riding. To access Dan's, turn off the Barnet at the Honda Dealership toward Heritage Mountain Blvd. / Ioco. As you go past the IGA mall onto Heritage Mountain Blvd. look for a trail on your right just after the bridge, this is **Dan's**

MOUNTAIN BIKING
BRITISH COLUMBIA
The Trail Guide

Backyard Trail. This climb literally brings you into people's backyards so refrain from yelling on the way up and especially on the way down. Dan's Trail has some testy sections and a few dismounts. Finding your way to the top of this urban trail will happen if you follow the tire tracks. As you enter the field at the top you can continue until an intersection with the old paved road to the Hydro Station. This is the entrance to The Wall Trail. This section is being bombed out for homes, —————————————— so finding what will remain of the Wall Trail *"These trails are all technical* will take a bit of tenacity. Once onto the Wall *descents with Randy's being* Trail be sure and veer right. Soon the power- *a tight challenging beauty of* line road brings you to the end of the Wall. *a downhill."* You can go left onto the powerline road and —————————————— look for the entrance to The Gutter Trail / Gutter Side Show / and Randy's Trail. These trails are all technical descents with Randy's being a tight challenging beauty of a downhill. You can retrace your steps down Dan's for a demanding 2 hours of 90% single track. Another access point to the powerline road is via the Academy Trail. This easier ride up is located off the first gravel parking lot on your right on the way to Buntzen Lake. Give yourself about 35 minutes to climb to the top of the Academy Trail. From the top a short ride on the powerline road will get you to the top of Gutter / Randy's, or for an easier descent try the Wall Trail, and ride back to the car on the road.

For those riders who want to access the top trails you have to ride on the powerline road and go left on the gas pipeline located above the paved road, or ride down to the paved road. If you chose the pipeline, inaccessible creek crossing may turn you back in the spring. This bumpy trail will get you to the pump station. Go around the pump station and look for a rocky left turn onto the Lungbuster off the paved road. If you simply go further down the powerline road onto the paved road the results are the same.

The Lungbuster is a bad-ass climb that requires power and skill to negotiate. Plenty of medium sized boulders bounce you around like a child on a proud grandfather's knee. The Dentist is the first trail to beckon you off the bumpy climb with the —————————————— Decapitator coming shortly *"This is all gnarly stuff that will test the* after a creek crossing. The *climbing stamina of most mountain bikers."* climb continues, and if you —————————————— go right onto an old double track, the Greaser is your reward. A further climb on the main road, and a left, gets you to the Chiropractor. This is all gnarly stuff that will test the climbing stamina of most mountain bikers. The descents are all technically difficult, but rideable. From the powerline road it is going to take a

(Continued on page 130)

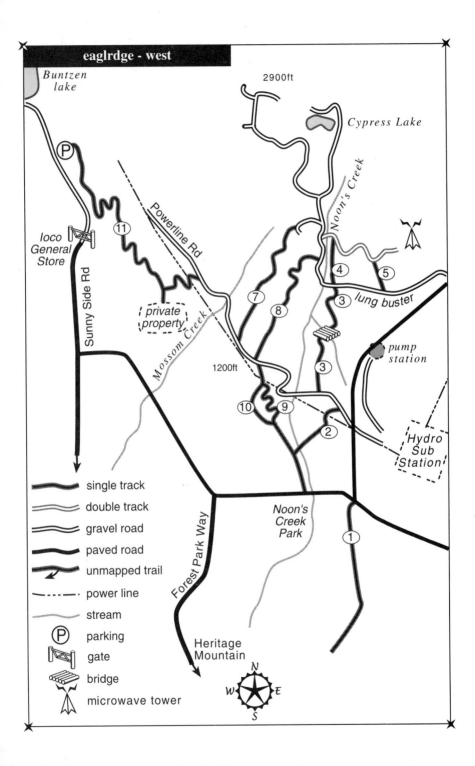

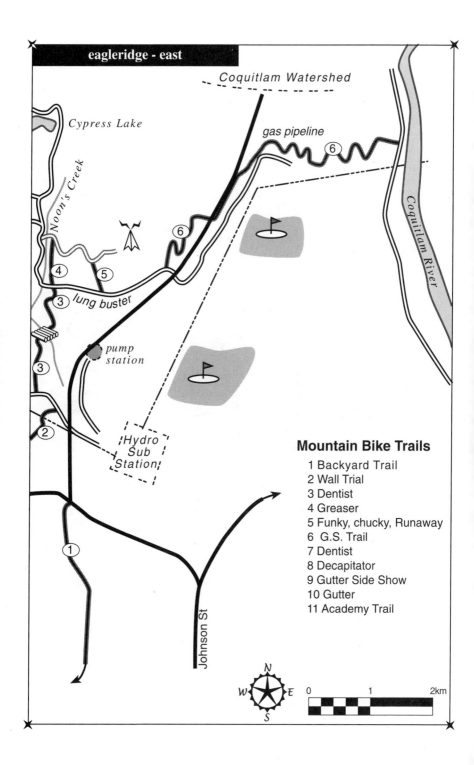

eagleridge - east

Coquitlam Watershed

Cypress Lake

gas pipeline

Noon's Creek

⑥

⑥

Coquitlam River

④ ⑤

③ lung buster

③

pump station

②

Hydro Sub Station

Mountain Bike Trails

1 Backyard Trail
2 Wall Trial
3 Dentist
4 Greaser
5 Funky, chucky, Runaway
6 G.S. Trail
7 Dentist
8 Decapitator
9 Gutter Side Show
10 Gutter
11 Academy Trail

①

Johnson St

N
W E
S

0   1   2km

(Continued from page 127)

minimum of 1 hour to get up the Lungbuster and down one of the trails, but most riders can count on it taking twice as long. A mixed group of elite women riders, 30 something keeners, and myself went up Dan's to the

Lungbuster, down The Greaser, the Dentist, and Randy's, and down Dan's in about 3.5 hours while I made scribbles on my note pad, and one of our riding partners broke everything on his bike. Look for the G.S. (golfers suck) trail to be resurrected in the summer of 1996.

MOUNTAIN BIKING
BRITISH COLUMBIA
The Trail Guide

Burnaby Mountain / Simon Fraser University Trails

If you believe that the act of riding a mountain bike is a metaphor for life, and that life is a perpetual lesson, then there is no better venue to combine learning and riding than on the Burnaby Mountain trails. For many Lower Mainland mountain bikers these trails were the introduction to technical single track riding; and the tradition continues.

Overall the trails are not as severe in pitch or technical difficulty as the North Shore, yet they have this gnarly, rideable flavor to them un-matched by many other venues. Unfortunately, the trails have always been of questionable legality. Various jurisdictions, and changing land authorities, continue to make S.F.U. a soap opera between bureaucracies and the mountain biking community. Today, the **Burnaby Mountain Biking Club** (President Eric Heidolf @ (604) 936-5172) is ac-tive in the enhancement of trails on the mountain . Their work has kept this popular area from de-teriorating, and many of the old favorites ride better then they did 10 years ago. All riders must obey posted signs when riding. And be aware that the printing of this information, and the Map, are not a green light to ride on the mountain. The land access may change at any time and the final responsibility rests with the individual, not anyone associated with this publication. Got It!

"This is one Colonel-sized bucket of single track fun, and the best example of Burnaby Mountain riding."

The best way to get a taste of the mountain is to park, or access, the trails from North Road. From here, take the powerline climb up to Joe's Trail, finishing at the gas station. Go through the school toward Naheeno Park, and the access to **Mel's Trail**. Mel's crosses **Ring Road** and begins to traverse across the slope. Shortly after the **Water Pipeline** downhill is the intersection for Nicole's. This is one Colonel-sized bucket of single track fun, and the best example of Burnaby Mountain riding. Other winners include: **Gear Jammer**, a touch steeper then the others, and the flat but technical challenges of **The North Road Trail**. The Lower portions of Burnaby Mountain have plenty of fun, un-named trails, but be careful not to go to far south into an area closed to mountain biking. Just watch for, and obey, the signs.

The climb up Joe's is one of the nicest double track climbs in the province with a perfect grade that will challenge the best to go fast. But it isn't steep enough to deter novices from reaching the top under their own power. With one climb up

(Continued on page 134)

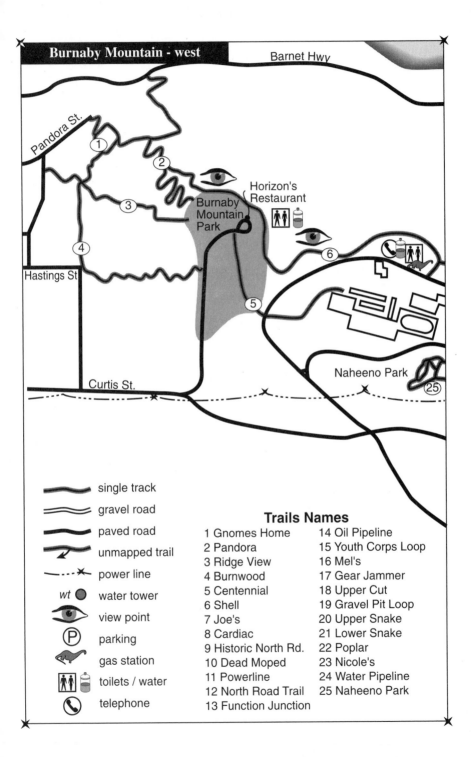

Burnaby Mountain - west

Barnet Hwy

Pandora St.

Horizon's Restaurant

Burnaby Mountain Park

Hastings St

Curtis St.

Naheeno Park

Legend

single track	
gravel road	
paved road	
unmapped trail	
power line	
wt ● water tower	
👁 view point	
Ⓟ parking	
gas station	
🚻 toilets / water	
☎ telephone	

Trails Names

1 Gnomes Home
2 Pandora
3 Ridge View
4 Burnwood
5 Centennial
6 Shell
7 Joe's
8 Cardiac
9 Historic North Rd.
10 Dead Moped
11 Powerline
12 North Road Trail
13 Function Junction
14 Oil Pipeline
15 Youth Corps Loop
16 Mel's
17 Gear Jammer
18 Upper Cut
19 Gravel Pit Loop
20 Upper Snake
21 Lower Snake
22 Poplar
23 Nicole's
24 Water Pipeline
25 Naheeno Park

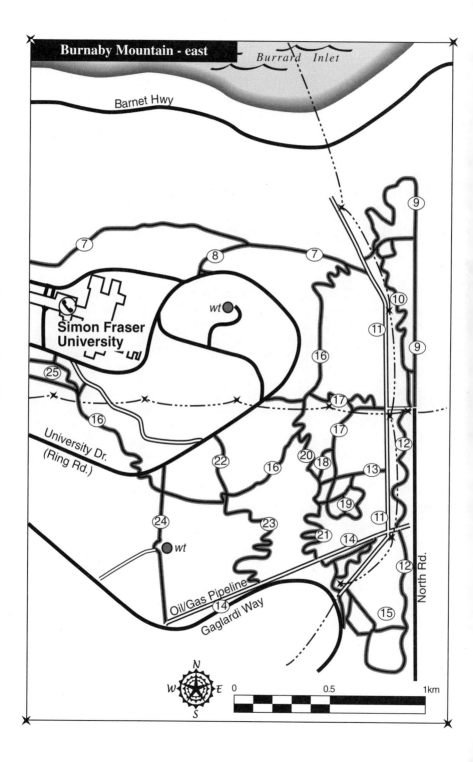

Burnaby Mountain - east

Burrard Inlet

Barnet Hwy

Simon Fraser University

University Dr. (Ring Rd.)

Oil/Gas Pipeline

Gaglardi Way

North Rd.

0   0.5   1km

MOUNTAIN BIKING
BRITISH COLUMBIA
The Trail Guide

(Continued from page 131)

Joe's you can get about 1.5 hours of riding, if you take advantage of the maze of lower mountain trails. With the single track access served by the powerline road, the gas pipeline road, and Joe's, it's easy to get around and explore,

dropping into single tracks when the need arises. If you find yourself at the bottom of the Oil / Gas Pipeline, dig in for another climb and drop into some of the single tracks accessed from Function Junction. The technical climb up Gear Jammer, and down under the steep downhill section, is a testy vertical route. These are a few recommended rides, but don't take my word for it. Go out and find your own favorites!

A good rip around Burnaby Mountain can make you forget that you are surrounded by a throbbing city. Despite its urban flavor the trails are not a 'white bread', bark-mulch-path type of ride, but the real thing packaged into a confined area. There are trails with good technical challenges, but not so dangerous that at day's end your bruises will out-number smiles. Nevertheless, a good riding buddy still lost two front teeth on the lower trails, so be careful and always ride with partners, or let someone know where you are riding.

Burke Mountain

Woodland Walk	135
Sawblade	135
Galloway	138

Introduction

Burke Mountain, located on the south facing slopes of Port Coquitlam, is one of B.C.'s newest Parks. As the area swells in population, its suburban location will surely enhance the value of this land, which has been set aside for recreational use. Residents of the Lower Mainland who have not discovered the Burke area for mountain biking or hiking will be surprised how the mountain can give any visitor a real wilderness experience only hours from their car.

"Residents of the Lower Mainland who have not discovered the Burke area for mountain biking or hiking will be surprised how the mountain can give any visitor a real wilderness experience only hours from their car."

As we went to print the park's recreational strategy was still in the planning stages. How mountain biking officially fits into the plans remains to be seen. Nevertheless, mountain bikers have been riding on a portion of Burke's trails for years. An existing network of

South West British Columbia

MOUNTAIN BIKING
BRITISH COLUMBIA
The Trail Guide

old logging roads, old skidder trails, and some single track primarily used by mountain bikers, add up to another outstanding mountain biking area for Lower Mainland riders to frequent. To access the Burke Mountain Trails, turn off the Lougheed Highway in Port Coquitlam onto Coast Meridian and follow it up until you reach Harper, then turn left. This gravel road will get you to the gate at the starting point for Burke Mountain rides.

The Burke Mountain Naturalists have done a great job signing the major trails on the mountain. Please keep this in mind when riding in the park, and be aware that the area may soon be a provincial park and mountain biking may be limited to certain trails. To date there are no 'official' restrictions or policies on mountain biking on these public lands.

Burke Mountain

Woodland Walk

This trail serves as a feeder trail back to the parking area after riding Sawblade, but can also be a nice flat beginner ride. It quickly takes a rider deep enough into the woods that they forget they're in the city. A waterfall marks the end of the trail. From the parking area at the gate, take the first left. The trail should be signed. Continue on this main wide trail under the powerlines, to the turn around point at the watershed. Return back the same way.

Woodland Walk (Map p.137)

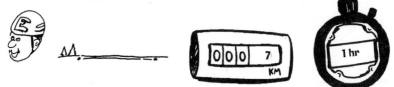

Burke Mountain

Sawblade

The Sawblade trail is the result of over 2 years of trail building efforts from two serious hard-core riders who simply wanted to have an off-the-scale, difficult trail in their backyard as an alternative to the typical North Shore scene. The result is a technical trail that will challenge all rider's slow, technical skills, balance, and guts. When I rode Sawblade I meant to count the number of tight switchbacks that come at you, but lost count after my face became buried in 6 inches of mud. If you can't do at least a partial track stand, and hop over foot high logs, the upper portions of Sawblade will eat you.

MOUNTAIN BIKING
BRITISH COLUMBIA
The Trail Guide

To access the upper portion of the trail, stay on the main old gravel road. This is not an easy climb due to it's grade and rough rocky surface. You will pass under the powerlines, then continue upward until the first flat spot and open space. The trail veers off left, passes a pile of saw dust, and becomes a single track that is rocky and climbs. Finding the actual entrance to Sawblades is not an easy task. While you are on the single track, at a small 'hump' on the trail you go left into the woods. The trail then slowly disappears. If you snoop around a bit further, however, you will (I promise) hit the trail head. From here this ultra-technical beauty cranks dips, rolls, turns, and drops-off to the Coquitlam Lake Trail.

"From here this ultra-technical beauty cranks dips, rolls, turns, and drops-off to the Coquitlam Lake Trail."

The tight slow technical stuff comes to an end as you are dumped onto the old road bed of the Coquitlam Lakeview Trail. Go left and down, as the trail works its way up and down the banks of the road bed. Don't miss the trail as it goes right off the road bed and into an awesome slightly less technical descent. This is my favorite portion of the ride, a nice soft, fast, single track that rips through the thickly forested second growth. Less skilled riders, or those with less time and less desire to crash, will want to access lower Sawblade from the Coquitlam Lakeview Trail. The ride up Coquitlam Lakeview Trail is a rocky challenge, but cuts out some time and gnarl factor from the upper section.

There are a few options on the lower portion of Sawblade. I recommend going right at all intersections until you hit Woodland Walk to maximize your downhill. Once onto Woodland Walk go left back toward the start. A short fun diversion into the woods occurs after the powerlines on your right. Just Prior to Pritchet Creek another trail goes down to the Coquitlam River. This trail will eventually bring a rider into Port Coquitlam along an easy path. The section of trail below Woodland walk should not be ridden in wet conditions. Nasty mud will damage your bike and your presence will damage the sensitive trail. (And a hostile land owner is something else to watch out for). Be patient and wait until summer to check out this lower trail. Sawblade is serious mountain biking. Expect to fall and have mechanical problems (nobody ever said the real fun stuff in life is safe or easy).

Sawblade (Map p.137)

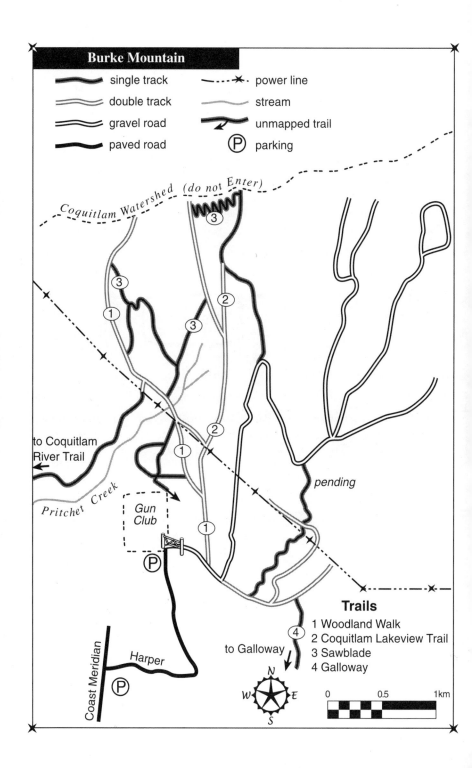

MOUNTAIN BIKING
BRITISH COLUMBIA
The Trail Guide

Burke Mountain

Galloway

The Galloway loop has some of the nicest rideable yet technical single track on Burke Mountain. This trail is known to very few riders in the Lower Mainland. To access the trail stay right at all intersections until you are climbing on an old skidder path. Start sniffing for the trail head on your right. If you hit the powerlines you've gone too far. The trail starts out steep, but soon settles into a very twisty trail that gently loses vertical in a perfect kind of way. You will eventually hit Galloway Rd., where you can ride up on the pavement back to the start.

Galloway (Map p.137)

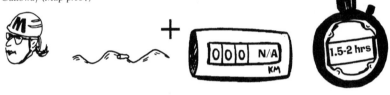

Belcarra Trails

The Belcarra area trails overlook Port Moody, the B.C Hydro Burrard Thermal Unit, and the Burrard Inlet. The extensive trail system developed by the Canadian Pacific Trials Association has brought out trials motorcycle riders onto these technical trails for around 30 years. The C.P.T.A. is a strong, well organized club that holds events and regular rides on this land. B.C. Hydro has authorized the trials club to manage the land. These riders are very courteous and do not *"This area is the host site for the Shaftebury* mind sharing their trails with *Classic mountain bike race put on by The* mountain bikes. Simply *Extreme Mountain Biking People."* respect their scene, and they will respect ours. The GVRD park area to the west is presently off-limits, but planning is underway to start developing trails for mountain biking in the near future. This area is the host site for the Shaftebury Classic mountain bike race put on by The Extreme Mountain Biking People.

To access the trails from Barnet Highway / St Johns, take the turn off to Loco Road near the Honda Shop then turn left at the IGA mall at the base of Heritage Mountain. Follow Loco Rd. to 1st Ave. and turn right at the site of an old school. Follow 1st Ave. as it winds up and becomes Bedwell Bay Rd. As the road passes by the turn off for Sasamat Lake, a steep downhill will bring you to the intersection with the B.C. Hydro Rd. Go left on this paved road and follow the map from here to the parking area.

Photograph by Blair Polischuk

One of the coolest aspects of riding here are the numerous hairy lines that can be had on the slick rock sections. There are lots of little trails and funky routes that riders can waste many an hour on. Plan on spending some time on the slick rock exploring the limits of your bike handling skills. If you're lucky, the trials riders will be on hand demonstrating how sick amounts of travel and power can propel an experienced pilot up and down some very gnarly trails.

Once you're able to break free from the slick rock playground a host of other trails await. All of the trails pop you out on a road under a power line. After a few hours, and a crash or two, they start to look the same. Just study the map and use a bit of common sense. Getting really lost should not be a problem. Or follow Dean McCay's advice and ride "away from the sun". Thanks for the tip Dean!

The Chute is the trail that will suck you out of Slick Rock down a loose, rocky downhill. This trail heads south under the powerlines where you can go around a gate and out toward Glassy Point. This short spur loop off the hydro service road loops around ————————————————— a big tower. Watch for broken glass. *"Getting really lost should not be a* Herman's Hill can be accessed by ei- *problem. Or follow Dean McCay's* ther road, climb to the north or de- *advice and ride "away from the sun".* scend to the south. While descending *Thanks for the tip Dean!"* veer left for some fun switchbacks. ————————————————— Herman's Hill will take you to the highest point in the area. The Stove Top trail is a super fun short loop that has a few testy drops that will get you giggling or screaming.

If you choose to ride Stove Top, a climb up The Crying Climb is required to do it again, or to get you elsewhere. This short steep grassy climb is an important artery that will get you to the top, of Ted's, Lower Jam Tart, Mom's, Sweet B and Oceanside. This little trail network is the guts of this area. To save you some bike pushing, keep in mind that Mom's is a technical climb while Ted's and Sweet B are downhills. Simply gain the necessary altitude via Ocean Creek or The Crying Climb. The Oceanside trail is the lowest point in the area. Be aware of private property after the creek.

Some of the smaller loops near the Slick Rock parking area include the Rainforest Amber Tr-ale, Turn Off, Sidewinder, and Deceptor. These loops are quite technical with drop-offs and steep sections.

The trails in Belcarra are generally rated technically difficult. The rating for physical difficulty depends ————————————————— on how long you ride. Those trails that are de- *"The trails in Belcarra* scribed as good single track climbs always haver easier *are generally rated* descents. Except for a few sections Ocean Creek is a *technically difficult."* more moderate downhill, but the climb is not easy. ————————————————— But you are never far away from the start, and the good trails always require some grunting to get to.

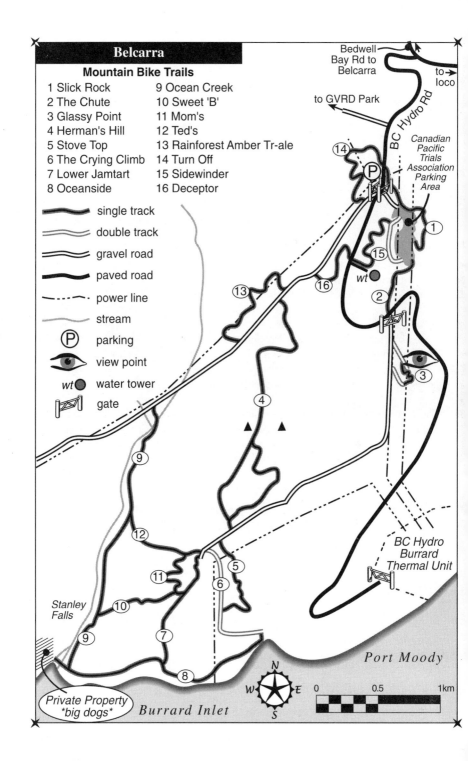

Belcarra

Mountain Bike Trails

1 Slick Rock
2 The Chute
3 Glassy Point
4 Herman's Hill
5 Stove Top
6 The Crying Climb
7 Lower Jamtart
8 Oceanside
9 Ocean Creek
10 Sweet 'B'
11 Mom's
12 Ted's
13 Rainforest Amber Tr-ale
14 Turn Off
15 Sidewinder
16 Deceptor

single track
double track
gravel road
paved road
power line
stream
Ⓟ parking
view point
wt● water tower
gate

Bedwell Bay Rd to Belcarra
to loco
to GVRD Park
BC Hydro Rd
Canadian Pacific Trials Association Parking Area

BC Hydro Burrard Thermal Unit

Stanley Falls

Private Property *big dogs*

Burrard Inlet

Port Moody

N W E S

0   0.5   1km

MOUNTAIN BIKING
BRITISH COLUMBIA
The Trail Guide

Blue Mountain

Introduction

Blue Mountain is Crown land that up until recently has been primarily used for logging, and by The Team Pagan Motorcycle Club. In 1995 there was a mountain bike downhill race held on the Humphill Trail, and although the conditions were wet and a bit greasy, the course held up and the times were very fast. The area has a soft organic soil bed and appears to be a victim of it's own popularity, and the forces of erosion. Because of the soft soils and frequent use, the trails vary in condition from soft and fresh, to nasty and severely rutted. While exploring this area I found some great downhill single tracks, but for every good trail I also found ruts that were literally over 3 feet deeper than the old trail surface. That said, most of these trails should be ridden downhill, and if you don't mind the empty beer cans and other trail side garbage, then a fun time can be had on this mountain.

To access the trails drive through Maple Ridge eastward on Dewdney Trunk Rd, and turn onto McNutt Rd. Follow McNutt till you see the sturdy gate at the bottom of Blue Mountain Forest Service Road. Park here. This main road is the way to gain elevation. The climb itself is challenging with plenty of cantalope-sized boulders to keep you on your toes when climbing. The omni-present power line is the other feeder trail, as well as a rocky double track that starts a few hundred meters above the powerline. All of these main roads, and a lower road, form the perimeter of most of Blue's good riding. Blue mountain road continues to climb beyond the area mapped and plenty of fun and boggy, exploring opportunities await.

Blue Mountain

Humphill Downhill

Finding the start of this trail is not easy, and took my trusty foul weather exploring partner and myself a few tries to get it dialed up. Ride up the main climb past the powerlines until an opening on the left, you will note the rocky double track adjacent to this flat open area. The trail starts at the end of the lot and appears to go east. Take the trail that goes down instead, and soon you'll be

(Continued on page 144)

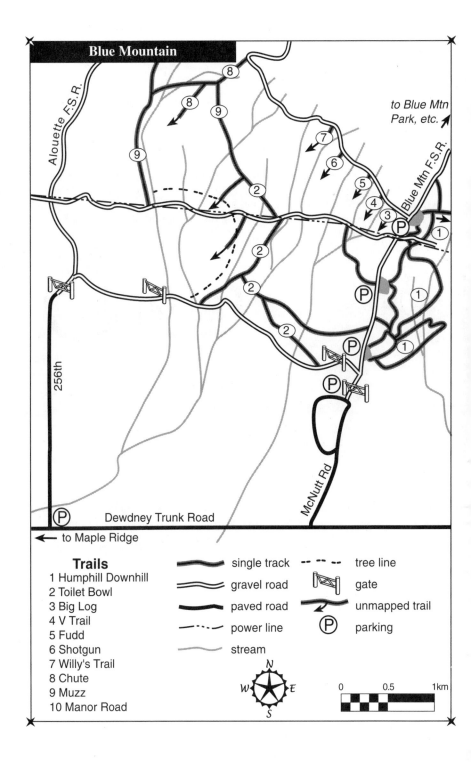

Blue Mountain

Alouette F.S.R.

to Blue Mtn
Park, etc.

Blue Mtn F.S.R.

256th

Dewdney Trunk Road

← to Maple Ridge

McNutt Rd

Trails
1 Humphill Downhill
2 Toilet Bowl
3 Big Log
4 V Trail
5 Fudd
6 Shotgun
7 Willy's Trail
8 Chute
9 Muzz
10 Manor Road

single track	- - -	tree line
gravel road	gate	gate
paved road		unmapped trail
power line	Ⓟ	parking
stream		

N
W E
S

0   0.5   1km

MOUNTAIN BIKING
BRITISH COLUMBIA
The Trail Guide

(Continued from page 142)
on a rocky downhill crossing under the powerlines. The trail continues until you are presented with many options to get off course. Be sure to take the trail that goes to the left, if you don't, you'll end up on a heinously eroded trail called The Duff Trail. Humphill has some brief flat portions, and one short uphill section. The bottom is fast, quite buffed, and a bit wider than the top; perfect, scary, fast, downhill stuff. The lower portions of the trail leave a big mud eating grin on your face, and beg you to do it again. So plan on being late for dinner. Climb up the trail, which is a good moderately technical climb, or on the main road push the reset button, and set yourself up for another ride on one of B.C.'s better downhill runs.

Humphill Downhill (Map p.143)

Blue Mountain

The Toilet Bowl Trails

This is a good single track descent but the condition of the trail could change due to nearby logging, and use by the moto bikers. In the fall of 95 the trail was soft and sweet, the type of trail that begs you to rail it, or as the folks in Smithers say, "color it outside the lines". To access the Toilet Bowl climb up the main road and go left at the powerlines. Ride past the first trail on the left, and start looking for the Toilet Bowl around the 3rd tower near an intermittent creek. If the trail you choose spits you into a cutblock it's the wrong one. Simply double back and take the next trail into the woods on your right. Once you are flushing your way down, the trail splits up into a couple of different options. Stay left, and take the next right to get the best ride. This trail makes for a fun technical climb as well.

The Toilet Bowl Trails (Map p.143)

MOUNTAIN BIKING
BRITISH COLUMBIA
The Trail Guide

Blue Mountain

The Muzz Trail

For those who want a longer tour of the area take the Muzz Trails, and get a good look at how loggers in years gone by dealt with the soft gooey soils on Blue; they built wooden sidewalks. These boardwalk type things called 'corduroy' roads keep you afloat over the mud and give the ride a haunting turn of the century feel. It doesn't take a huge imagination to see the ghosts of flannel clad loggers munching on their beef sandwiches among the trees and stumps. Then again, I was starting to bonk on the cold wet day The Muzz Trails were explored.

To access this ride you must climb up the main Blue Mountain road past the powerline go- ing left onto the rocky dou- *"These boardwalk type things called 'corduroy'* ble track. This trail crosses *roads keep you afloat over the mud and give* several creeks and teases you *the ride a haunting turn of the century feel."* with trails on the left. Trust me, the trails #3 - #7 are deceptive, and appear better than they are. Unless it's dry mid-summer conditions, most of them will disappoint.

Continue on the rocky trail as it slowly climbs upward. At an intersection the trail will either go right and up sharply, or left and stay flat. Go left. You are now on the Chute Trail which branches into Muzz East and West. Stay right and have fun riding over the corduroy. You will be deposited onto the powerline trails from which you can go left toward the Toilet Bowl Trails, or, if you've had enough, out to the main road.

The Muzz Trail (Map p.143)

MOUNTAIN BIKING
BRITISH COLUMBIA
The Trail Guide

Mission Abbotsford Area

Mission Abbotsford Area

The Buttafouco / McKee Peak Trails

Ask Bruce at Wenting's Cycle Shop about why Joey Buttafouco's name is associated with the challenging loop located above the Ledgeview Golf Course. The last time I rode **Buttafouco, McKee** road was under construction, so access to the old double track climb might be different. You are surrounded by old, second growth, deciduous forest that is quite different from the heavily forested norm on the west coast. In the fall, after the leaves have fallen, the atmosphere is almost eerie in the absence of our little green friends. Be careful on the main climb, it can be deceptively slick with a combination of moisture and some slimy green stuff of unknown origin.

The climb starts on your right just past the golf course and you quickly settle into a *little ring* climbing pace. The climb itself is about 3 km long and will most likely take your average keen rider around 30 minutes depending on the route taken. The climb is on an old deteriorated service road that has a unique concrete like surface that as much as I can tell is hard rock, but looks like old concrete. The quickest way to the top is to take this main road ignoring all possible turnoffs. To lengthen the climb, and add a bit of variety, turn right just when the old ———————————————————— gravel-like surface turns into *"This is a short trail with plenty o' challenges."* the firm rock bed. Your next ———————————————————— left will spit you back out onto the main climb. To further stretch out the climb take the next right, and then a left at an old fence line. Again this will deliver you onto the finishing sections of the climb. The single track starts at the top and drops abruptly away, starting out with a couple of testy drop-offs that are rideable but require some skill and guts. The rest of the trail rolls back around the mountain giving riders great views of the Fraser Valley. The trail gets exposed in a few spots and has some interesting steep chutes to negotiate. Eventually the trail

146   *South West British Columbia*

joins up with the climb near the start. This is a short trail with plenty o' challenges. It will ride much easier in dry conditions, with the inevitable opposite occurring in the wet.

The Buttafouco / McKee Peak Trails (Map p.148)

Mission Abbotsford Area

Lower McKee Peak Trail

This trail is accessed by turning right at the noticeable change in the climb's surface from gravel and dirt, to firm rock bed. Once you turn right and start to descend, an option of a single track right or a rocky double track will confront you. Go right. This trail will take you to a grassy open area where you go left and after a few dips another right. This trail will shoot you onto Purcell Rd. where you can ride the blacktop back to the start.

Lower McKee Peak Trail (Map p.148)

Mission Abbotsford Area

Red Mountain

Red Mountain has been the sight of a good local cross country race for the last couple of years. Typical of a B.C. race course, this loop has just the right combinations of challenging double track climbs, fast single track, and tight, technical single track climbs and descents. All of this is woven into a loop with easy access and another possible circuit (Bear Mountain) right across the street.

The riding is located just north of Mission on Dewdney Trunk Rd. To get to the riding you have to go through gun club property. Access is allowed, but make sure to park at Mill Pond and not on Rod 'n' Gun Club property.

(Continued on page 150)

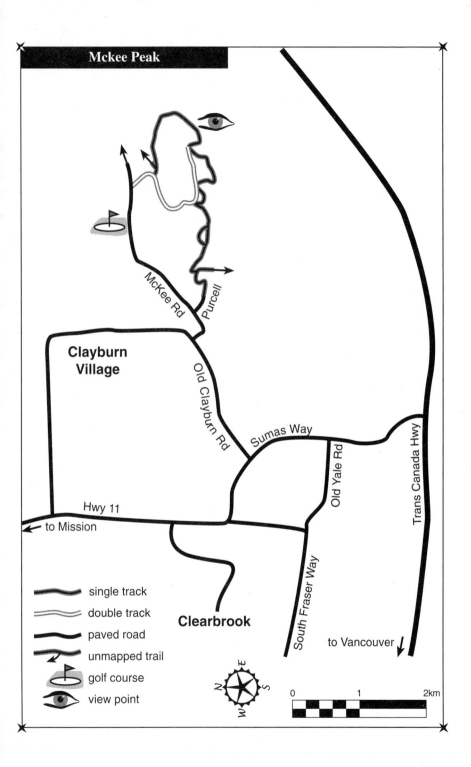

Mckee Peak

Clayburn Village

McKee Rd

Purcell

Old Clayburn Rd

Sumas Way

Old Yale Rd

Trans Canada Hwy

Hwy 11

← to Mission

South Fraser Way

Clearbrook

to Vancouver ↓

single track
double track
paved road
unmapped trail
golf course
view point

0   1   2km

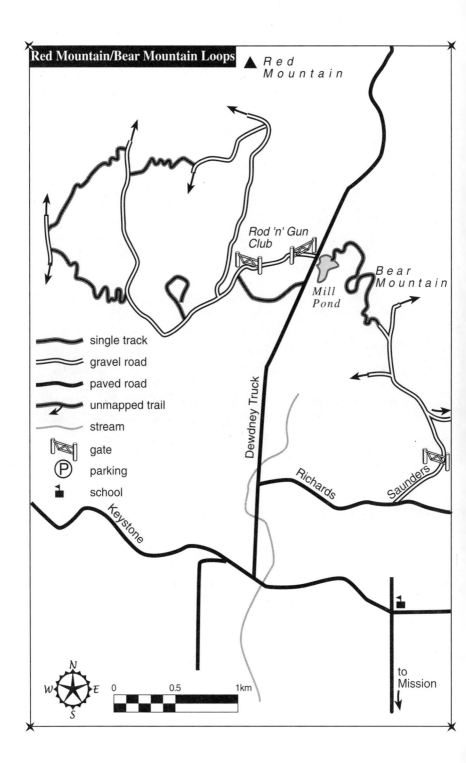

Red Mountain/Bear Mountain Loops

▲ Red Mountain

Rod 'n' Gun Club

Bear Mountain

Mill Pond

single track
gravel road
paved road
unmapped trail
stream
gate
Ⓟ parking
school

Dewdney Truck

Keystone

Richards

Saunders

N
W E
S

0   0.5   1km

to Mission

MOUNTAIN BIKING
BRITISH COLUMBIA
The Trail Guide

(Continued from page 147)

Riding up the main gravel road you take the right fork and climb up the steepish road. Once you are in a clearing at the top take a left onto another old road which slowly becomes an overgrown double track. This trail leads you to a single track descent with a rocky chute dropping you onto a main road. Go right, and 100 meters _____ later left into some more single track fun. *"This series of climbs are short* This portion of the loop is very wet in the *and quite steep."* off season or after substantial rainfall. Once _____ you are on the main road again look for a trail on your left that climbs upward. This series of climbs are short and quite steep. The trail will veer left onto a section of new single track that is the most technical part of the loop. This portion will challenge the best climbers with steep grades and tight corners. Once onto the main road, a single track option appears on your left over a small bridge. This mini loop is a good challenge, and when combined with the big loop can make for an ideal

Red Mountain (Map p.149)

Mission Abbotsford Area

Bear Mountain

This trail is accessed by turning right at the noticeable change in the climb's surface from gravel and dirt, to firm rock bed. Once you turn right and start to descend, an option of a single track right or a rocky double track will confront you. Go right. This trail will take you to a grassy open area where you go left and after a few dips another right. This trail will shoot you onto Purcell Rd. where you can ride the blacktop back to the start.

Bear Mountain (Map p.149)

MOUNTAIN BIKING
BRITISH COLUMBIA
The Trail Guide

Mission Abbotsford Area

Mt. Mary Ann / Glen's Gift

Go and pay your respects to the gods of technical riding on the **Mt Mary Ann, Monastery Trails**. This small area is filled with the type of technical riding where reputations are made and bones are broken. Rumor has it *"This small area is filled with* that some of the sections have yet to lose *the type of technical riding* their fat tire virginity. So go out and give it a *where reputations are made* try. Hopefully, if you are the first to clean a *and bones are broken."* section, the divine location won't have you rushing off to the confessional. Even tough trails have to be tried. After that, all others are easier and more pleasurable.

Park at the **Heritage Park** lot. Ride across the fields, over the creek, and across the second field. Look for the trail on the left. To ride the entire loop ignore the cut off loop which is the first left. The second left will give you the whole loop. If you take your right the trail will take you up to the monastery.

Expect steep drop offs, triple log piles, and diagonal log sections that will test the balance of the most dialed riders. Some of the descents have good jumps, and tricky off camber corners. If you are looking for a technical challenge bit don't have the fitness, time, or desire for the long climb, come and prey to these trails in Mission.

Mt. Mary Ann / Glen's Gift (Map p.152)

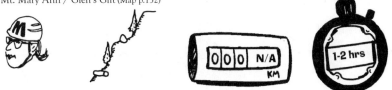

Mission Abbotsford Area

Vedder Mountain

Vedder Mountain is a B.C. Demonstration Forest Site with a well maintained gravel road which borders the riding area and serves as an access road to some of the great double and single track trails which this area is famous for. Vedder Mountain is the home of B.C.'s longest running mountain bike race, and apart from a few changes at the top of the course, it has virtually stayed the same since 1982. The large Vedder loop is a B.C. mountain biking classic, combining

(Continued on page 154)

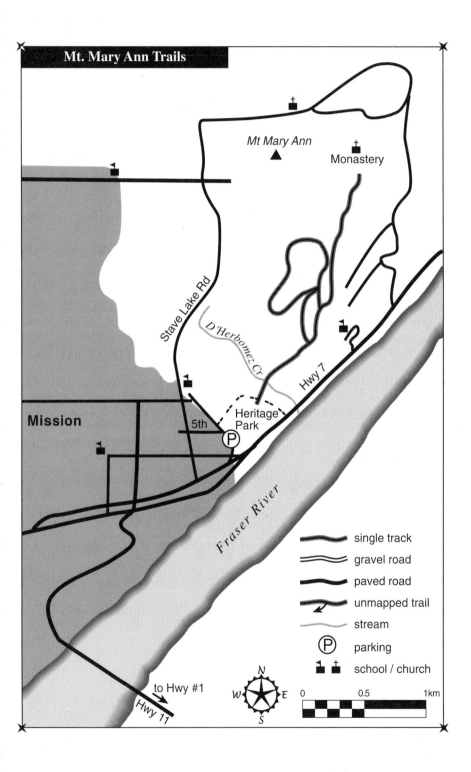

Mt. Mary Ann Trails

Mt Mary Ann

▲

Monastery

Stave Lake Rd

D'Herbomez Cr

Hwy 7

Mission

5th

Heritage
Park

Ⓟ

Fraser River

to Hwy #1

Hwy 11

≈≈≈ single track

══ gravel road

▬▬ paved road

↙ unmapped trail

～ stream

Ⓟ parking

▟ ✝ school / church

N
W ✦ E
S

0   0.5   1km

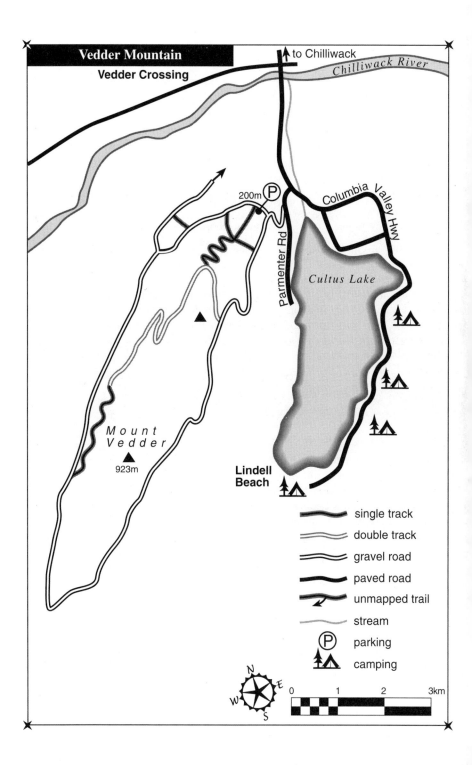

MOUNTAIN BIKING
BRITISH COLUMBIA
The Trail Guide

(Continued from page 151)
rolling gravel roads, steep double and single track climbs, and an outstanding, hand-numbing, downhill single track that seemingly goes on forever.

To access the Vedder Mountain trails, turn off Highway #1 at the Cultus Lake / Yarrow turnoff. Follow the road into Yarrow and turn right at the lights up to Cultus Lake. Turn right again onto Parmenter Rd. Take the first right fork,

Mission Abbotsford Area

The Race Loop

From the parking area, ride up the main gravel road which will slowly climb. A flatter open area about 15 minutes into the ride is where the start/finish area for the annual race is located. There is a short single track on the right, which, if you go left at the bottom of, rejoins the main road. Continue along the main road for about 7 km until an abrupt left turn doubles you back westward on a series of steep single track climbs and descents. The single track continues until a right turn at the bottom of a fast descent. From here the serious climbing begins on a super steep double track. You'll switchback once before the grade gets ugly. Yes, people do climb this stuff, although 2 or 3 times in a race humbles the most goat-like of mountain bikers. As you crest the summit, a trail to the left gives

"Yes, people do climb this stuff, although 2 or 3 times in a race humbles the most goat-like of mountain bikers."

you a well deserved break and a great view. The downhill starts out fast on a double track, interrupted by a few more climbing sections before the real descent begins. On the downhill, be sure and go left onto the single track where the going gets steep and more technical. At the base of a rocky straight section go left, onto some welcoming bermed-up trails. This trail splits into two parts, the course on the left, and a slightly longer section on the right. The car should be less than 1 km away if you go right. Pro racers can do one lap of this exact course in 1 hour at full throttle, while fit, average riders can ride at a social pace and finish a loop in under 2 hours. If you're not fit, the climbing could make this an all day thing, but the sweet downhill is worth the grunt up.

The Race Loop (Map p.153)

MOUNTAIN BIKING
BRITISH COLUMBIA
The Trail Guide

Mission Abbotsford Area

Lower Vedder Options

If you don't have the time for a full loop, but want to taste the great lower section single tracks, then this option will work for you. From the same parking area take the steeper left fork up the main gravel road. If you're real short of time, take a right at about 1.7 km and it will connect you to the last small single track sections. I recommend riding further up and going right at about 3 km. This trail will be a double track climb and will bring you up to the top of the steep single track about 4 km from the start of the ride. While taking less time, the climbing is as demanding as the race loop. If you have an appropriate vehicle, and are feeling lazy, you can shuttle up to the turnoff and cut out some of the nasty climbing.

Lower Vedder Options (Map p.153)

Golden Ears Provincial Park

Introduction

Golden Ears Provincial Park, Alouette Lake Area Trails, are located north of Maple Ridge approximately 45 km east of Vancouver. Follow the road signs once you are in Maple Ridge and they will lead you to the park. The area was once a logging site, and remnants of its operation over 60 years ago are still visible. Today the park is filled with mature second growth forest, and the trails have dense vegetation and a west coast flavor without the steep gnarl factor of the North Shore.

Alouette Lake is the primary recreational focus of the park. In regard to trail use, the local horse group has been involved in trail projects throughout the park and mountain bikers may feel as thought the park is a trail monument to our methane-producing friends. Mountain biking is definitely a new user group in the park. Today the efforts of the Golden Ears Trail Preservation And Restoration Committee (Getparc) are working toward the "enhancement of opportunities for all user groups in the park". As this book went to print, the riding was limited to the Alouette Mountain Access Road and the East Canyon

(Continued on page 158)

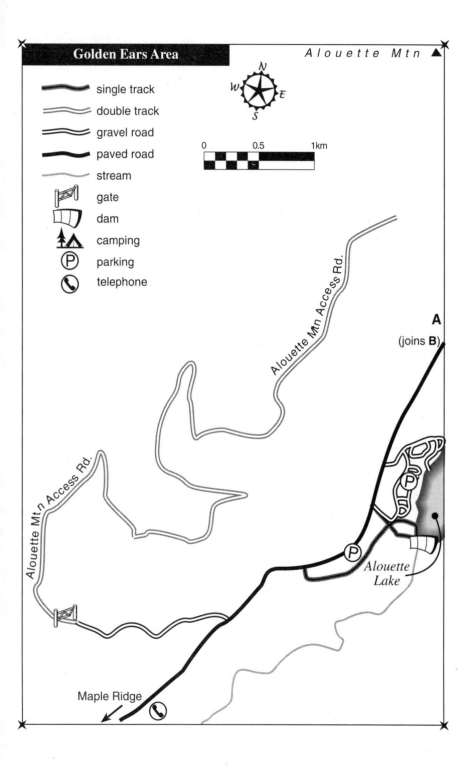

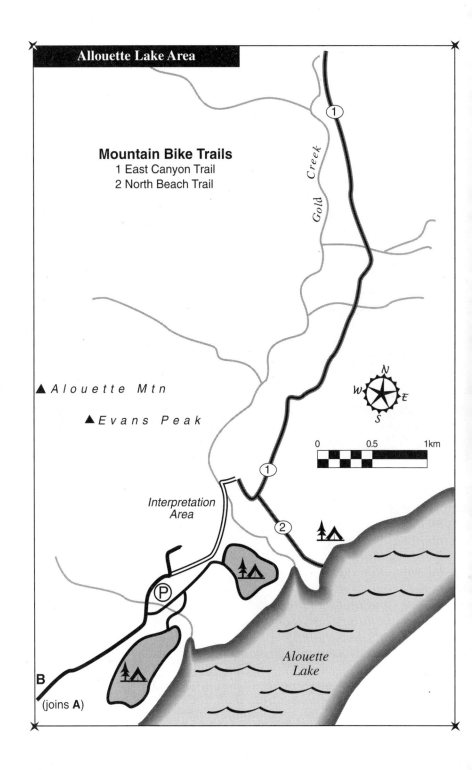

MOUNTAIN BIKING
BRITISH COLUMBIA
The Trail Guide

(Continued from page 155)

Trail. The North Beach Trail is also open to mountain bikers, but it only gives you a short ride to the beach. This park is full of potential for mountain bikers, and those who want to see more opportunities are encouraged to get involved in the efforts of Getparc. Contact the park office for details.

Golden Ears Provincial Park

East Canyon Trail

The East Canyon Trail is an out and back ride that skirts along the eastern side of Gold Creek. The trail starts as an old logging road and slowly transforms into a single track horse trail. The trail has a slight climb up and down to the creek bank, some sandy sections, and a few technical portions with cabbage sized boulders to navigate through. The trail eventually deteriorates about 14 km from the start. Once the trail becomes unrideable, turn around and head home. This ride quickly takes you into a wilderness valley and riders should plan accordingly. A solitary dip in the creek will quickly adjust your core body temperature on a hot day making the return trip as enjoyable and refreshing as the way out.

East Canyon Trail (Map p.156)

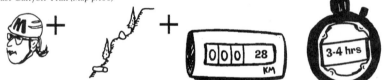

Golden Ears Provincial Park

Alouette Mountain Fire Access Road

This old logging and fire road provides a gentle grade for mountain bikers to climb. The trail is an out and back ride that can be confidently tackled by all levels of cyclists. The trails that you see starting out from the main trail are not open to riding. The road stops at a dead end. Mountain bikers may want to combine a hike to the top of Alouette Mountain and grab a view from the 1371 meter peak. Descend down the road, and enjoy the rewards of your labor.

Alouette Mountain Fire Access Road (Map p.157)

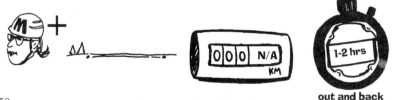

out and back

MOUNTAIN BIKING
BRITISH COLUMBIA
The Trail Guide

Sunshine Coast

Photograph by Blair Polischuk

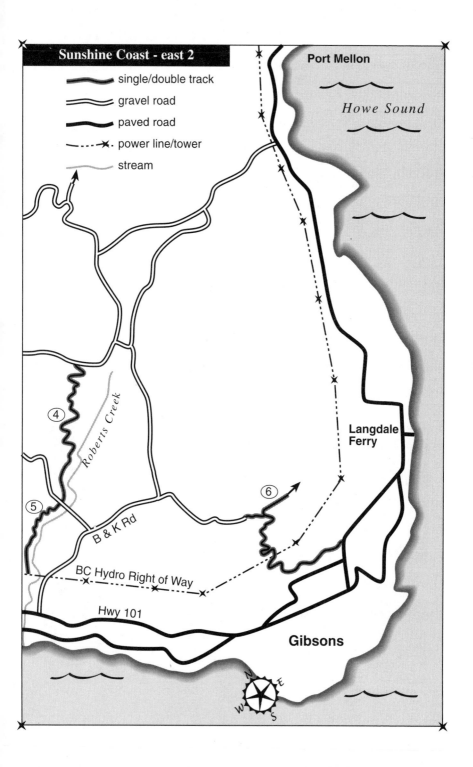

Sunshine Coast - east 2

	single/double track
	gravel road
	paved road
	power line/tower
	stream

Port Mellon

Howe Sound

④

Roberts Creek

⑤

Langdale
Ferry

⑥

B & K Rd

BC Hydro Right of Way

Hwy 101

Gibsons

N
E
W
S

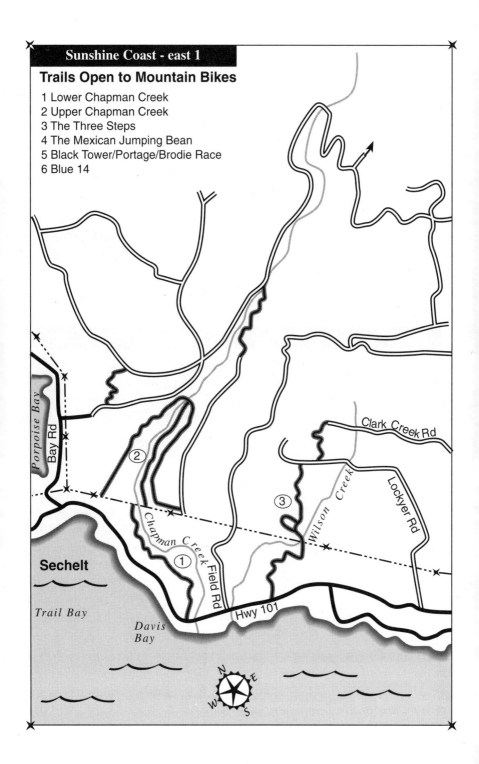

Sunshine Coast - east 1

Trails Open to Mountain Bikes

1 Lower Chapman Creek
2 Upper Chapman Creek
3 The Three Steps
4 The Mexican Jumping Bean
5 Black Tower/Portage/Brodie Race
6 Blue 14

Porpoise Bay

Bay Rd

Clark Creek Rd

Wilson Creek

Lockyer Rd

Chapman Creek Field Rd

Sechelt

Trail Bay

Davis Bay

Hwy 101

N
E
W
S

MOUNTAIN BIKING
BRITISH COLUMBIA
The Trail Guide

Sunshine Coast

1. Lower Chapman Creek Trail (east trails)

A steep hill in the center, some tricky technical sections beside the creek, and a few hikers, will confront the rider on this route. The section is best ridden from top to bottom.

Lower Chapman Creek Trail (east trail)

1. Lower Chapman Creek Trail (east trails)

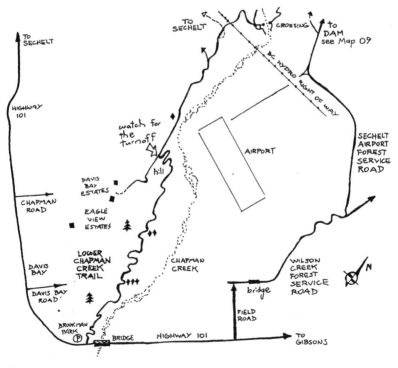

MOUNTAIN BIKING
BRITISH COLUMBIA
The Trail Guide

Sunshine Coast

2. Upper Chapman Creek Trail (east trails)

The trail starts at the top of the dam just above the falls. Expect a moderate ride down after a difficult ride up. There is a challenging creek crossing at the bottom end. Continue on to Lower Chapman Creek for a longer ride with some more difficult technical sections.

Upper Chapman Creek Trail

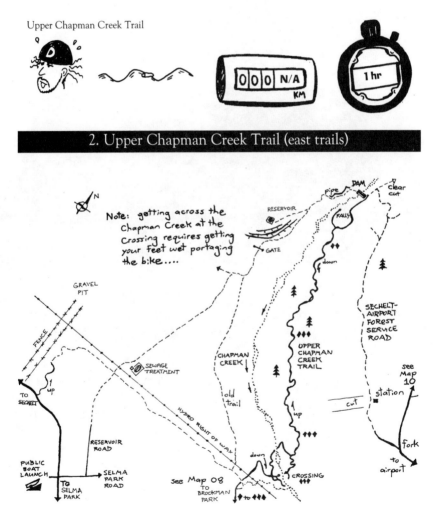

2. Upper Chapman Creek Trail (east trails)

Photograph by Blair Polischuk

Photograph by Darrin Polischuk

MOUNTAIN BIKING
BRITISH COLUMBIA
The Trail Guide

Photograph by Blair Polischuk

MOUNTAIN BIKING
BRITISH COLUMBIA
The Trail Guide

Sunshine Coast

3. The 3 Steps (east trails)

Riding up The 3 Steps is a difficult   lung-stretching process. Riding down from the top of Clack Creek Forest Service Road is a blast, with each step getting progressively faster as each large cedar looms ahead to keep the sane from going too fast.

The 3 Steps

3. The 3 Steps (east trails)

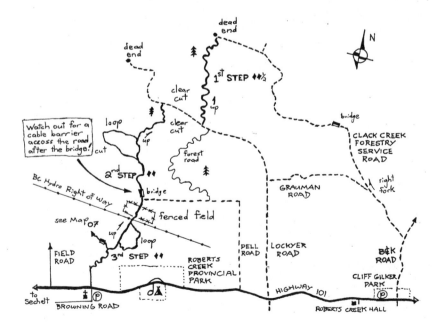

South West British Columbia

Significant
Adrenaline
Overdose

Get A feel FOR it

When it's so much fun,
it hurts

NORCO®

Look in the Yellow Pages
for a Dealer near you

ROCKY MOUNTAIN PRO RACE TEAM

PRO RIDERS (CLOCKWISE FROM TOP): WADE SIMMONS, BRUCE SPICER, ERIC TOURVILLE, ANDREAS HESTLER, KEITH STARK, ELLADEE BROWN, CHRISSY REDDEN, NEIL GROVER.

WORLD CLASS BIKES DEMAND WORLD CLASS DEALERS
B.C.'S AUTHORIZED ROCKY MOUNTAIN DEALERS

LOWER MAINLAND

AMBLESIDE CYCLE, 1852 MARINE DR. WEST, WEST VANCOUVER, BC 604-926-6242
BIKES ON BROADWAY, 620 EAST BROADWAY ST., VANCOUVER, BC 604-874-8611
CAPS PRO WORKS, 420 E. COLUMBIA ST., NEW WESTMINSTER, BC 604-524-8655
CARLTON CYCLE, 3201 KINGSWAY ST., VANCOUVER, BC 604-438-6371
JACKS CYCLE, 5628 VEDDER RD., VEDDER CROSSING, BC 604-858-3011
LIFE CYCLES BIKE SHOP, 104-1520 MCCALLUM RD, ABBOTSFORD, BC 604-859-2453
NEWTON ROCKY CYCLE, 7143 KING GEORGE HWY, SURREY, BC 604-591-5333
RIDGE BIKE & BOARD, 2605 B ST. JOHN'S ST., PORT MOODY, BC 604-976-8885
SIMONS BIKE SHOP, 608 ROBSON ST., VANCOUVER, BC 604-602-1181
TAILWIND CYCLES, 136-4800 NO. 3 ROAD, RICHMOND, BC 604-273-8050
WEST POINT CYCLES, 6069 W. BOULEVARD, VANCOUVER, BC 604-263-7587
WEST POINT CYCLES, 3771 W. 10TH AVE., VANCOUVER, BC 604-224-3536
WHITE ROCK CYCLES, 1465 JOHNSTON ROAD, WHITEROCK, BC 604-531-8111

VANCOUVER ISLAND

ARROWSMITH MOUNTAIN CYCLE, 11-425 E. STANFORD AVE, PARKSVILLE, BC 604-248-5575
EXPERIENCE CYCLING, 482 TRANSCANADA HWY, DUNCAN, BC 604-746-4041
JR'S CYCLEDELI, 3646 DENMAN RD., DENMAN ISLAND, BC 604-335-1797
OZZIE SPORT 'N' CYCLE, 3787 3RD AVENUE, PORT ALBERNI, BC 604-724-6556
PACIFIC RIM BICYCLES, 6-6404 METRAL DR., NANAIMO, BC 604-756-1783
PEDAL PUSHER CYCLE, 137 5TH ST., COURTENAY, BC 604-334-4845
PEDAL YOUR WORLD, 465 BIC MERECROFT ROAD, CAMPBELL RIVER, BC 604-287-2453
RIDER'S CYCLE, 1092 CLOVERDALE AVE., VICTORIA, BC 604-381-1125
RUSS HAY BICYCLE SHOP, 650 HILLSIDE AVE., VICTORIA, BC 604-384-4722
RUSS HAY SIDNEY, 2480 BEACON AVE., SIDNEY, BC 604-656-1512

OKANAGAN

FERNIE SPORTS, BOX 1538 401 HWY 3, FERNIE, BC 604-423-3611
FRESH AIR EXPERIENCE, 18-2070 HARVEY AVE., KELOWNA, BC 604-763-9544
OLYMPIA CYCLE & SKI, 3102-31ST AVE., VERNON, BC 604-542-9684
SACRED RIDE, 347 B BAKER ST., NELSON, BC 604-354-3831
THE BIKE BARN, 300 WESTMINSTER AVE. WEST, PENTICTION, BC 604-492-4140
VERNON BIKE WORLD, 3106 32ND ST., VERNON, BC 604-545-8775

COAST

COMPLETE CYCLE, 142-4801 JOYCE AVE., POWELL RIVER, BC 604-485-9817
CORSA CYCLES, 38128 CLEVELAND AVE., SQUAMISH, BC 604-892-3331
GLACIER SHOP, 4573 CHATEAU BLVD., WHISTLER, BC 604-933-7744
TRAILBAY SPORTS, 5504 TRAIL AVE., SECHELT, BC 604-885-2512
VERTICAL SKI & CYCLE, 212 3RD AVE. WEST, PRINCE RUPERT, BC 604-627-1766

INTERIOR

COLUMBIA MOTOR SPORTS, 380 LAURIER ST., INVERMERE, BC 604-342-6164
DAWSON CYCLE & SKI, 416 4TH ST. N.E., SALMON ARM, BC 604-832-7368
KEENS SPORTS, 273 REID ST., QUESNEL, BC 604-992-2724
100 MILE SPORTSHOP, 409 HWY FRONTAGE, 100 MILE HOUSE, BC 604-395-4812
RED SHEDS B & B, 95 SOUTH 1ST AVE., WILLIAMS LAKE, BC 604-398-7873
SILVER BARN, HWY #3 WEST, GRAND FORKS, BC 604-442-8006
SPOKE 'N' MOTION, 194 WEST VICTORIA ST., KAMLOOPS, BC 604-372-3001
SPOKETACULAR MTN SPORTS, 111 MACKENKIE AVE., REVELSTOKE, BC 604-837-2220
ULTRA SPORT, 1237 4TH AVE., PRINCE GEORGE, BC 604-562-7930

FOR A FREE CATALOG, CONTACT US AT:

Rocky Mountain Bicycle Co. Ltd. 1322 Cliveden Ave, Delta, B.C., Canada V3M 6G4
Tel: (604) 527-9993 Fax: (604) 527-9959
Web: www.rocky-mountain.com

MOUNTAIN BIKING
BRITISH COLUMBIA
The Trail Guide

Sunshine Coast

4. The Mexican Jumping Bean (east trails)

This trail is an extremely technical climb up, but it is more fun to ride up The Wilson Creek or B&K Forest Service Roads and descend from the top. The rough creek beds and technical sections in the middle portion of the 'bean', and the fist-sized boulders on the 10 km climb up B&K Road make this a challenging overall ride. You earn your 'burritos' on this one.

The Mexican Jumping Bean

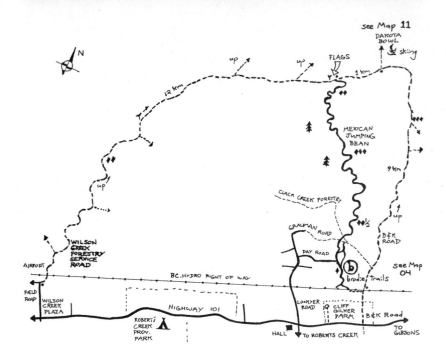
4. The Mexican Jumping Bean (east trails)

MOUNTAIN BIKING
BRITISH COLUMBIA
The Trail Guide

Sunshine Coast

5. Black Tower / Portage / Brodie Race (east trails)

This is the area that is really littered with trails. Advanced riders will want to head east from the 'start', and go north up on Black Tower, down B&K about 100 meters, cut right to Portage trail, and back all the way down to the Hydrolines, up the Brodie Race Trail, out to B&K again, up to Black Tower, and down Black Tower to the 'start'. A good hard ride.

Black Tower / Portage / Brodie Race

5. Black Tower / Portage / Brodie Race (east trails)

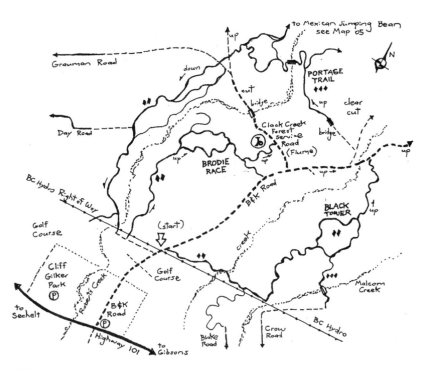

MOUNTAIN BIKING
BRITISH COLUMBIA
The Trail Guide

Sunshine Coast

6. Blue 14 (east trails)

This trail can be ridden in either direction, via the Sechelt Dump Road or the Sechelt Airport Forest Service Road. It is recommended to ride up to the Blue 14 sign and bomb down the trail. Be aware of the log bridges and water bars on your trip down.

Blue 14

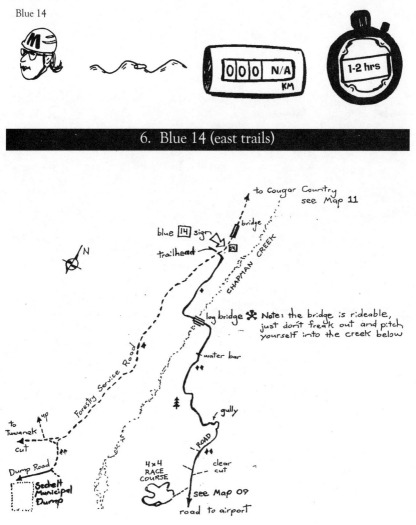

6. Blue 14 (east trails)

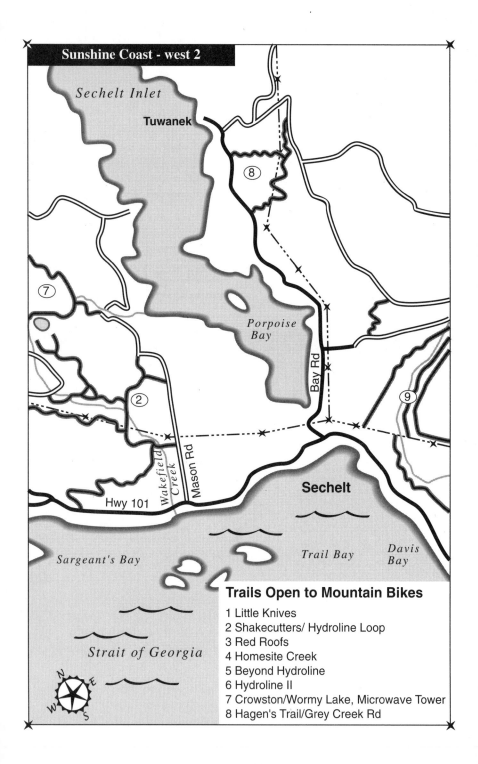

Sunshine Coast - west 2

Sechelt Inlet

Tuwanek

⑧

⑦

Porpoise Bay

Bay Rd

②

⑨

Wakefield Creek

Mason Rd

Hwy 101

Sechelt

Sargeant's Bay

Trail Bay

Davis Bay

Strait of Georgia

N
W E
S

Trails Open to Mountain Bikes

1 Little Knives
2 Shakecutters/ Hydroline Loop
3 Red Roofs
4 Homesite Creek
5 Beyond Hydroline
6 Hydroline II
7 Crowston/Wormy Lake, Microwave Tower
8 Hagen's Trail/Grey Creek Rd

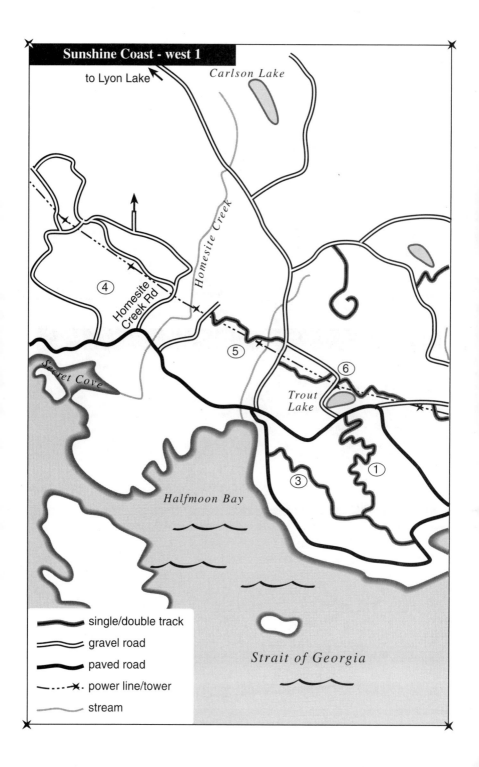

MOUNTAIN BIKING
BRITISH COLUMBIA
The Trail Guide

Sunshine Coast

1. Little Knives (west trails)

This trail is best ridden from the top of Trout Lake down to Sargents Bay. Wipe out on this trail and you risk being skewered by one of the many saplings which are cut about 6 inches from the ground. These "knives" are leftover from a recent trail clearing.

Little Knives

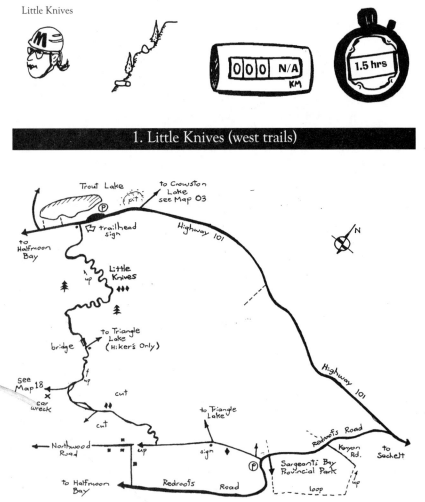

1. Little Knives (west trails)

MOUNTAIN BIKING
BRITISH COLUMBIA
The Trail Guide

Sunshine Coast

2. Shakecutters / Hydroline (west trails)

This is an enjoyable loop in either direction with a good climb at the start. It is recommended to ride up **Shakecutters** first. While bombing down the forest road make sure not to miss the sharp left hairpin turn which will put you back onto the Hydroline Trail.

Shakecutters / Hydroline

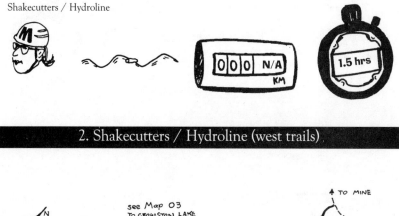

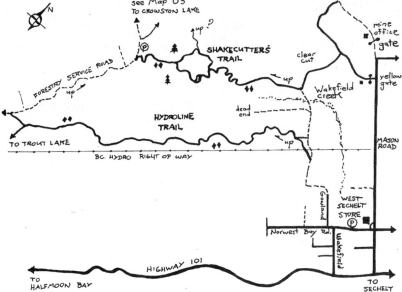

2. Shakecutters / Hydroline (west trails)

MOUNTAIN BIKING
BRITISH COLUMBIA
The Trail Guide

Sunshine Coast

3. Redroofs (west trails)

This trail has been groomed by hikers, and local riders looking for technical challenges now ride elsewhere. For new mountain bikers, or those not "up" for a hard ride, this one will please.

Redroofs

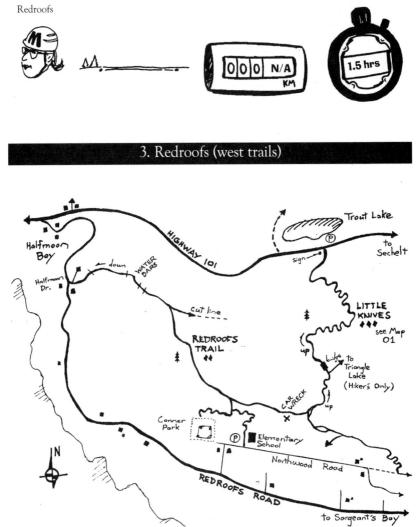

3. Redroofs (west trails)

MOUNTAIN BIKING
BRITISH COLUMBIA
The Trail Guide

Sunshine Coast

4. Homesite Creek (west trails)

This is a great area for intermediate riders to rip it up and feel at 'home'. A good uphill crank with lots of riding under the lines, and a downhill that will make your eyeballs bleed.

Homesite Creek

4. Homesite Creek (west trails)

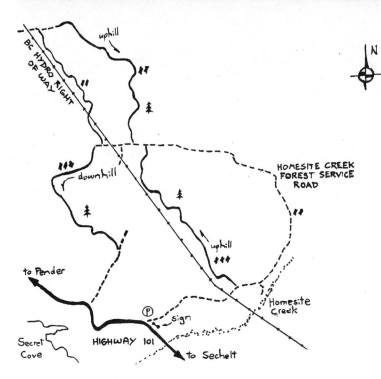

MOUNTAIN BIKING
BRITISH COLUMBIA
The Trail Guide

Sunshine Coast

◢ 5. Beyond Hydroline (west trails)

This ride ducks in and out of the woods along the B.C. Hydro right-of-way.
The ride arrives at a gravel road which provides a great downhill to the highway, or a less travelled that route continues to the Homesite Creek Road.

Beyond Hydroline

5. Beyond Hydroline (west trails)

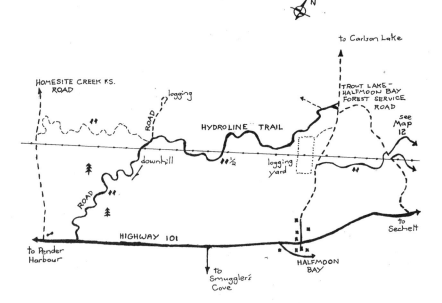

South West British Columbia

MOUNTAIN BIKING
BRITISH COLUMBIA
The Trail Guide

Sunshine Coast

6. Hydroline 2 (west trails)

This extension of the Hydroline trail increases in difficulty as you proceed west. After arriving at the Trout Lake Forest Service Road, it is best to take this road to the next hydroline section above Halfmoon Bay.

Hydroline 2

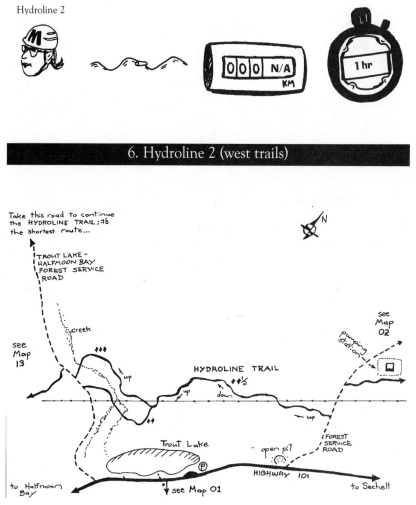

6. Hydroline 2 (west trails)

MOUNTAIN BIKING
BRITISH COLUMBIA
The Trail Guide

Sunshine Coast

7. Crowston / Wormy Lake / Microwave Tower (west trails)

A multitude of old roads, skidder trails, and dead ends make getting lost in this area a definite possibility. It is best to combine this ride with others like Shake-cutters or Hydroline.

Crowston / Wormy Lake / Microwave Tower

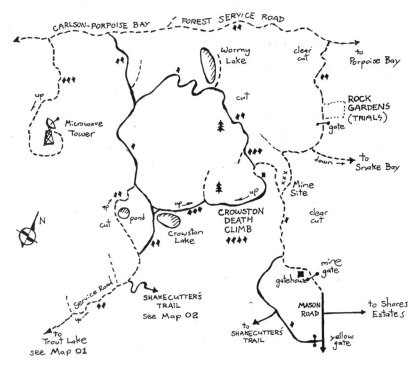

7. Crowston / Wormy Lake / Microwave Tower (west trails)

MOUNTAIN BIKING
BRITISH COLUMBIA
The Trail Guide

Sunshine Coast

8. Hagen's Trail / Gray Creek Road (west trails)

Hagen's Trail is accessed by taking the cut from the Tree Farm Trail / Road west to the hydroline and proceeding about 100 meters towards Gray Creek. The trail head is in the bush about 200 meters from the Gray Creek Ravine. Since you can't ride up Hagen's, you have to start from the Hydroline and ride down this truly nasty technical downhill.

Hagen's Trail / Gray Creek Road

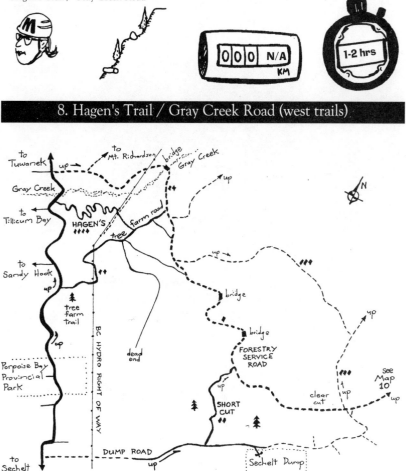

8. Hagen's Trail / Gray Creek Road (west trails)

MOUNTAIN BIKING
BRITISH COLUMBIA
The Trail Guide

Sunshine Coast

Sprockids Mountain Bike Park

Doug Detwiller is the pioneer of mountain biking within the B.C. school system. He has done an amazing job of designing and implementing mountain biking into the schools. Part of the work done by students, the community, the school, and Doug has involved building a mountain bike park. This park has plenty of short fun loops for younger riders to enjoy. Access the mountain bike park from the ferry terminal, by taking either the new By-pass, or North Rd. to Stewart Rd. At the end of Stewart go left, park, and ride.

Photograph by Blair Polischuk

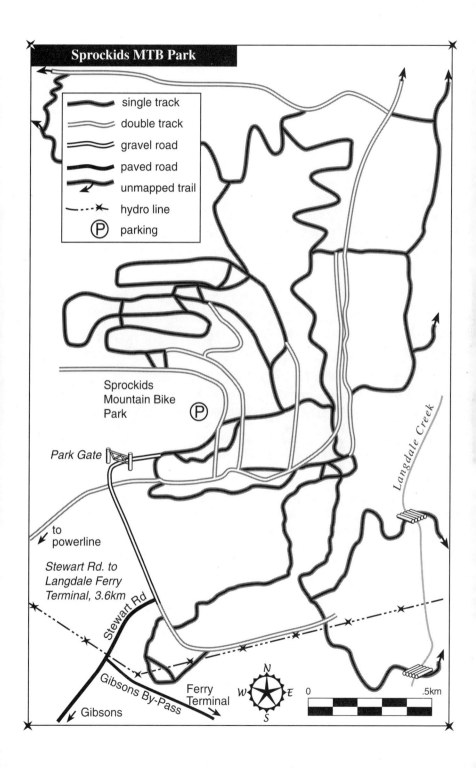

Sprockids MTB Park

single track
double track
gravel road
paved road
unmapped trail
hydro line
Ⓟ parking

Sprockids
Mountain Bike
Park Ⓟ

Park Gate

to
powerline

Stewart Rd. to
Langdale Ferry
Terminal, 3.6km

Stewart Rd

Langdale Creek

Gibsons By-Pass

Ferry
Terminal

Gibsons

N
W E
S

0   .5km

MOUNTAIN BIKING
BRITISH COLUMBIA
The Trail Guide

Powell River Trails

Powell River Trails

Introduction

The upper Sunshine Coast / Powell River area is accessed from the Lower Mainland by taking the ferry from Horseshoe Bay to Langdale, driving up the coast, and taking the ferry from Earls Cove to Saltry Bay. The final push to Powell River is along Highway 101. Ferry service is also available from Comox on Vancouver Island. The trip may sound epic, but for mountain bikers who want unlimited riding that rises up from the ocean and opens into a small town setting, it's well worth it.

Powell River is renowned for sport fishing, but according to the boys at **Taws Cycle and Sport** in Powell River, the riding that stretches deep into the Coast Mountains is right on par with that other world class recreational opportunity. Bringing your moun-site, but you may want ing, or a canoe trip on Canoe Route that has tween a chain of eight area is built upon an ated by the forest in-roads and single tracks

"The trip may sound epic, but for mountain bikers who want unlimited riding that rises up from the ocean and opens into a small town setting, it's well worth it."

tain bike is a prerequi- to consider some div- the Powell River Forest portage trails in be- lakes. The riding in this infrastructure first cre- dustry. Old logging weave around the hills,

lakes, and valleys near Powell River. The information and maps are included because the Sushine Coast Forest District have done a great job in mapping, describing and signing mountain bike routes. Cheers to all who worked on the mountain bike mapping project.

MOUNTAIN BIKING
BRITISH COLUMBIA
The Trail Guide

Powell River Trails

Bunster Hills Loop

This counter clockwise loop features a long 12 km grind up 750 meters, but the rewards are views of Okeover Inlet and Georgia Straight that make the big push less of a chore. Follow Wilde Road north-east for 2 km to where the road becomes Theodosia Forest Service Road. Once on this forest road, the climb begins. 8 km up from High- *"...the rewards are views of* way 101 you will pass the Appleton Creek *Okeover Inlet and Georgia* Trail, but stay on the main road. The Apple- *Straight that make the big* ton and Marathon Trails cut across the *push less of a chore."* big loop. Once you crest the climb a long 6 km descent will bring you to an intersection, turn left and follow the road for 3 km to a fork. The right fork is Southview Road. Follow this road for 3 km to Highway 101 and then turn right onto the start of the loop. This loop is on old logging road and is marked with the white mountain bike symbol, or double orange band of paint.

Bunster Hills Loop (Map p.186-7)

Powell River Trails

The Inland Lake Loop

This wheel chair accessible loop around Inland Lake is an easy ride for all levels of mountain bikers. The crushed limestone surface has gentle grades and passes by picnic sites and fishing wharfs that beg you to stop and relax. Be aware that this is a busy multi-use trail and ride slowly with caution. The Inland Lake area has a trail leading to Powell Lake as well as a trail leading from Inland Lake Road to Person Lake.

The Inland Lake Loop (Map p.186-7)

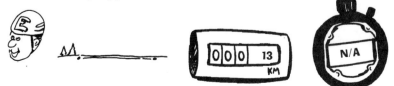

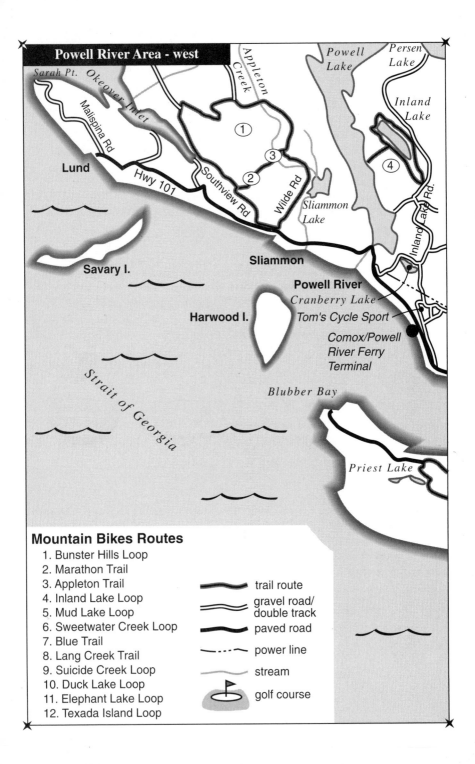

Powell River Area - west

Sarah Pt.
Okeover Inlet
Malispina Rd
Lund
Hwy 101
Southview Rd
Appleton Creek
① ③ ② Wilde Rd
Sliammon Lake
Powell Lake
Persen Lake
Inland Lake
④
Inland Lake Rd.

Savary I.

Sliammon

Powell River
Cranberry Lake
Tom's Cycle Sport

Harwood I.

Comox/Powell
River Ferry
Terminal

Strait of Georgia

Blubber Bay

Priest Lake

Mountain Bikes Routes
1. Bunster Hills Loop
2. Marathon Trail
3. Appleton Trail
4. Inland Lake Loop
5. Mud Lake Loop
6. Sweetwater Creek Loop
7. Blue Trail
8. Lang Creek Trail
9. Suicide Creek Loop
10. Duck Lake Loop
11. Elephant Lake Loop
12. Texada Island Loop

‖‖‖ trail route
═══ gravel road/
double track
━━━ paved road
-·-·- power line
~~~ stream
⚑ golf course

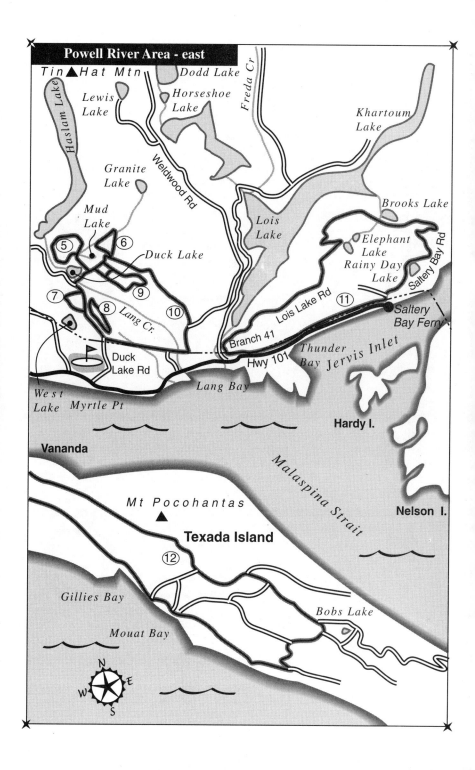

MOUNTAIN BIKING
BRITISH COLUMBIA
The Trail Guide

Powell River Trails

Mud Lake Trail System

Access to the **Mud Lake Trail** is found by following Highway 101, 4 km south of Powell River and then left on Duck Lake Road. Drive or ride 7.5 km to Duck Lake. Turn right at the intersection just before Duck Lake and you'll find a small parking area after 1.5 km. The trail is a circular system at the end of a 2 km access spur.

Mud Lake Trail System (Map p.186-7)

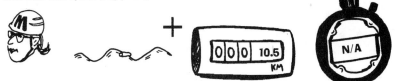

Powell River Trails

Sweetwater Creek Loop

To access this loop from Duck Lake Road, turn right just before Duck Lake and left at the first intersection about 2.5 km from the right turn. Take the next left fork and look for the trail head on the right. The start of the trail follows an old railroad grade to Sweetwater Creek. The trail narrows and continues to follow Sweetwater Creek toward MacGregor Falls. Approximately 1 km up the trail it crosses a logging road and continues, following along the creek to the summit where Donnelly Falls cascades down the grade. Return down the hill following the same trail but take the branch to the left, and follow the old railway grade back to the main road.

Sweetwater Creek Loop (Map p.186-7)

Powell River Trails

Blue Trail

To access this short loop drive or ride 7.5 km up Duck Lake Road to the middle of a recently cut area. You can also access this ride from **Fred's Trail** in Pleasant Valley. From the recently cut area, backtrack along the road south for 1.5 km.

MOUNTAIN BIKING
BRITISH COLUMBIA
The Trail Guide

On the right, just before a small quarry you will see a trail leading into the woods, and a short distance later the old rail bed. Turn right and follow the rail bed 1.5 km past **Fred's Trail** on the left. Turn right on the marked trail and follow the single track 500 meters to a recently cut area. Stay on the trail when it becomes a skid road and descend back to the start. Trail markers should lead the way. This trail was built by the Ministry of Forests in conjunction with a federal government employment assistance program. Signs along the trail were provided by the local Junior Forest Warden Club which relate to the " The Powell River Demonstration Forest Blue Tour" brochure.

Blue Trail (Map p.186-7)

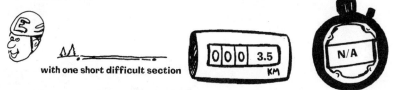

with one short difficult section |0|0|0| 3.5 KM   N/A

Powell River Trails

Lang Creek Loop

Drive or ride 6 km up Duck Lake Road to a trail marker on the right. You can also access this ride from Fred's trail via the Blue Trail. This ride has some of the best single track in the area and has a few steep pitches leading down to the Lang Creek Recreation Site. The southern part of the trail features easy shallow grades on an old rail bed. This looped is marked with a double band of orange paint. Be sure and look for the returning salmon in September and October.

Lang Creek Loop (Map p.186-7)

|0|0|0| 6.5 KM   1 hr

Powell River Trails

Suicide Creek Loop

To access the trail, turn at the intersection just before Duck Lake and follow along to a small parking area about 1.5 km further. This route heads in a southeast direction following an old railway grade. Two connector re-routes have been built to avoid two bridges and rough terrain. Two waterfalls and a picnic site will tempt you off your bike. The route is marked with orange squares and the small mountain bike symbol.

MOUNTAIN BIKING
BRITISH COLUMBIA
The Trail Guide

Powell River Trails

Duck Lake Loop

This longer loop combines the power lines with Duck Lake Road and makes for a long non-technical ride where you can explore many of the area's shorter loops. From the power lines on Duck Lake Road ride to the intersection just before the lake. Keep right at the next 3 forks, and left onto the main road 300 meters after the gravel pit. The next turn will be right onto the power line and a return to the start.

Duck Lake Loop (Map p.186-7)

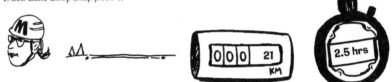

Powell River Trails

Elephant Lake Loop

For those mountain bikers who want a long day tour with outstanding views, while riding exclusivly on old logging roads, this is your ride. Access the loop at the Saltry Bay ferry terminal, or at the intersection of Highway 101 and the M&B main.

From the ferry terminal follow the Saltry Bay Forest Service Road west 300 meters until a steep fork goes left. This is the start of an 8 km climb. Keep right at the first fork. Continue past Rainy Day Lake and the steep rocky switchback until the view of Jervis Inlet forces you off the bike. At the bottom of a steep downhill turn left and stay on the main road. Views abound on the long downhill. At the bottom there is a gate, go left onto the M&B mainline. If you go right it leads to Lois Lake Forest Service Recreation Site. Go left at the mainline and left again onto highway 101 to return the Saltry Bay. If this sounds confusing follow the bike symbol or a double band of yellow or red paint.

Elephant Lake Loop (Map p.186-7)

MOUNTAIN BIKING
BRITISH COLUMBIA
The Trail Guide

Powell River Trails

Texeda Island

This all day off road tour of the island is accessible by ferry. It is possible to camp overnight at Bob's Lake or Shingle Beach and make this a two day tour. It is recommended that you leave your car in Powell River.

Start at the Esso station and ride northeast into Vanada. Leave the town on High Road and ride 16 km past Pochontas Bay intersection and School Road where the road becomes Bell Road. Follow Bell 4 km to an intersection marked B.C. Hydro Reactor and follow the right fork for 5 km to another intersection. Take the right fork to a Hydro Sub-station. Bob's Lake Recreation Site is accessible by the left fork. At the sub-station keep left around the fence and follow for 5 km. This is a steep and sketchy section. At the bottom the left fork leads to Shingle Beach. To continue the loop stay on the main road. Finish the loop by following Davie Bay Road through Gillies Bay 21 km to the Esso station.

Texeda Island (Map p.186-7)

MOUNTAIN BIKING
BRITISH COLUMBIA
The Trail Guide

Squamish

Squamish

Sea To Sky Corridor

The fact that Whistler B.C. is a world class year round resort is no fluke. The area has all the natural elements that make people want to play, or just hang out and spend money. Something amazing happens as you swing around the corner from West Vancouver and enter the famous Sea to Sky Highway; you fully realize just how beautiful British Columbia really is (despite the fact that this is the phrase printed on our licence plates). You can slag Whistler all you want for its up-scale image and run-away development, but no one can deny that the reason people flock here is because it is an awesome place to play, regardless of your sport or the season.

> *"Something amazing happens as you swing around the corner from West Vancouver and enter the famous Sea to Sky Highway..."*

While Whistler is the famous hub of the Sea to Sky corridor, the smaller, less famous recreational havens of Squamish and Pemberton, do more than hold their own when the activity is mountain biking. The trails in each center have a unique flavor. In Squamish and Pemberton the rides are not as rough in comparison to Whistler. All the trails however, share the steep, narrow, Pacific Northwest flavor that makes mountain biking in this area challenging, fun, and never boring.

Squamish

Sea To Sky Trail

This is the type of trail that could put British Columbia on the mountain biking map of the world. It has the catchy name, potential epic distance, and

(Continued on page 194)

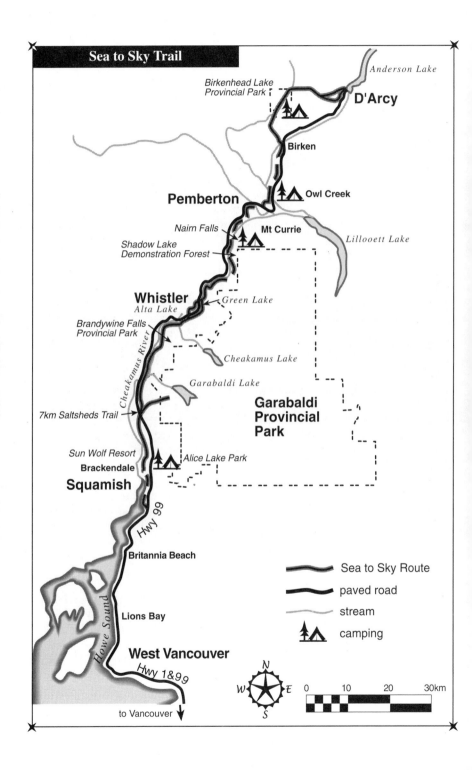

Sea to Sky Trail

Anderson Lake

Birkenhead Lake
Provincial Park

D'Arcy

Birken

Owl Creek

Pemberton

Nairn Falls

Mt Currie

Shadow Lake
Demonstration Forest

Lillooett Lake

Whistler
Alta Lake

Green Lake

Brandywine Falls
Provincial Park

Cheakamus Lake

Garabaldi Lake

Garabaldi
Provincial
Park

7km Saltsheds Trail

Sun Wolf Resort

Brackendale

Squamish

Alice Lake Park

Hwy 99

Britannia Beach

Lions Bay

West Vancouver

Hwy 1&99

Howe Sound

to Vancouver

Sea to Sky Route

paved road

stream

camping

N
W E
S

0   10   20   30km

MOUNTAIN BIKING
BRITISH COLUMBIA
The Trail Guide

(Continued from page 192)

untouchable views and terrain in the coastal mountains. The catch about this dream trail is that it is a work in progress. There are plenty of completed sections, most of which follow the fall, Cheakamus Challenge race route. So before you get too excited and plan a continuous off-road ride from Squamish to D'Arcy read on, and plan on riding some paved sections if you want to complete the entire sea to sky corridor.

The Whistler to Squamish route begins at the Sun Wolf Resort where you take a right fork into Paradise Valley. This paved road follows the Cheakamus River gradually changing _____ from paved to gravel to double track to cart *Expect some hiking sections* trail. A steep climb brings you out of the *and great views.* " valley. Expect some hiking sections and _____ great views. Once onto Highway 99, a downhill cruise takes you past the salt sheds where you look left for a logging road and a bridge over the Cheakumus River, go right after the bridge.

This next section is a bit confusing with multiple spurs. You should end up riding along a dike and beside a lake. The trail crosses a foot bridge, then through a Forest Service Campsite to the Hydro Lines. Go left on the Hydro Road for about .5 km and you should pop out at Pinecrest Estates. Follow Highway 99 to Brandywine Falls. Use the trail description in the Whistler section to find the route from Brandywine Falls to Whistler.

The section of trail from Whistler to Pemberton doesn't exist yet, sorry. From Pemberton to D'Arcy, follow the Highway from Pemberton through Mt. Currie and stay on the main road (do not take the right turn towards Lillooet). At Owl Creek a double track heads up the west side of Birkenhead River. A paved road crosses and follows the south east side. The old logging road is part of the Sea To Sky route but it currently dead ends at Gramsons where a bridge must be built. About 6 km north of Mt.Currie turn left off Portage Road and follow the description of the Birkenhead Lake Loop to D'Arcy.

This trail is moreso a work in progress than an actual set ride. It is without a doubt a noble undertaking and as mountain bikers and citizens of B.C. we should support it with donations or trail building time. For further information and on update or completed sections contact: Sea To Sky Trail Society, Box 2539 Squamish, B.C. V0N 3G0, Canada. Phone (604) 892-5467 or Highline Cycles in Pemberton at (694) 894-6625.

MOUNTAIN BIKING
BRITISH COLUMBIA
The Trail Guide

Squamish

The forest town of Squamish (from the Indian Squohomish, or 'strong wind') is famous for its howling wind and the Stawamus Chief. The wind attracts boardheads to what is now considered the 'Gorge North', and the Chief and surrounding 'bluffs' attract sport, and big wall climbers from all over the world. The most recent recreational group to converge on this resource-based town are mountain bikers who come for the unlimited riding on the valleys and slopes that surround Squamish. A comprehensive mountain biking guidebook on this area is available for those who want to explore further.

Squamish

Alice Lake Provincial Park

The terrain around Alice Lake, named after the first white woman to see the lake in 1893, offers some excellent single track riding without having to endure super steep climbs. Here, a network of trails snake their way through a beautiful second growth forest that stretches from the park to Garibaldi Highlands in Squamish. The park can be very busy during peak summer months, and is best avoided on weekends. Once July and August have passed, Alice Lake comes alive with great riding, right into the early winter.

> *"Here, a network of trails snake their way through a beautiful second growth forest that stretches from the park to Garibaldi Highlands in Squamish."*

In the spring the trails are often too wet to ride and are actually closed for that reason. Check at Corsa Cycles for up to date information on spring trail closures.

Squamish

Four Lakes Trail / Cheekeye Loop

To access the trails in Alice Lake drive north from Squamish 9.5 km along Highway 99 to the Alice Lake turnoff. The turnoff is well marked with blue and white Provincial Park signs. Turn right off the highway and drive a short distance to where the road splits at the main entrance to the park. I recommend going left, towards the RV sani-station, where a small parking lot sits near the Four Lakes Trailhead.

At this point, a small map will show you a rough idea of where you are going. The Four Lakes Trail lies entirely in the park boundaries, and is well marked with direction signs. The trail runs from the parking lot up to Stump Lake, where it splits, with a branch running along both shores. You can take either one, as they meet again at the far end of the lake. At this point a sign will indicate the route to the second of the four lakes, Fawn Lake. When you reach Fawn Lake, the single track pops out on a small dirt lot. From this point signs will indicate that the Four Lakes Trail runs to the right, down the dirt road, but you should consider a small detour to the Cheekeye Loop before continuing.

Squamish

The Cheekeye Loop

This loop starts at the end of the dirt lot, just beyond the boulders. The trail follows an old logging road through the forest for about a kilometer, until you arrive at a clearing under some powerlines. Continue past the powerlines, back into the forest. Immediately start to look on the right for a single track, head up the single track and follow it to the bank of the Cheekeye River. Here the trail turns left, and follows the river bank for awhile, until it reaches an old "corduroy" road, so named because they were made by lying lengths of timber side by side. This road leads back to the powerlines, but the single track continues to the right. It follows the river a bit longer, then heads back to close the loop under the powerlines. Turn right and head back to Fawn Lake.

Continue to follow the signs to the third of the lakes, Edith Lake. Here you will have to make another decision: whether to continue to Alice Lake, or head out of the park towards Garibaldi Highlands. If you choose to head to the Highlands, continue along the shore of Edith Lake and you will find yourself on another corduroy road. This road is short, washed out in spots, and may require some bushwhacking. Soon the trail arrives at another dirt road, turn right, and head down the road. At one point you will have to cross a small bridge over a wash out, ———————————————————————— then continue down *"The left fork takes you directly to Garibadli High-* the road. After the *lands, while the right fork begins a long beautiful* bridge, keep your eyes *descent through a moss covered forest."* peeled for a small metal ———————————————————————— post on the right, at the top of a dip in the road. Beside the post, on the right side of the road, a single track climbs up into the woods. Go up this trail. The left fork takes you directly to Garibadli Highlands, while the right fork begins a long beautiful descent through a moss covered forest. This trail ends at an intersection of trails. From here a trail goes left to the Highlands, while Jack's Trail continues straight into the forest. Jack's Trail used to run back to Alice Lake, but its middle section has been logged. It may be rebuilt in the future, but as of

(Continued on page 198)

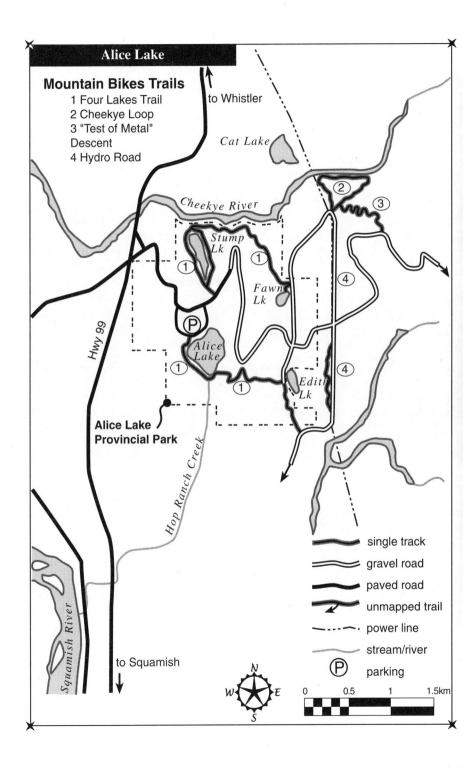

Alice Lake

Mountain Bikes Trails
1 Four Lakes Trail
2 Cheekye Loop
3 "Test of Metal" Descent
4 Hydro Road

to Whistler

Cat Lake

Cheekye River

Stump Lk

Fawn *Lk*

Hwy 99

(P)

Alice Lake

Edith Lk

Alice Lake Provincial Park

Hop Ranch Creek

to Squamish

Squamish River

~~~~~ single track
——— gravel road
▬▬▬ paved road
↙ unmapped trail
–·–·– power line
⌇⌇⌇ stream/river
(P) parking

N
W ✦ E
S

0   0.5   1   1.5km

MOUNTAIN BIKING
BRITISH COLUMBIA
The Trail Guide

(Continued from page 196)

the fall 1995 its status was uncertain. If you elect not to ride Garibaldi Highlands from Edith Lake, continue down the Four Lakes Trail towards the final lake on the loop. This section of trail is the most technical on the Four Lakes Trail, and will provide an entertaining descent. When you reach the lake, go left and follow the shore back to the parking lot.

The Cheekeye Loop (Map p.197)

for both trails

Squamish

Diamond Head Alpine Trail

This trail is a high alpine ride and the only trail open to mountain bikers in Garibaldi Provincial Park. It is an out and back ride that follows an old jeep road and features stunning vistas of jagged peaks, hanging glaciers, Howe Sound, and acres of wild flowers. You can expect about 2500 vertical feet of climbing from the parking lot or a whopping 5800 ft. if you ride from the valley floor. This trail can be very busy in the summer, so keep your bike under control on the descent, and try to plan your high alpine ride on a weekday if possible.

To access the trail from downtown Squamish, head north on Highway 99 for about 4 km to the blue and white 'Garibaldi Provincial Park' sign reading: 'Diamond Head ————————————— 16 km'. Turn right and follow *"It is very important to stay on the main* this road as it runs past the golf *trail while in the alpine, and avoid riding* course and be- comes hard- *on the side trails as the meadows are very* packed dirt for 16 km to the *fragile and can be easily damaged. "* parking lot. The road is well ——————————————— marked with signs. If you are into climbing the whole shot to the alpine, then ride the entire 16 km to the parking lot.

For most mortals the ride will start at the trail head area where relevant trail information will be posted. From the start, the trail switches up through old growth forest that steadily thins as you approach the treeline. Soon you will reach the red Heather Hut, located at the treeline on the edge of the meadows.

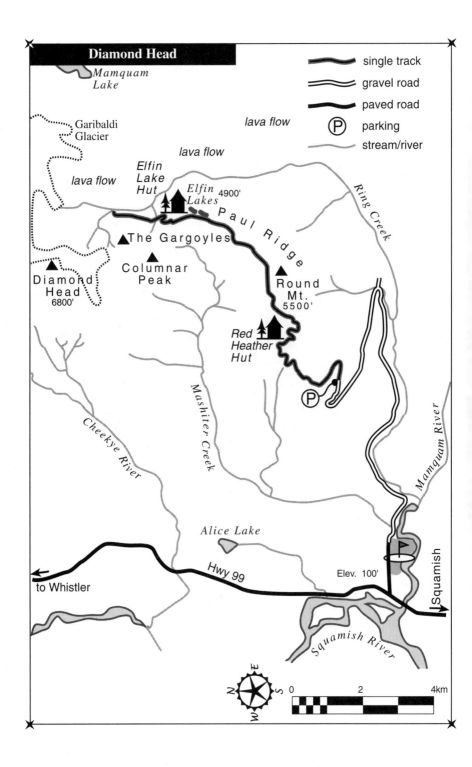

MOUNTAIN BIKING
BRITISH COLUMBIA
The Trail Guide

From here the trail climbs into the alpine areas of Round Mountain. It is very important to stay on the main trail while in the alpine, and avoid riding on the side trails as the meadows are very fragile and can be easily damaged .

As the trail reaches its crest on the flank of Round Mountain you are presented with a stunning panorama of the interior of Garibaldi Provincial Park. From this point, the trail continues for another 5 or 6 km to the Elfin Lakes Hut along the ridge ahead of you. The trail drops into the lake, necessitating a short climb back out. The legal bike route ends at the Elfin Lakes Hut, but hiking routes extend further into the park. Retrace your steps back and be aware of other riders and hikers on the trail.

Diamond Head Alpine Trail (Map p.199)

Brandywine Falls

This moderate ride follows old logging roads along the valley floor from the village of Whistler to Brandywine Falls Provincial Park and back. Most of the riding is technically easy, but includes a modest single track section just past the suspension bridge at the Cal-Cheak Forest Service Site. The route also traverses the Lava Lakes area above Brandywine Falls, on a great high speed double track through stands of Lodgepole pine. This is a popular early season ride and is usually the first ride of any length to be free of snow.

To access the trail, ride south from the village on Highway 99 for 7.5 km past Whistler Creek to Function Junction, which is marked with a large wooden sign. Turn left into the Whistler Interpretive Forest and ride up the paved road towards the dump. After crossing the single lane bridge over the Cheakamus ———————————————— River the road splits. The left *"This section can be a little foul on a hot* fork is marked as Westside *day but hey, it's your garbage! "* Main and the right fork leads ———————————————— into the dump. This section can be a little foul on a hot day but hey, it's your garbage! Follow the right fork into the heart of the landfill. You will pass a building on your left, and on your right a road that goes deeper into the dump. Keep riding for about 100 meters and you should see another road on the right that leads away from the stench. A Brandywine Falls sign was there once, but may be

South West British Columbia

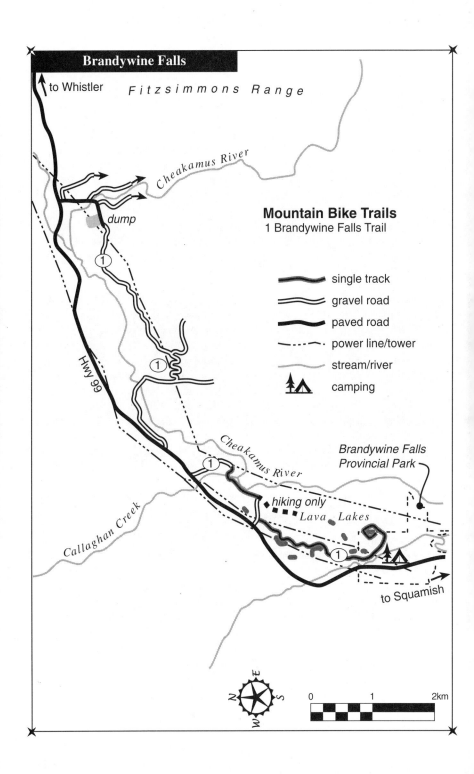

Brandywine Falls

to Whistler

Fitzsimmons Range

Cheakamus River

dump

Hwy 99

Cheakamus River

Callaghan Creek

Mountain Bike Trails
1 Brandywine Falls Trail

single track
gravel road
paved road
power line/tower
stream/river
camping

Brandywine Falls Provincial Park

hiking only
Lava Lakes

to Squamish

0   1   2km

missing. Follow this road as it rolls through the hills south from the dump. There is a basalt quarry about 1 km from the dump so be aware of heavy vehicles.

After a couple of km, just past the crest of a hill, the road forks, with the right branch dropping downhill, while the main road continues off to the left. Take the right branch and begin the rough, rocky descent down the Cheakamus River. Along the way you pass another road heading left. Ignore it and keep descending to the bridge.

After crossing the bridge the road rolls along to an area known as the Basalt Columns. This is a volcanic formation of hexagonal pillars just off the highway.

"This is a volcanic formation of hexagonal pillars just off the highway."

Here you must ride down the highway a short distance to the Cal-Cheak Forest Service Site. The turnoff is on the left just before a bridge and is marked with a small sign. If you reach the four lane section of highway you've gone too far.

After entering the Cal-Cheak site (named for the confluence of the Cheakamus and Callaghan Rivers), ride past the first campsite down to the hydro lines. The entrance to the suspension bridge is through the second campsite on the right. This is a large site and you may have to search around for it. Once across the bridge there is a section of single track that follows the riverbank for about 1 km. This trail emerges briefly beside some railway tracks. From here the trail heads back into the woods, but do not ride it if you want to ride to the falls because it becomes unrideable from this point. Just ignore the Brandywine sign.

The route for mountain bikers crosses over the railway tracks and briefly along a dirt road to the hydro lines. From here a double track runs up into the pine trees on the left beside the powerlines. This section is known as Lava Lakes. This entire area is an ancient lava flow, and in the depressions rainfall collects forming many small ponds. This winding section of trail is slightly downhill and is great fun. Be aware of a short steep section just before the entrance to the park. This hill has a nasty drop-off on the right so be careful. The park, with plenty of hikers and Brandywine Falls, awaits. Retrace your steps back, or take the highway back to Whistler.

Brandywine Falls (Map p.201)

MOUNTAIN BIKING
BRITISH COLUMBIA
The Trail Guide

Whistler

Introduction

The Resort Municipality of Whistler lies in a valley at the crest of a gentle pass between Squamish and Pemberton. At the low altitude of 2200 ft. above sea level, the terrain surrounding Whistler maintains an alpine feel to it in spite of its low elevation. The tree-line in the valley can be found around 5000 ft. and glaciers can exist as low as 6000 ft. The actual valley stretches for about 25 km and is home to five lakes, from north to south called: Alpha, Nita, Alta, Lost, and Green Lakes.

Like much of B.C., the Whistler Valley was home to gold fever in its early days, however, the color that turned Whistler into a world famous mega-resort is white. While skiing is still the main winter activity, the resort is now humming in all the seasons. Today, mountain biking is one of many 'off-season' activities that draw people to the valley. The history of mountain biking in Whistler goes hand in hand with the development of skiing. It was some ski bums from North Vancouver who first *"The history of mountain biking in Whistler goes hand in hand with the development of skiing."* brought their bikes up to check out the local terrain. What they found was a variety of tough rocky single tracks and an unlimited network of old logging roads to take you into the backountry. The great views, high alpine riding, and uncrowded trails, have become a Whistler hallmark. Today, through the efforts of The Whistler Off-Road Cycling Association (WORCA), trails have been cut and the valley is now covered with outstanding single track.

Whistler

Green Lake / Parkhurst

This ride begins with a 10 km spin before crossing the Green River, and returning to Whistler Village on a series of old logging roads, hydro access roads, and a brief section along the railway track. Besides the great views of Green Lake, and the Rainbow Glacier, this trail provides an opportunity to ride a single track loop through the ghost town of Parkhurst, on the shores of Green Lake.

To access the trail from the village, go north on Highway 99 and begin the 10 km road spin to the trail. This will take you past Green Lake, Emerald Estates,

MOUNTAIN BIKING
BRITISH COLUMBIA
The Trail Guide

and the heli-port. At the bottom of a long downhill, where the road and the Green River parallel briefly, look for a road that branches right from the highway, over railway tracks, and into a small parking lot with a sign reading 'Wedgemont'.

After turning into the parking, lot ride through it and over the bridge that crosses the Green River. The road forks here. Take the right fork that heads back to Whistler up some steep hills which characterize much of this ride. The left fork is closed to mountain bikes. After cresting the first hill, the road drops down into a large open area that is the eroded remains of a gravel pit. Continue along the road until ——————————————— you hit a small creek and a washed out *"These trails are well marked and* road. Cross the creek and go right *return to the village. "* off the main road, and ride toward the ——————————————— railway tracks. Follow the tracks over the bridge and continue past for about 200 meters until a single track on your left beckons you into the woods. This trail soon widens, and you'll ride down a washed out spot. Keep to the right and shortly you'll see a road climbing to the right under the powerlines. From here the road begins a long, sandy climb, then a short descent to a flat section. Ride across the flats, and when the trail begins to climb again, look right for a well worn single track. This is the Parkhurst Trail.

The Parkhurst Trail is a short loop that branches off the main trail and is well worth exploring. After leaving the main trail Parkhurst drops down a steep rocky hill, crosses a small creek, and then splits into two. Take either fork, as the trail loops back, and soon you will come across the old townsite of Parkhurst. This small logging operation was abandoned in the 1930's, though in recent years a few of the buildings have been fixed up. Remember to respect this private property. Return to the main Green Lake Trail and retrace your steps up the rocky trail you entered on.

When you have rejoined the Green Lake Trail turn right and ride towards Whistler. From here the trail takes you high above Green Lake looking down on Emerald Estates. After a rocky descent, the trail ends at an intersection. The right fork leads to the Valley Trail and the left fork heads into the Lost lake Trails. These trails are well marked and return to the village. Try Hydro Hill and stop for a swim.

Green Lake / Parkhurst (Map p.205)

South West British Columbia

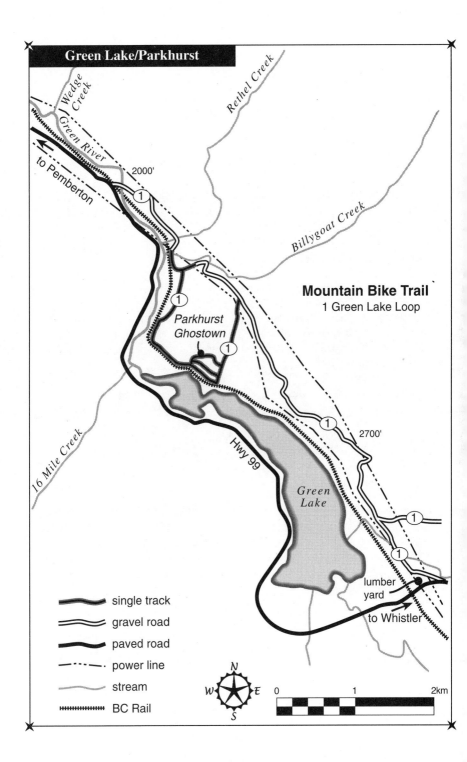

MOUNTAIN BIKING
BRITISH COLUMBIA
The Trail Guide

Whistler

Ancient Cedars / Cougar Mountain

Surrounding yourself with the splendour found in a grove of old growth trees can quickly re-attach you to the natural world . The cappuccino bars and shopping frenzy of the village contrasts sharply with the atmosphere amid the trees. After rid-ing about 6 km up a logging road *"The trees are estimated to be about 800* the trail becomes a smooth single *years old and are simply awesome."* track that a rider can slowly glide through. The trees are estimated to be about 800 years old and are simply awesome. This moist microclimate acts like a giant pitre dish for breeding mosquitos, so plan ahead if you want to spend some time with these grand-daddy trees. The fishing on the Showh Lakes are the another reason to ride into this area.

To access the trail ride north about 6 km on Highway 99, past Green Lake and the Emerald Estates subdivision. Just past Emerald, look for a gravel logging road on your left with a sign reading 'Cougar Mountain, Showh Lakes'. If you reach the heli-port turn around. Once on the Forest Ser-vice Road the valley starts to narrow. Af-ter the creek crossing ride up the north side of the valley and tak-ing the next right fork around the switch-backs go right at the following fork. The left fork takes you to the lakes. These forks should all be marked. The final section of road slowly

gets rougher, ending up with a loose, challenging climb to the crest. The short single track quickly brings you to the cedar grove. Stay to the trail as cedar roots are sensitive to being trampled. It would be sadly ironic if these old trees were killed by their admirers.

Ancient Cedars / Cougar Mountain (Map p.207)

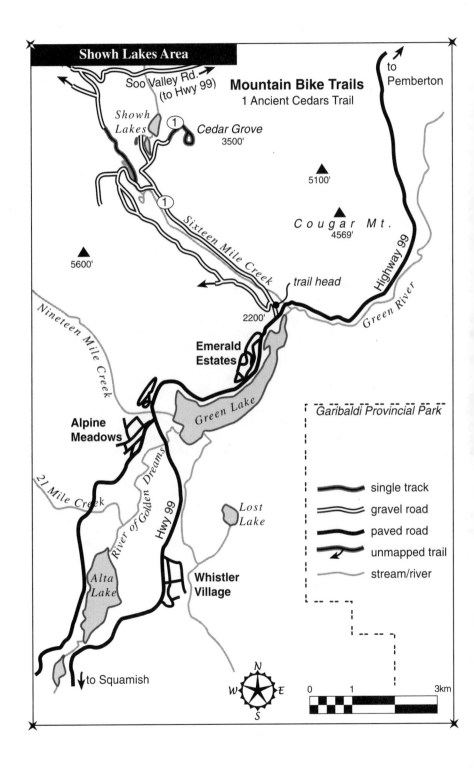

MOUNTAIN BIKING
BRITISH COLUMBIA
The Trail Guide

Whistler

West Side Trail System

Mel's Dilemma / Bart's Dark Trail / Rebob / Rainbow Trail
Whip Me Snip Me / A River Runs Through It

This is serious single track territory where the most experienced riders will be tested by the nasty drop-offs, and non-stop challenges. This is an area new mountain bikers should avoid until their skills and confidence are capable of taking an esteem beating. Most of these trails are open by mid April. All of these famous single tracks can be found branching off a short section of Alta Lake Rd., which runs north to south along the west side of Whistler Valley. Some involve long climbs up renovated road beds, followed by heart-in-mouth descents, and intense slow technical obstacles.

Several routes can be taken to Alta lake Road. The one described utilizes the paved Valley Trail network, and delivers a rider to the north end of the West Side Trail System. From the Village, ride out on Whistler Way to the Highway 99 underpass. This underpass leads to the parking lot of the Whistler Golf Club. The Valley Trail heads both north and south from here. The south branch heads left from the parking lot away from the highway and beside the golf course. Take the north branch, through the on the main lows the golf *"Some involve long climbs up renovated road beds, followed by heart-in-mouth descents, and intense slow technical obstacles. "* straight lot, and stay trail as it follows the golf course. Just after passing the golf course, the trail takes a slight jog through a residential area known as Tapley's Farm, then crosses the River Of Golden Dreams and the B.C. Rail Line. Continue to follow the paved main trail as it travels alongside the river until you reach a fork. The right fork goes to Meadow Park and a water fountain. Take the left fork that leads up a short steep hill to Alta Lake Road. At the intersection of the Valley Trail and Alta Lake Road. you will find the trail head of the first of the west side single tracks.

This first trail is Mel's Dilemma. This trail climbs up the mountain side into a maze of trails which loop back to down to Alta Lake Rd. Like most of the single tracks at Whistler, Mel's is challenging but not off-the-scale difficult. After returning to Alta Lake Road., continue your tour by heading south on the road. After passing a gravel road on the left, Alta Lake Rd. climbs a short steep hill that curves to the left. About halfway up the hill look on the left for a trail that drops into the forest. This is A River Runs Through It. A long, beautiful,

(Continued on page 210)

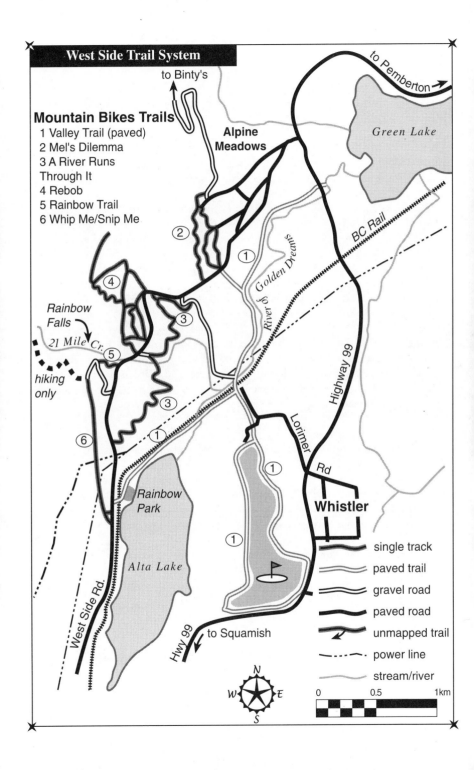

West Side Trail System

Mountain Bikes Trails
1 Valley Trail (paved)
2 Mel's Dilemma
3 A River Runs Through It
4 Rebob
5 Rainbow Trail
6 Whip Me/Snip Me

to Binty's

Alpine Meadows

Green Lake

River of Golden Dreams

BC Rail

to Pemberton

Rainbow Falls

21 Mile Cr.

hiking only

Highway 99

Lorimer Rd

Whistler

Rainbow Park

Alta Lake

West Side Rd.

Hwy 99

to Squamish

single track
paved trail
gravel road
paved road
unmapped trail
power line
stream/river

N
W E
S

0   0.5   1km

MOUNTAIN BIKING
BRITISH COLUMBIA
The Trail Guide

(Continued from page 208)

technical trail that includes a crossing of Twentyone Mile Creek . This trail gains no altitude, but is still one of the more difficult trails on the west side. The trail climbs up, over, and sometimes along huge downed trees, across creek beds, through old logging structures, and down sheer embankments before finally looping back to Alta Lake Rd., just before the cemetery. The soft, mossy soil will cushion any falls that will inevitably occur.

A short distance up from A River Runs Through It lies Bart's Dark Trail. The entrance to Bart's is just before the crest of the hill on the left side, as it drops away from the road. This short entertaining blast down an old road bed has a tricky section at the half way mark. Bart's briefly joins A River Runs Through It, then leads back toward the road again, ending at a small, gravel parking lot. There is a nice short trail to a *"There is a nice short trail to a swimming hole in* swimming hole in *Twentyone Mile Creek out of the corner of this lot."* Twenty-one Mile Creek out of the corner of this lot. Almost directly across Alta Lake Rd. from the lot's driveway, just north of the river, lies another single track known as Rebob. Head up Rebob as it follows along an old logging road that has been reclaimed by WORCA. There are many descents that drop-off from the Rebob climb. Some are high speed, while others are slow, scary, and technical.

Another option from the gravel parking lot is to ride the lower sections of the Rainbow Alpine Trail. This trail is well marked and provides some wonderful single track climbing. Follow the trail up from Alta Lake Rd. to a point just past the small pump house, then look for the marked trail that descends back to Alta lake near Rainbow Park. This trail is called Whip Me Snip Me. This route is often ridden in reverse, allowing a single track descent. The Whip Me Snip Me trail touches the north end of the Lower Sproat Trail system as well.

Thus ends your suggested tour of the north end of Alta Lake Rd. From here ride down to Rainbow Park, swim in Alta Lake, or rejoin the Valley Trail back to the Village. If you've got some stuff left in your legs, check out the Lower Sproat Trails.

West Side Trail System (Map p.209)

ROACH

handcrafted
bags,
clothing,
and
body armour

**STURDY
CONSTRUCTION,
FOR RUGGED
PLAY**

ROACH
IDENTIFICATION
ENT.
(604) 669-9032
fax:(604) 684-7433

Trail Info
Group Rides
Large Rental Fleet
Full Service Bike Shop
*Exclusive **Giant** & **Dekerf** Dealer*

The Whistler Bike Company
4050 Whistler Way
Whistler, B.C. V0N 1B4
(604) 938-9511
bikeco@whistler.net

MOUNTAIN BIKING
BRITISH COLUMBIA
The Trail Guide

Whistler

Whistler Interpretive Forest

The Whistler Interpretive Forest is a working demonstration forest in the upper Cheakamus Valley at the southern boundaries of Whistler. In the past two years a fantastic network of mult-use trails have been developed. The riding is generally wide, fast, and smooth, with a few technical challenges.

To access the trails ride or drive 7.5 km south from the village past Whistler Creek to Function Junction, which is marked with a large wooden sign. Turn left off the highway and you will see a large info sign and parking lot. There are trails leading directly from the parking lot that lead to the bridge over the Cheakumus River. Cross the bridge, and on the left another trail is visible. The Riverside Trail follows the river up the valley for several km with occasional sections along the East Side Main Rd. Eventually you will arrive at a parking lot from which trails head in all directions. The Riverside Trail continues to parallel the river, while directly across a gated road climbs steeply up to Loggers Lake and the Ridge Trail. Also across the road, a new trail heads off below the cliffs of the Crater Rim until it reaches Basalt Spur Rd. Logger's Lake sits in the crater of an extinct volcano.

At this point, there is an option of continuing on the single track, directly across the road (it climbs up to meet the East Side Main Rd. then goes on to the valley at Helm Creek), or turning right on the Basalt Spur Rd. for a steep climb up the back of the crater to join the Crater Rim Trail. This technical single track follows the narrow crater rim then descends to Logger's Lake. From the lake the Ridge Trail provides a fast, fun blast back to the dump at the bottom of the hill.

On the other side of the valley, Westside Main Rd. climbs up the Cheakumus Lake Trail, one of the few legal single tracks in Garibaldi Provincial Park. Along the way several new loops have been cut that drop down to the river then back to the road. There is also a new trail that wins the trail name award called the 'Biogeoclimatic Loop Trail'.

The Interpretive Forest is still under construction and new trails are always being added, so be sure and compare our map to the posted map at the trail heads for updates.

Whistler Interpretive Forest (Map p.214)

1-3 hrs

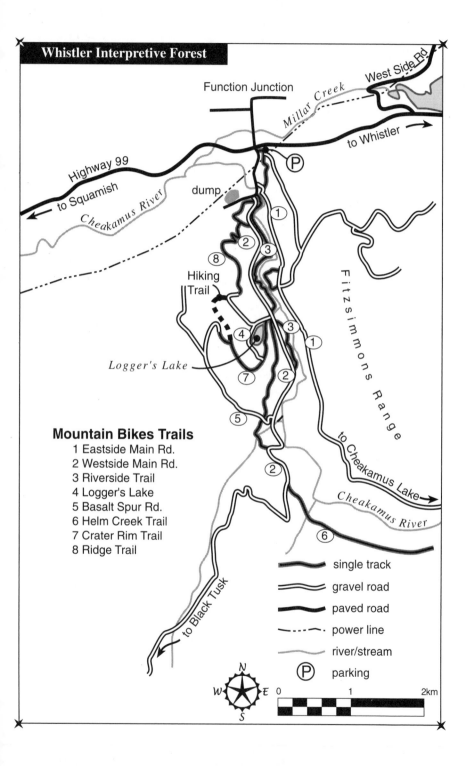

Whistler Interpretive Forest

Function Junction

Millar Creek

West Side Rd.

to Whistler

Highway 99

to Squamish

Cheakamus River

dump

Fitzsimmons Range

Hiking Trail

Logger's Lake

to Cheakamus Lake

Cheakamus River

to Black Tusk

Mountain Bikes Trails
1 Eastside Main Rd.
2 Westside Main Rd.
3 Riverside Trail
4 Logger's Lake
5 Basalt Spur Rd.
6 Helm Creek Trail
7 Crater Rim Trail
8 Ridge Trail

single track
gravel road
paved road
power line
river/stream
Ⓟ parking

N W E S

0 1 2km

MOUNTAIN BIKING
BRITISH COLUMBIA
The Trail Guide

Pemberton

Pemberton

Mosquito Lake / Ramble On / Ridge Trail / Lake Loop

Directly across the Pemberton Valley from spectacular Mt.Currie lies a small (at least compared to Mt. Currie) knoll that provides some of the best singletrack in the Sea to Sky Corridor. The Forest Service Recreation Site at Mosquito Lake can be accessed by several different routes, and a maze of trails descend back to the valley floor. By connecting different routes, it is possible to ride this area for two to three hours.

To access the trails from Pemberton, ride about two kilometers east towards the town of Mt. Currie. After crossing a bridge the highway turns to the right, and a road branches sharply to the left (look for the massive log home on the corner). Take the left spur, and in a few hundred meters the road enters a small gravel pit. Follow the road through the pit and cross the B.C. Rail lines to a fork. The left fork, the Ivey Lake Road, marks the beginning of the climb.

From the railway tracks follow the Ivey Lake Road as it climbs up about 600 ft. through several switchbacks. The road crests behind some Hydro lines, then drops slightly to an intersection. Ride straight through on this wide, well graded section onto another short climb. Just after this second crest, the road to Mosquito Lake (marked with a Forest Service sign) branches to the right. The main road dead-ends a hundred feet further along. Ride down Mosquito Lake Road, and soon _____ you will see one end of the Ridge   *"Go ahead and take a plunge, but if you*   Trail climbing up to your right.   *are riding here in May or June, remember*   This trail climbs steeply up to the   *that there is a reason why it is called*   top of the ridge, then drops down   *Mosquito Lake."*   to the main Mosquito Lake _____ single track descent. If you continue on the Mosquito Lake access road it will turn to the right, and pass a cut block below on the left. Soon a gravel, hydro road will appear on the left, and just past this, a fainter road bed will be visible with a single track running up it. This is the Lake Loop, which climbs up under the hydro lines, then snakes through the trees behind Mosquito Lake back to the access road once more. Riding a little past the turn-off to the Lake Loop will lead you to

(Continued on page 217)

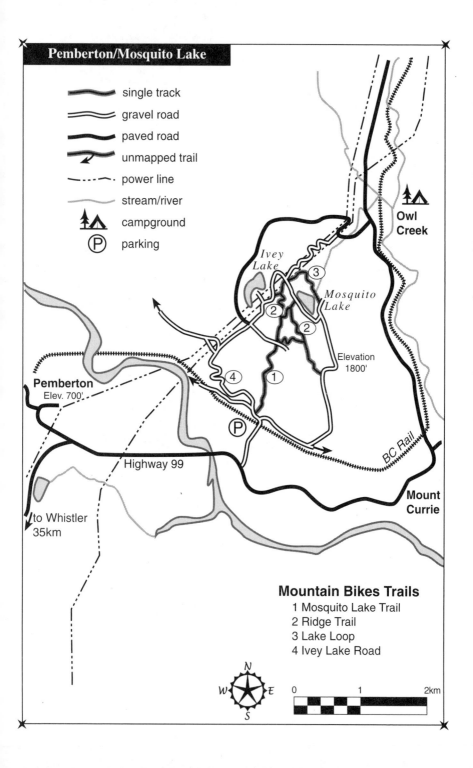

Pemberton/Mosquito Lake

- ~~~ single track
- ≈ gravel road
- ▬ paved road
- ➤ unmapped trail
- –·–·– power line
- ~~ stream/river
- 🏕 campground
- Ⓟ parking

Ivey Lake

Mosquito Lake

③

②

②

①

④

Elevation 1800'

Owl Creek

Pemberton
Elev. 700'

Ⓟ

Highway 99

BC Rail

Mount Currie

to Whistler 35km

N
W · E
S

0   1   2km

Mountain Bikes Trails
1 Mosquito Lake Trail
2 Ridge Trail
3 Lake Loop
4 Ivey Lake Road

MOUNTAIN BIKING
BRITISH COLUMBIA
The Trail Guide

(Continued from page 215)
Mosquito Lake itself. There is a picnic table, dock, and a rope swing to fool around on. Go ahead and take a plunge, but if you are riding here in May or June, remember that there is a reason why it is called Mosquito Lake. Sometimes it's best to just keep moving.

The Mosquito Lake single track descent begins a hundred meters or so back down the road from the dock. Backtrack from the lake, looking up the hill to your left. The first trail you see should lead to outhouses. The second climbs steeply up from the road into the forest. You will likely have to push your bike the first few meters, then ride this section of technical uphill until it crests and begins the descent. The first section drops through an old clear-cut, then joins an overgrown double track road. Turn left on the road and climb for a short distance. The _____ trail branches into the forest *"You will likely have to push your bike the first* on the right in about 100 *few meters, then ride this section of technical* feet. From here the trail *uphill until it crests and begins the descent."* drops back to the valley, _____ eventually popping out onto the Ivey Lake Road near the railway line. The Ridge Trail, and another descent known as Ramble On, can also be accessed from the Mosquito Lake area. Ride past the lake, and in a short distance you will come upon a road that climbs up to the right. Ride up this road for about a kilometer, at which point it turns right and climbs three short steep hills. Then turn left and begin to descend. At this point you will see a single track climbing into the trees straight ahead, this is the other end of the Ridge Trail. The Ridge Trail makes its way along the top of the ridge towards the main Mosquito Lake descent. Along the way it forks at least twice, taking different lines across the hill.

If you decide to ride Ramble On, go down the logging road past the Ridge Trail for a few hundred meters or so. As you descend, look on your right for a single-track that drops into the woods. Ramble On winds through forest and meadow before it pops out onto a double track. Follow the double track down to the railway tracks, turn right and follow the train tracks to the bottom of the climb. Both the Mosquito Lake and Ramble On descents have numerous side trails to explore, and the trails can be linked together in different combinations.

Mosquito Lake / Ramble On / Ridge Trail / Lake Loop (Map p.216)

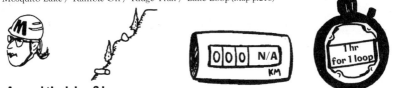

Around the lake, 3 hrs.

MOUNTAIN BIKING
BRITISH COLUMBIA
The Trail Guide

Pemberton

Birkenhead Lake Loop

About a 30 minute drive north of Pemberton lies Birkenhead Lake Provincial Park, a beautiful spot nestled in some of the most striking mountains in the corridor. This long loop takes the rider through unlogged stands of Lodgepole pine along the west shore of Birkenhead Lake. This ride contains only one major climb (the 3 km grunt from the highway), and the rest consists of rolling hills and a final 7 km descent on a smooth dirt road. This is the area where numerous side trails are being built as part of the Sea To Sky Trail project. Contact a local bike shop for trail details.

To access the trail from Pemberton, drive east on Highway 99 approximately 6 km to the village of Mt.Currie. In Mt.Currie, Highway 99 splits to the right, over the Duffy Lake Rd. to Lillooet, while Portage Rd. continues straight through town north towards D'Arcy. Drive north towards D'Arcy for about 17 km at which point you should see a map reading "Birkenhead Lake Provincial Park Turnoff 16 km". It is important to note this spot, as you will be riding back down the highway to a turnoff at this sign. Continue driving north past Gates Lake until you reach the main turnoff for the park, marked with a blue and white Provincial Park sign reading "Birkenhead Lake 17 km".

"This long loop takes the rider through unlogged stands of Lodgepole pine along the west shore of Birkenhead Lake."

From the parking spot, backtrack south along the highway past Gates Lake for about 16 km toward the sign you passed earlier reading 'Birkenhead Lake Provincial Park Turnoff 16 km'. You're now getting close when you pass the new subdivision called Poole Creek. Look for a spot where one of the large hydro lines crosses the road, and you should find a gravel logging road branching right (west) from the highway.

Turn right onto the logging road, ride over the train tracks and you will see a sign reading,"Birkenhead Lake Forest Service Road", and another reading, "No Access to Birkenhead Lake". Don't worry about this second sign, as it is designed to keep vehicles, not mountain bikers, out of the park. This road runs straight and flat for a short distance, then turns sharply to the left and begins the only big climb of the ride (a 3 km hill through a series of switchbacks). At the crest of the hill the road levels out and runs along the north side of Birkenhead River Valley. Just past the crest, another road branches to the right that leads to a section of the Sea to Sky Trail that is marked and parallels the

(Continued on page 220)

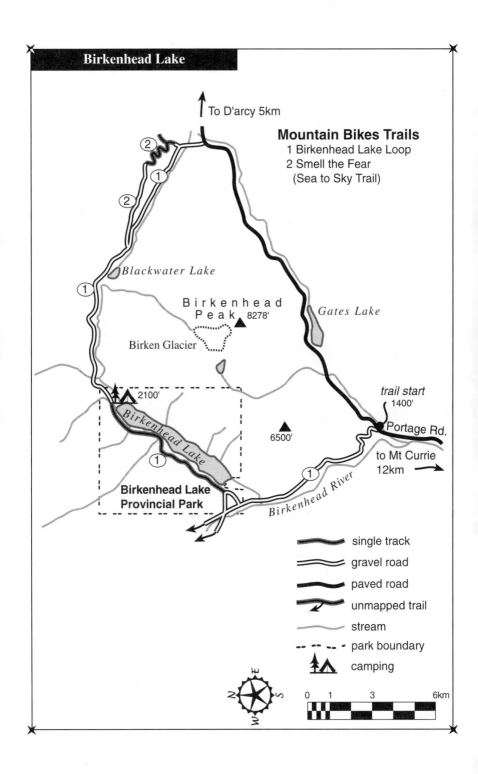

Birkenhead Lake

To D'arcy 5km

Mountain Bikes Trails
1 Birkenhead Lake Loop
2 Smell the Fear
(Sea to Sky Trail)

Blackwater Lake

B i r k e n h e a d
P e a k 8278'

Gates Lake

Birken Glacier

2100'

trail start
1400'

Birkenhead Lake

6500'

Portage Rd.

to Mt Currie
12km

**Birkenhead Lake
Provincial Park**

Birkenhead River

single track

gravel road

paved road

unmapped trail

stream

park boundary

camping

N E S W

0   1   3   6km

MOUNTAIN BIKING
BRITISH COLUMBIA
The Trail Guide

(Continued from page 218)

road. This new trail goes to the same place, so the choice is yours. The main road is signed with orange kilometer markers, and just past kilometer 8 you will come to a small bridge that crosses Taillefer Creek at its confluence with the Birkenhead River. Shortly after crossing the bridge you will come to a road that

branches right from the main logging road. Head down this right branch, and soon you will come to a gate marked "Private Property Birkenhead Lake Estates Ltd.". From this point on a double track road branches to the left running through the forest parallel to the fence marking the private property. Follow this road and soon you will come upon several signs that mark the park boundary. Keep riding along this double track until it makes a sharp left. At this point look to your right *"After taking in the sights return to the main trail and continue the ride north around the lake. "* and you will see a fainter road, blocked by a couple of large mounds, that are meant to prevent vehicles from entering the park. This is the main trail that runs along the west shore of Birkenhead Lake. If you miss this turn the double track will end at a gravel logging road. Head back the way you came!

After turning right onto the Birkenhead Lake Trail, ride a short distance and you will find 2 trails branching to the right. The first returns to the private property, ignore it. The second provides a short detour down to a small campsite on the shore of the lake, a nice spot for a snack and a swim. After taking in the sights return to the main trail and continue the ride north around the lake. This section of the trail gently rolls along climbing above the lake then smoothly descending for about 8 to 10 km eventually popping out on the main access road near the campsite and beach at the north end of the lake. This is another great spot for a swim.

When you are ready for the final section of the loop, ride out of the park onto the park access road and start the 17 km ride back to the highway. The first 10 km of this smooth, hard-packed sand road leads gently upwards through rolling farmland towards the Forest Service Recreation Site at Blackwater Lake. Just after passing Blackwater Lake the road begins a high speed, 1200 foot descent over the last 7 km, completing the loop at your parked car.

Just as the descent begins there is an option to ride another section of the Sea To Sky Trail. Just after passing Blackwater Lake look on the left for a road, and ride up a short distance to a fork. Take the right fork and follow the road as it climbs gently for about 4 km. A single track named Smell The Fear branches to

MOUNTAIN BIKING
BRITISH COLUMBIA
The Trail Guide

the right and begins a long, loose surf-fest to Portage Road and the town of D'Arcy. The bottom sections of Smell The Fear branch in several directions, but all eventually reach the valley. Signs will improve as the trail system is further developed. Basically, you just keep descending. If you end up in D'Arcy, on the shore of Anderson Lake, you will have to backtrack down the Portage Road to your car.

Birkenhead Lake Loop (Map p.219)

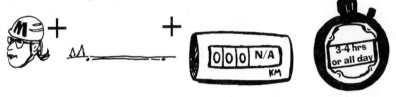

Pemberton

Blowdown Creek

This epic out and back ride climbs from the parking area at 3500 ft. to its crest at an altitude of 7100 ft. The trail follows logging and mining roads high above the Duffy Lake Road. Blowdown Creek presents the rider with some amazing views, and a first class wildlife viewing opportunity. You can expect to see deer, mountain goats, and of course, bears. From Gott Pass the road drops into South Cottonwood which is part of the drainage system for the Stein Valley.

To access the trail from Pemberton, drive east to the village of Mt. Currie, then turn right onto the Duffy Lake Road at the mileage sign reading 'Lillooet 96'. The first 8 or 9 km follows the meandering Birkenhead River. Then the road begins its long 4000 ft. climb up and out of the Pemberton Valley. Several km after reaching _____ Cayoosh Pass comes Duffy *"You can expect to see deer, mountain* Lake, and just after passing the *goats, and of course, bears."* lake you will drive over two _____ small bridges. About 3 km past Duffy Lake you will reach a pullout beside a winter snow gate with a mileage sign just beyond it. Park at the mileage sign where the Blowdown Creek Road (marked 'Not A Through Road') climbs to the right.

From the Duffy, The Blowdown Creek Rd. climbs at a good middle-ring grade for about 45 minutes to an hour. The road is a smooth, double-track. Ignore all overgrown spurs. As you approach the end of the valley and the mountains are towering overhead, you'll reach a fork with the right one following the valley floor, and the rougher left one starting a steep, granny gear climb through an unlogged side valley to Blowdown Lake and Gott Pass. Head up the left fork and you will find that this road is loose and rideable all the way into the alpine

(Continued on page 223)

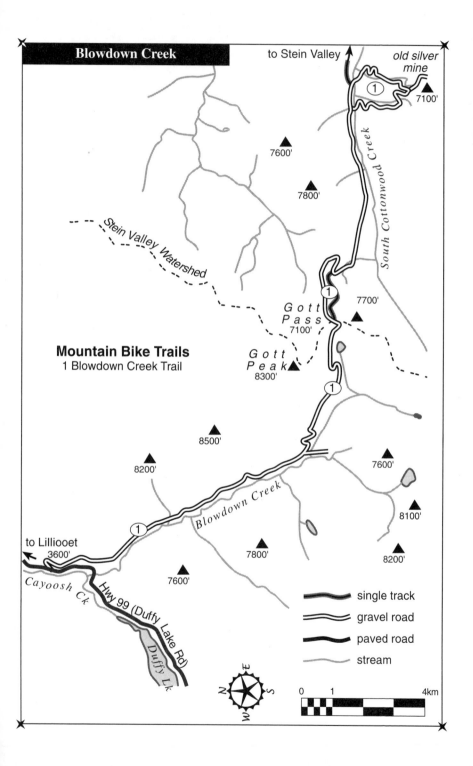

Blowdown Creek

to Stein Valley

old silver mine

▲ 7100'

①

South Cottonwood Creek

▲ 7600'

▲ 7800'

Stein Valley Watershed

①

Mountain Bike Trails
1 Blowdown Creek Trail

Gott Pass
7100'

▲ 7700'

Gott Peak ▲
8300'

①

▲ 8500'

▲ 8200'

▲ 7600'

Blowdown Creek

▲ 8100'

①

to Lillooet
3600'

▲ 7800'

▲ 8200'

Cayoosh Ck

Hwy 99 (Duffy Lake Rd)

▲ 7600'

Duffy Lk

━━━ single track
━━━ gravel road
━━━ paved road
━━━ stream

N E S W

0   1   4km

MOUNTAIN BIKING
BRITISH COLUMBIA
The Trail Guide

(Continued from page 221)

meadows and beyond. Just as you reach the treeline, the road switchbacks hard to the left, and from this corner a rough, muddy track continues straight on through some marshy meadows to Blowdown Lake. If you want to explore the lake, walk it to avoid damage. The main road switchbacks once more, then begins the final grind up Gott Pass. From this point one can see down into South Cottonwood Creek, and, if you have the energy and time, you can explore this area also.

The main road descends into South Cottonwood, gradually wrapping around the left or north side of the valley, while a rougher road drops straight into the marsh below. These two trails eventually join, forming a short loop where you can descend the rougher trail, or ride down the valley on the main road and follow the old _____ mining roads that run *"If you choose to ride into the South* throughout the area. If you *Cottonwood be prepared, because this is* choose to ride into the South *serious backcountry riding."* Cottonwood be-prepared, be- cause this is seri- ous backcountry riding. The main road drops a long way into this valley, then turns and climbs back up to the treeline, before looping down to the main road again. Then you have to ride back up the pass as there is no other way out. How about 6900 ft. of total climbing in one day! I get tired just thinking about it. When you are ready to descend simply retrace your steps from the pass to Duffy Lake Road.

Blowdown Creek (Map p.222)

Pacific Spirit Regional Park

Pacific Spirit Regional Park, commonly referred to as the University Endowment Lands, is an amazing 763 hectare park made extra special by its location just west of Vancouver. This park is literally bordered by the city, The University of British Columbia, and the Pacific Ocean. Pacific Spirit was created as a regional park in 1989, and to date is one of the best examples of a multi-use urban parks that seem to function for all groups concerned.

One ride through this urban gem and you cannot help but discover the healing qualities that a good ride in a beautiful setting has, especially when contrasted with the nearby stale grey concrete of the city. However, the city is very much

(Continued on page 226)

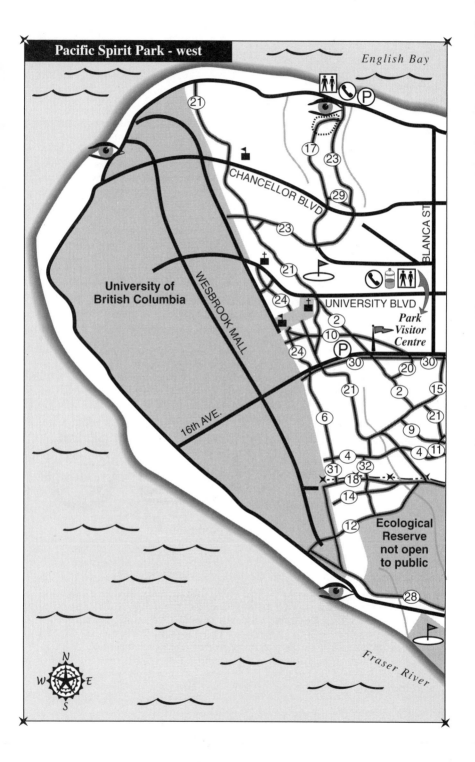

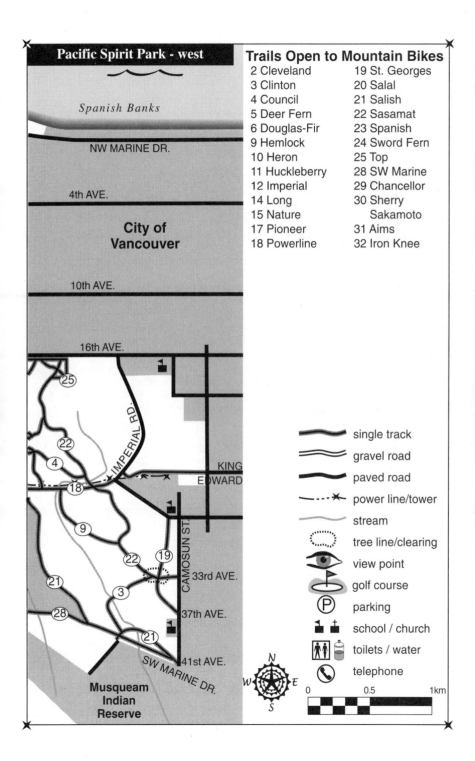

Pacific Spirit Park - west

Trails Open to Mountain Bikes

2 Cleveland	19 St. Georges
3 Clinton	20 Salal
4 Council	21 Salish
5 Deer Fern	22 Sasamat
6 Douglas-Fir	23 Spanish
9 Hemlock	24 Sword Fern
10 Heron	25 Top
11 Huckleberry	28 SW Marine
12 Imperial	29 Chancellor
14 Long	30 Sherry
15 Nature	Sakamoto
17 Pioneer	31 Aims
18 Powerline	32 Iron Knee

Spanish Banks

NW MARINE DR.

4th AVE.

City of Vancouver

10th AVE.

16th AVE.

IMPERIAL RD.

KING EDWARD

CAMOSUN ST.

33rd AVE.

37th AVE.

SW MARINE DR.

41st AVE.

Musqueam Indian Reserve

single track
gravel road
paved road
power line/tower
stream
tree line/clearing
view point
golf course
(P) parking
school / church
toilets / water
telephone

N
W E
S

0   0.5   1km

MOUNTAIN BIKING
BRITISH COLUMBIA
The Trail Guide

(Continued from page 223)
part of the backdrop of this area, and finishing a ride with a cruise down Spanish Banks looking at the emerging night skyline adds a unique urban feel to riding in this park.

The trails are generally a wide type of single track and are either flat or rolling. There are a few hilly sections, but no serious climbs. The only noteworthy ascents are the Spanish and Salish Trails, located off N.W. Marine Dr. The gentle year around riding in Pacific Spirit means that the area experiences a great deal of multi-user traffic. The park offers a welcome relief from the technical trails of the North Shore, and has riders of all abilities enjoying the trails day and night.

Any mountain biker who uses the park is responsible for upholding a basic social contract between the park, pedestrians, and equestrians. The two primary terms of the contract involve reckless riding (public safety), and off trail riding (poaching). Both of these concerns are addressed by following the basic rules of the trail, however, the importance of riding responsibly, and in control, is more critical than usual because of the high traffic in the park. In regard to poaching trails. Don't Do It!! The simple, respectful act of staying on the main trail is a crucial component of the social contract. If you need something a bit more technical, then ride elsewhere. Leave this area to those who want to ride the fun, easy trails. Failure to uphold the terms of the contract by riding too fast around blind corners, could result in the loss of mountain biking in this area for everyone. If the act of one irresponsible rider causes the unthinkable to happen, the only suitable punishment should be a public flogging by all riders who need this area to help make living in the city more bearable. This notion of a social contract applies anytime, anywhere you ride. Perhaps nowhere else in B.C. do you have to be as conscious of this contract as when you ride in Pacific Spirit Regional Park.

The trails in Pacific Spirit Regional Park are well signed with most trail heads telling you of the type of use allowed, and the name of the trail. While you ride in the park you will cross major intersections, and pass by very noticeable landmarks such as schools, the golf course, etc. To effectively navigate your way around the park for the first few times, briefly study the map, or bring it along, and remember key points you pass. With basic route finding skills it would be quite difficult, but not impossible, to get lost. Consequently, no detailed descriptions of specific routes will be provided. Having to study a map and follow a description is an unnecessary distraction from what is a generally safe, and getting-lost-proof mountain biking experience.

Pacific Spirit Regional Park (Map p.224-5)

MOUNTAIN BIKING
BRITISH COLUMBIA
The Trail Guide

South Central British Columbia

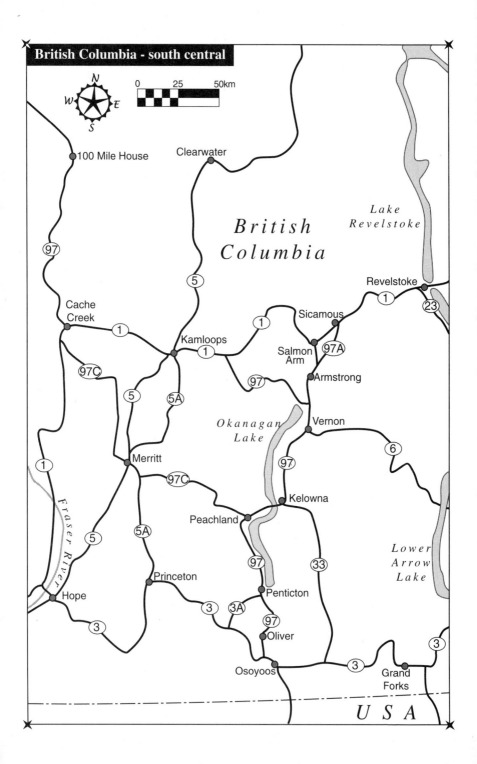

British Columbia - south central

MOUNTAIN BIKING
BRITISH COLUMBIA
The Trail Guide

Oliver / Osoyoos Area

The Trails
The International Bicycling And Hiking Society Trail
Osoyoos Trails

Oliver / Osoyoos Area

The International Bicycling And Hiking Society Trail

The southern Okanagan towns of Oliver and Osoyoos offer up some great desert style riding and endless opportunities to explore and soak up some serious summertime heat. This ride in Oliver is great for all levels of cyclists who want an easy spin along a meandering river. The trail has many access points and can be ridden back and forth in about an hour. This isn't a mountain bike ride, but more of a gravel path ride that is simply too nice to leave out of this book.

Oliver / Osoyoos Area

Osoyoos Trails

A great trail network of beat up old jeep roads and single track is located on the east facing slopes overlooking the Osoyoos Golf and Country Club, and the town of Osoyoos. To access the trails follow the signs toward the golf course, turn left on Fairwinds, and park at the first cattle gate. The trails are generally steep double track that _____ are scattered all over the hillside. The higher *"The trails are generally steep* you climb the steeper the trails become. *double track that are scattered* Some of my favorite routes are on this map, *all over the hillside."* but it's the type of area where you just ride ——————————— and explore. Many of the climbs are testy short ones that serve up a fast return trip. The constant up and down riding can tire you out in a couple of hours, in which time you'll know this area as well as I do.

Osoyoos Trails (Map p.231)

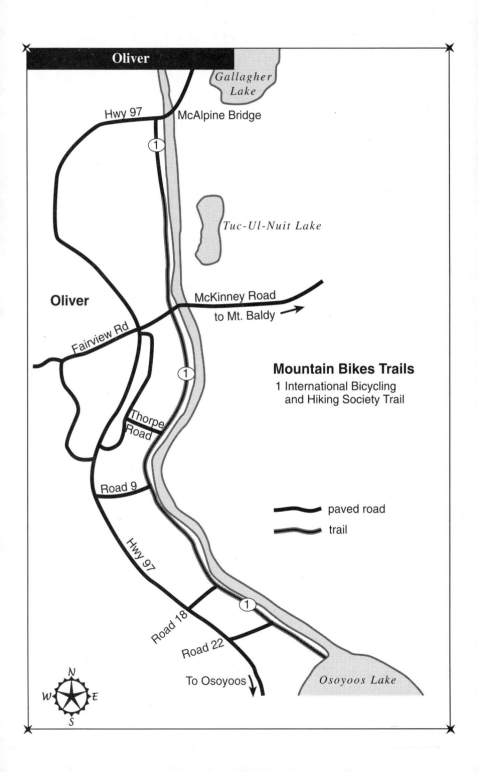

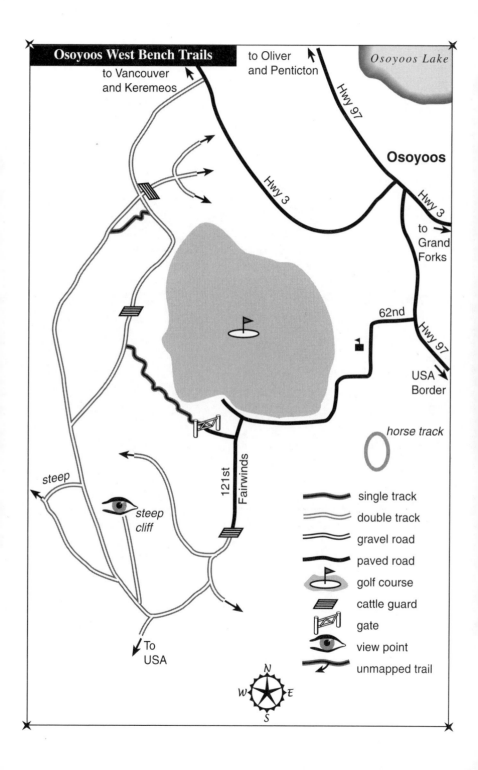

MOUNTAIN BIKING
BRITISH COLUMBIA
The Trail Guide

Introduction

This parched little Okanagan town has a lot more to offer other than just Apex Alpine, Peachfest, and Ironman. The town also has some great riding on Ellis Ridge, Campbell Mountain, and on the Three Blind Mice trail systems. The latter is getting rave reviews from the local hardheads who frequent the area. Check out the Okanagan Mountain Biking Trail Guide to get a beter idea of where else to ride in Penticton, or drop by one of the local shops and ask for directions. Better yet, join in on one of the group rides. Look for the second edition of the local trail guide for updated maps on local riding secrets.

Penticton

Ellis Ridge

Anyone who has a bike strapped to the roof of their car, or can beg or borrow a bike for the day, has to ride Ellis Ridge located high above Penticton. This is an impeccable single track that skirts the south facing canyon wall high above Ellis Creek. The trail has some exposed sections and a few steep drop-offs and climbs. If novices take it easy on the trail's difficult sections there is no reason that most mountain bikers can't enjoy this truly divine ride.

To access the trail, turn left onto Carmi Ave at the Dairy Queen on Main St. Turn Right at the XC ski area sign and park your car (if you drive) at the open area on the right just prior to the cattle guard. Ride up about 3 km to the large parking area on the right. The trail takes off from here and a left turn puts you onto the single track. You will quickly realize why this is an awesome trail, so take your time and enjoy the impeccable views and brilliant meandering single track. After a steep climb be sure to go left because there is more trail to enjoy. The ride will finish at the cattle guard where you parked.

Ellis Ridge (Map p.233)

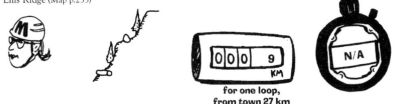

for one loop,
from town 27 km

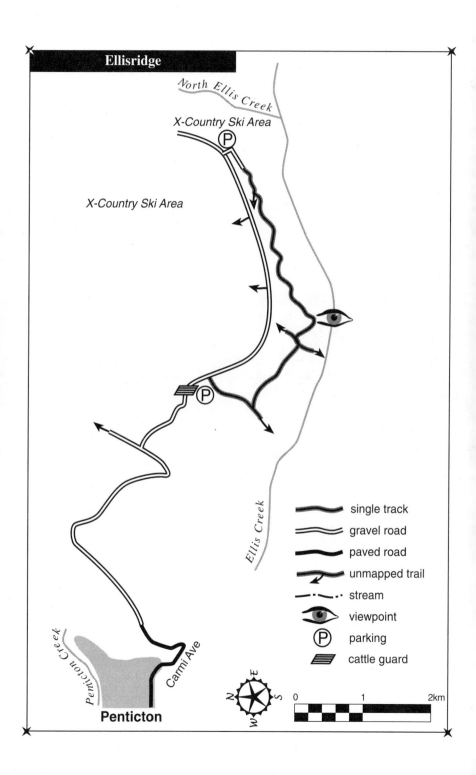

MOUNTAIN BIKING
BRITISH COLUMBIA
The Trail Guide

Kelowna Area Trails

Introduction

The last time I checked Kelowna was the fastest growing city in Canada. Generally people come here for the warm friendly lakes, world class alpine recreation, and some of Canada's most consistent weather. The enlightened individuals among us gravitate to the valley for the above mentioned reasons, and more importantly, because the mountain biking is awesome and limitless. Escape the crowded trails and continual rain of the Wet Coast and ride in the valley that has it all. From desert-like valley bottom rides through sage and ponderosa pine, to heavily wooded trails in the high country, the variety will open the eyes of all who ride here.

For the longest time the only mountain biking talked about outside the Central Okanagan/ Kelowna was the famous Kettle Valley Railway. The railway is a great easy ride, and the trestles are very cool, but as far as the actual riding is concerned the K.V.R is simply an old rail bed, and as such it is a well maintained and per- _____ fectly graded gravel road. Mountain bikers *"A few of the great riding areas* tend to want a bit more than a gravel *in Kelowna include: Knox* road, and Kelowna can satisfy the needs of *Mountain, the Crawford area,* all mountain bikers from the hard core to *Okanagan Mountain Park,* timid novices. As a resident of the Okana- *and a host of others."* gan and author of the local guide book, I had _____ a tough time selecting a sample for you. A few of the great riding areas in Kelowna include: Knox Mountain, the Crawford area, Okanagan Mountain Park, and a host of others. I have selected some satisfying appetizers for your tires to munch on, for the complete menu pick up a copy of the Okanagan Mountain Biking Trail Guide, available at cool bike shops and book stores. Now for the first course...

MOUNTAIN BIKING
BRITISH COLUMBIA
The Trail Guide

Kelowna Area Trails

Casa Loma Trails

How does an easy evening ride along side a sparkling blue lake sound? Who can say no. More ambitious cyclists will want to access this ride on bike from anywhere in Kelowna, or use it as a short cut between Westbank and Kelowna. To access the trail on the top side go south on Highway 97 from Kelowna to Boucherie Rd. Turn left on Boucherie and left again on Sunnyside. To access the bottom side, ride across the Bridge from Kelowna and take Campbell Rd. left for about 1.5 km. Take the single track to the right just before the Casa Loma Resort. The trail is a nearly flat single track, perfect for a family ride, or as a place to introduce new riders to the joys of mountain biking.

Casa Loma Trails (Map p.236)

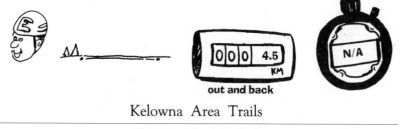

out and back

Kelowna Area Trails

Okanagan Mountain Park

Okanagan Mountain Park is the first thing to pleasantly assault your vision as you speed off the Coquihalla Connector. This impressive rocky park sits on the eastern shores of Okanagan lake, and stretches from Kelowna to Naramata near Penticton. This is low elevation riding, and the kind of place where one can feel what real Okanagan "melt your helmet heat" feels like. Rumor has it that local cyclists bring raw omelets in a plastic container and cook them on the rocks in mid summer. To access the park take Pandosy St. South from Highway 97 to Lakeshore Dr. and park about 1 km after the pavement ends.

Kelowna Area Trails

Boulder Trail

The Boulder Trail is a short steep loop which is mostly rocky technical single track. The trail features short steep challenging climbs, heart pounding drop-offs, and numerous too gnarly to ride sections. The Boulder trail is common with the Commando Bay Trail until the top of Dead Horse Creek Hill. The Commando Bay Trail goes straight while the Boulder Trail goes left looping

(Continued on page 238)

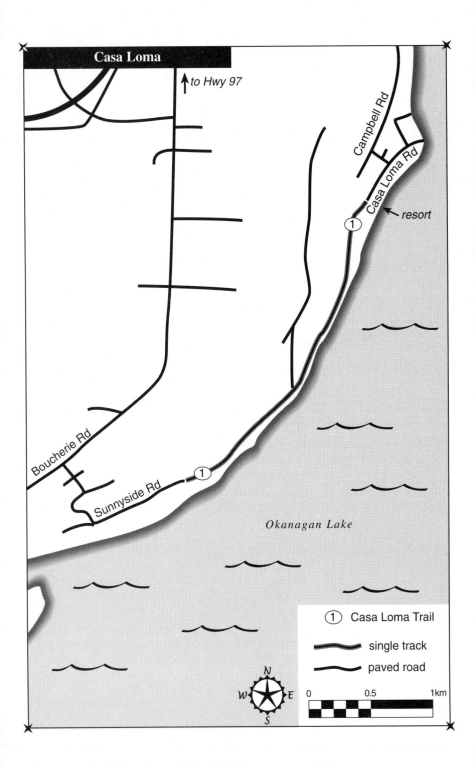

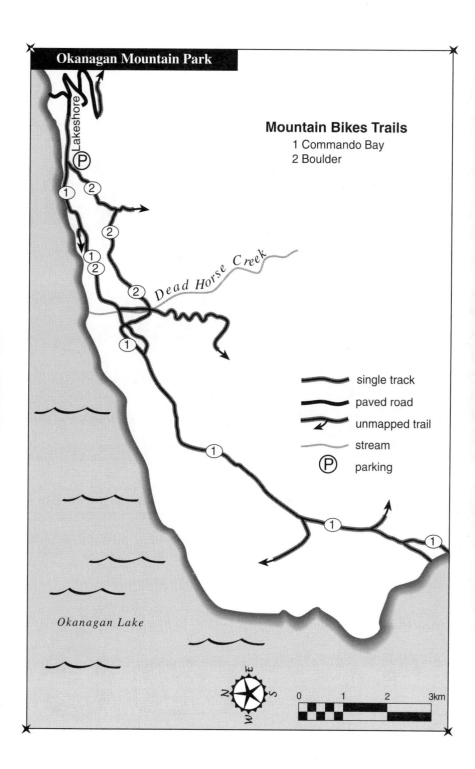

MOUNTAIN BIKING
BRITISH COLUMBIA
The Trail Guide

(Continued from page 235)

back to where you started. This is a popular hiking trail so ride accordingly.

Boulder Trail (Map p.237)

Kelowna Area Trails

Commando Bay Trail

This is a long out and back ride that takes you into the heart of Okanagan Mountain Park. The ride is mostly on loose rocky double track with the last 1.6 km's being technical single track. Sections of Wild Horse Canyon can be very hot in the summer and flooded in the spring. Despite the flooding it is usually possible to make it through.

From the parking lot ride down the road 1.7 km's and turn where you see a mettle gate on the left. This rocky double track is an old pioneering road that was used to connect early valley residents. At Dead Horse Creek turn right to cross the bridge and climb the long hill. At the top go straight, or take the single track to the right which loops back to the road. From here the trail goes through Wild Horse Canyon and is fast, rolling, and yes you guessed it, FUN!. At the end of the canyon go right toward Buchan and Commando Bays. The single track to Commando Bay is on the left. This trail is steep and rocky down to the beach. Explore the First Nations petroglyphs on the rocks above the beach. Also check out the plaque at the end of the beach commemorating the role this area played in W.W. II.

Ride options include staying on the double track down to Buchan Bay. Also check out the view from the Rim Trail which is on the right about three quarters of the way through Wild Horse Canyon. On the return trip the Boulder Trail can add some distance and technical challenges to the ride.

Commando Bay Trail (Map p.237)

MOUNTAIN BIKING
BRITISH COLUMBIA
The Trail Guide

Kelowna Area Trails

McDougal Rim

The McDougal Rim Trail is a great ride with challenging climbs and winding single track that snakes through typically varied Okanagan terrain. The first half of the ride is steep double track climbing that will test your endurance, but remember that what goes up most rip down. Snow will linger until late May and and possibly appear in early October.

To access the trail take Highway 97 south from Kelowna and turn right at Bartly Rd. Park at the McDougal Rim trailhead and ride down the road. Turn right on the double track just before the bridge on McDougal Creek. At the 3rd switchback, about 8.5 km's up, take the double track straight ahead. Continue past the first double track to the right which comes in at a 45' angle, and take the second overgrown double track to the right. This double track comes to a junction after .4 km and changes to a single track. At the junction, turn right and continue past the weather recording station on the left and downhill until you reach the next major viewpoint where the trail briefly turns to a double track. Shortly past the mudholes take the single track to the left. This section of the trail will descend to the trailhead and is likly to have hikers on it so please don't do your Missy Giove impersonation on this one.

McDougal Rim (Map p.240)

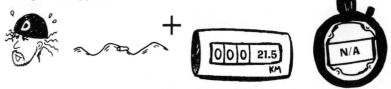

Kelowna Area Trails

Kettle Valley Railway / Myra Canyon Section

Mountain bikers of all abilities will want to ride on the old railbed and check out the trestles, tunnels and great views from this historic railway. If you are only going to ride on the K.V.R. once, then make sure you do this section. Because it is an old railgrade the ride is flat, on an easy gravel surface. The Myra Canyon Trestle Restoration Society have worked to re-deck most of the old bridges and put up hand rails so safety is no longer a concern if you use common sense. A complete guide book to the Kettle Valley Railway is available for those who want to go beyond Myra Canyon.

(Continued on page 241)

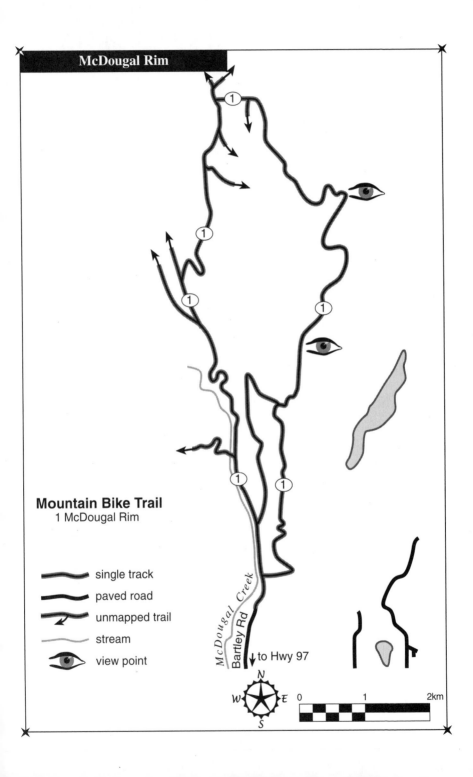

MOUNTAIN BIKING
BRITISH COLUMBIA
The Trail Guide

(Continued from page 239)

To access the K.V.R from Orchard Park in Kelowna, take Benvoulin Rd. to
K.L.O. Rd., then McCollough Rd. to June Springs Rd. When the pavement
ends, June Springs Rd.becomes Little White Forest Service Rd. While driving
or riding up this road be sure and veer left 3 km from the end of the pavement,
and in about 1.2 km you can park. The K.V.R. is on your left. Myra Canyon
begins about 4 km from the starting point. Since the K.V.R. is at 1200 meters,
be prepared for sudden changes in the weather and dress accordingly.

Kettle Valley Railway / Myra Canyon Section

but you can turn back any time

MOUNTAIN BIKING
BRITISH COLUMBIA
The Trail Guide

Vernon

Mountain biking in the North Okanagan is all about consistent weather and diverse geography. As you move north up the valley the parched, desert-like slopes gradually give way to more temperate forests, and north facing slopes with fairly dense vegetation. Nevertheless, when you combine the right elevation and slope exposure, the open fast single tracks in this desert-like setting are still plentiful. This diversity is what makes riding in the Vernon area such a blast. Despite the lack of trail development, the area has great early season riding on the slopes of Bella Vista, the constant visual candy of Kalamalka Lake Provincial Park, _____ and excellent mid-summer riding in *"This diversity is what makes riding in* the trees and sub-alpine on Silver *the Vernon area such a blast."* Star Mountain and the BX Creek ——————————————————— drainage area. Mountain bikers who sample our rides always rant about the open spaces and fast riding full of amazing views. After living in Vernon for years I never tire of the visual aspect of riding in the North Okanagan. The poor souls who ride all day under the forest canopy on the West Coast owe themselves one visit to our valley to experience the long climbs and fast descents with a postcard view around every corner. And how about feeling the warmth of the sun while on a ride, try that in Vancouver!

Vernon

Spanky's

How about an eye popping 800 meter plunge, in 13 km, to get the adrenaline circulating through your body? This trail starts directly across from the Sovereign Lakes XC ski area turn off of Silver Star Rd. Once you ride through the grassy area, a testy little drop-off lets you know that Spanky's has begun. The trail follows an old powerline for a while and is generally a well worn path because of consistent rider traffic in the past few years. It is next to impossible to get lost on the first section of trail because there are no intersections or confusing portions until the trail nears the first paved switchback of Silver Star Rd. So relax, and try to soak up the bumpy ride.

Once you pass the washed out creek where the trail hugs the side, you will come up on an open loose gravel area. Here you can go left, down a short loose chute, and follow the double track that veers close to a creek and on toward Silver Star Rd. Just before the road, the single track drops off to your left. The other option

MOUNTAIN BIKING
BRITISH COLUMBIA
The Trail Guide

is to go straight at the loose gravel area toward the switchback, ride up the Silver Star Rd. for about 200 meters, and drop off left into a new single track. This trail will bring you back to Silver Star Rd. where you can hook up with the single track across the road on your right. This single track is perfect, but be careful crossing _____ the log bridge. The trail will *"This is the finishing rip of what is slowly* shoot you onto Forsberg Rd., *becoming Vernon's most popular ride."* where a double track continues _____ almost straight ahead. This fast double track will take you over BX Creek, up a muddy short climb, and onto a very fast wooded double track downhill. Follow the main path and tire marks to a short climb up onto a log landing, and from here, follow out the main road as it joins up with Dixon Dam Rd. This is the

finishing rip of what is slowly becoming Vernon's most popular ride. Since this is a long downhill you may want to shuttle up to the start to avoid the arduous road climb up Silver Star Rd.

So what's with the name Spanky's? Since corporal punishment is no longer allowed, the Wednesday night crew have been longing for a periodic tap on the bum. Since the rough trail gets the butt a little bruised it reminds riders of their childhood spankings; hence the name.

Spanky's (Map p.246)

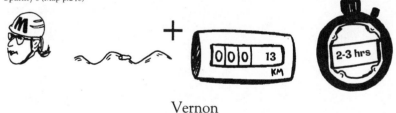

Vernon

Noah's

Noah's is a local hot weather favorite as the area feels like a refrigerator in the forest on a hot summer day. This trail combines some nice double track climbing with a tight single track descent. The whole loop is not that long, and really is best enjoyed if you do several laps.

To access the trail from Vernon drive or ride up Silver Star Rd., and turn right on Tillicum Rd. Follow this road to the next left and up to the end of the paved road. You should pass an old, paved, race car track. Ride up this double track road for about 2.6 km and take a right at the fork in the road. Take another right, and start the steeper climb to the top of the single track. The trail

MOUNTAIN BIKING
BRITISH COLUMBIA
The Trail Guide

is on the left, at the top of some steep climbing. This tight trail dumps you out on the retaining wall of Dixon Dam. Scoot off the steep left chute, midway across the dam, and ride the road back to the beginning of the steep climb. Push the reset button for another lap.

Noah's (Map p.246)

from the beginning of Dixon Dam Rd.

Silver Star Mountain Trails

The snow comes in early October and stays until June at this Okanagan ski resort, but in between, the summer season is a mountain biker's dream. Silver Star hosted the Grundig World Cup Finals in 1994 on a course that was well received by all. The downhill is fast, turny, and considered a peddler's course, while the cross country is a perfect combination of double and single track climbs, with good technical sections. "A solid test of mountain biking" according to two time world champion Allison Sydor. Apart from these world class trails there are plenty of other trails to challenge all levels of riders. The main road up to the top is an easy grade and is paved part way up. Once riders reach the summit, which can also be done by chairlift , a host of rippin fun options await. Ride toward the 'bus runs' and explore some of the area's steeper descents and hook up with the Gold Mountain Trail, or continue on to the Sovereign Lakes XC Ski Area, but be careful of wet bogs and killer mosquitos. Good single track sections are located off the Silver Queen climb in 'Doryland'. Plenty of riding in the alpine is what you can expect. The altitude makes the climbs a little more testy than usual, but it's nice to know a chairlift is there to keep the fun going after your climbing legs have given up.

The best part of mountain biking on Silver Star is the moderate temperatures. The trails range from 4000 to 6280 ft., so obviously the stinking hot weather in the valley will be easier on the systems of all riders who like to go at it all day. But, if you plan on a day at Silver Star bring clothes for all weather conditions because it can turn cool and wet any time at this altitude.

The trails are great, the weather is usually nice, and you can go rollerblading, have a great lunch, and ride downhills all day among the alpine flowers at this great summer resort. If you drive up for the day, draw straws on who gets to ride Spanky's down to town.

the best way

to see
the
back country.

Silver Star Mountain has incredible biking terrain for all levels of riders. Take a bike to the top. Chairlift open 10 am to 5 pm everyday. Guided rides, bike & gear rentals on-mountain at Brian James Ski & Sport.

MORE INFO:
1-800-663-4431
OR 604-542-0224
SUMMER SEASON:
JUNE 22 - OCTOBER 14.

August 17 & 18, Silver Star Mountain plays host to the BRIKO CANADA CUP MOUNTAIN BIKE Cross country and Downhill Race

June 23 - August 18
TECHNICAL MOUNTAIN BIKE CAMPS
$199. includes 2 nights accommodation and 3 meals daily.
Sponsored by Silver Star Mountain & Skedaddle Cycle Tours.
INFO: call 1-800-663-4431

SILVER STAR MOUNTAIN
A CANADIAN CLASSIC

JUST 20 KM. FROM VERNON, B.C.
EXIT EAST AT 48TH AVE.

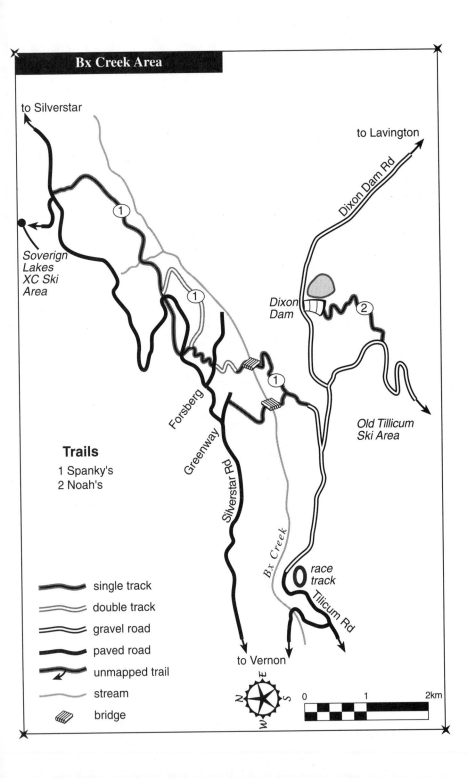

MOUNTAIN BIKING
BRITISH COLUMBIA
The Trail Guide

Salmon Arm

The Trails

Salmon Arm

Introduction

The town of Salmon Arm, nestled at the southern tip of Shuswap Lake, has plenty to offer the mountain biker. Travellers often view this town as a pit stop enroute to the Rockies, or as a place to rent a house boat and float away the summer. However, the word is now spreading that mountain biking enthusiasts can have a great time checking out the uncrowded trails, warm lakes, and groovy hospitality of Salmon Arm. The area already has a trail guide book published, and I used the book to give you the best of Salmon Arm. So, without any further adieu . . .

Salmon Arm

The Rubberhead

So what if they borrowed the name from Rossland, it is still a gnarly ride that can crush egos or create new ones, depending on how you, and the gravity gods, are coexisting. Hit it on a dry day and you will probably shake a little and laugh a lot. On a wet day you will shake, laugh, and probably crash a lot. On a trail like this, if you fight the pull of gravity the switchbacks and drop-offs will haunt you. On the other hand, if you allow the bike to flow down the hill giving you a few seconds of pure, free falling joy, and regain control later, then the trail will become your best friend. And people and babies will adore you!

To access the trail head, drive north east of Salmon Arm on Highway #1 until the Co-op Lumber Mill parking lot. The second gravel lot has a grassy road that climbs up into the _____ fun zone. Ride up onto an old road bed *"On a trail like this, if you fight* that veers left of a gravel pit. This climb *the pull of gravity the switchbacks* is gentle, on a canopied road which *and drop-offs will haunt you."* leads to a right turn onto a main forest _____ service road. If you end up at the TNT shack you turned right to soon. This wide, well maintained forest service road is your home as you climb upward for about 25 minutes. Near the 4 km mark you will notice a single track on the left, and a few meters

MOUNTAIN BIKING
BRITISH COLUMBIA
The Trail Guide

later, another on your right. This is the downhill that awaits. Continue the climb until a right onto an old narrower road bed approximately 5 km from the start. The downhill is now 1 km ahead on the right. The first few drop-offs are fairly indicative of the rest of the trail. Be sure to check out the single track diversion on the route back, shortly after the gravel pit, on the return trip to the parking lot.

The Rubberhead (Map p.251)

Salmon Arm

Prudential

This single track area is located close to town on the lower western facing slopes of Larch Hills. The low elevation will give you good early season conditions, and the variety of single track will please mountain bikers of all abilities. Access the trail, drive up 10th Ave. and park at the bottom of the Larch Hills Canoe Creek Forest Service Road. The best tour of the area requires you to ride up the main road 1.5 km until a right turn, where a convergence single track going off very sweet trail that 2 km later. From the tions can make some

"You can easily blow off an entire day here, and as a bonus there is great exploring to be done on the upper slopes of Larch Hills."

of old roads has a to the left. This is a reaches a gully about gully, a couple of options nice loops. Return back on the same single track. Once you are onto the main road, you'll find another trail directly across the road. This trail has multiple branches and will lead you into the watershed area. These lower trails are loose and dusty and can have multi-use traffic on the weekends. Please obey all posted signs in this area. You can easily blow off an entire day here, and as a bonus there is great exploring to be done on the upper slopes of Larch Hills.

Prudential (Map p.250)

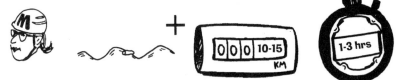

Photograph by Blair Polischuk

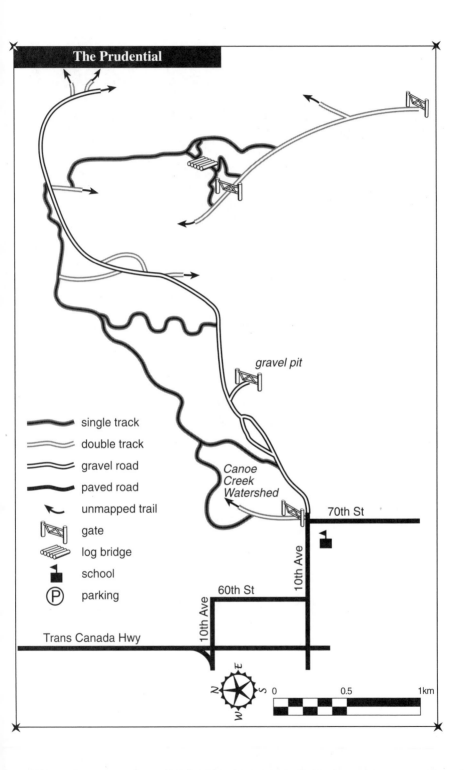

The Prudential

single track
double track
gravel road
paved road
unmapped trail
gate
log bridge
school
Ⓟ parking

gravel pit

Canoe Creek Watershed

70th St

10th Ave

60th St

10th Ave

Trans Canada Hwy

N
E
S
W

0   0.5   1km

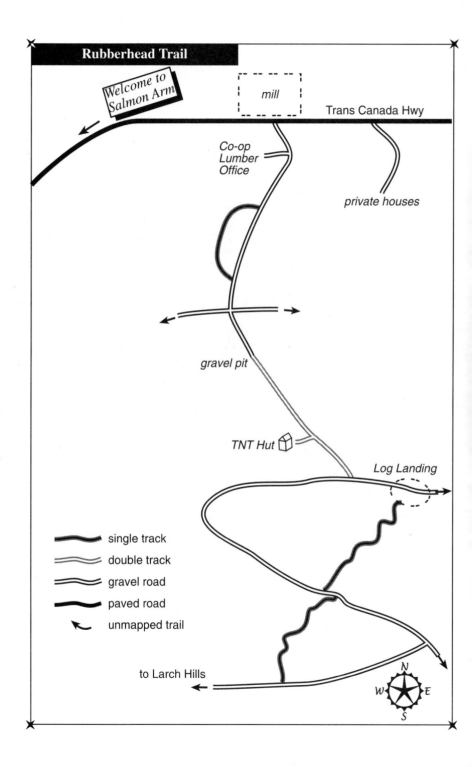

MOUNTAIN BIKING
BRITISH COLUMBIA
The Trail Guide

Kamloops

Kamloops

Mount Dufferin Trails

Mount Dufferin is the most popular mountain biking area in Kamloops because of its easy access and satisfying terrain. Parched, semi-arid land, with thinly spaced trees and scrub brush on an old network of double track roads and ultra buffed single track is what riders can expect. The riding on the southern exposed slopes and valley bottoms is very desert-like, contrasting sharply with higher elevation rides and slopes with hidden northern exposures. The riding here is fast, and the climbing sometimes steep, but always short. Novice riders have plenty of room to explore the lower trails and take the gentle main climb up to the communication tower.

> *"The riding here is fast, and the climbing sometimes steep, but always short."*

To access the fun on Mount Dufferin you have to climb to the tower. The 2 km climb up the main road is a gentle grade, but power climbers will want to check out the steep pitches accessed east of the main climb. This killer ride will deposit you gasping on the last switchback near the top. Go past the tower and look for a right turn downhill shortly after. This will spit you out on one of the best sections of fast, turny, single track I have ever ridden. If you go left, the trail snakes its way through sparse trees, and lets you go fast but checks your ability and speed with quick, testy turns. Once onto the double track veer left at the intersections, ride past the jail and up a gradual climb back to the main climb. Scamper to the top and push the reset button for another session.

You can become familiar with the area and easily dial up a great couple of hours of mountain biking with the weakest of route-finding skills. Picturesque views of the Thompson River Valley and the city of Kamloops are found throughout the area because of the thin forest cover. Mount Dufferin is a Biological Weed Control Area, and riders should, as always, stick to well established routes. For a larger sample of the trails in this area pick up a copy of the Kamloops / Shuswap Mountain Bike Guide.

Mount Dufferin Trails (Map p.253)

one loop as described

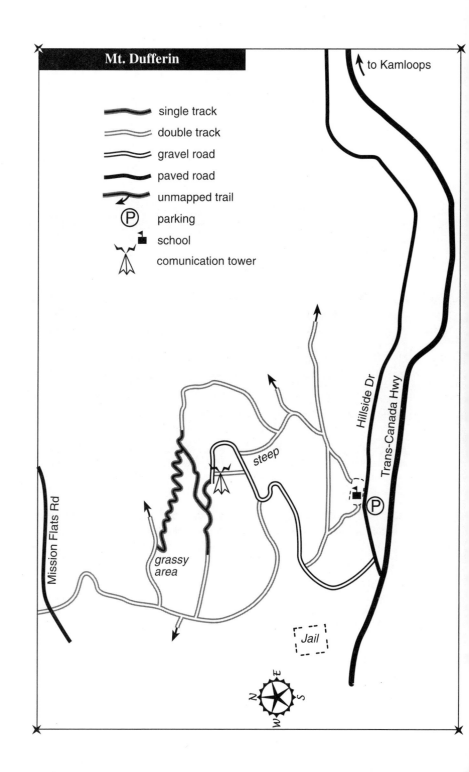

MOUNTAIN BIKING
BRITISH COLUMBIA
The Trail Guide

Revelstoke

Revelstoke B.C. is a quiet mountain town with awsome four season recreational opportunities. Despite the area's natural environment, it is most often recognized for its human-made landscape, specifically the huge dams that dot the Columbia River forming the Arrow Lakes. However, a further look and you'll see one of the best rides in the province, Keystone Standard Basin, and a host of other riding opportunities in The Begbie Falls Forest Service Area. Good riding on double track, and the odd sneaky single track, is also found in the Mt MacPherson XC Ski Area. With all of these mountain biking possibilities, riders of all abilities can't help but stop and check it out when passing through Revelstoke. Drop by Spoketacular to find out what the locals are keeping a secret, I'm sure it's worth it!

"Good riding on double track, and the odd sneaky single track, is also found in the Mt MacPherson XC Ski Area."

Revelstoke

Keystone Standard Basin Trail

High alpine single tracks are a rare species in the mountain biker's taxonomy of fun zones. Throughout my travels in B.C. the thought of this trail became the benchmark from which all other rides were judged, and few compare to the total package of mountain biking fun that can be had on the Keystone Standard Basin Trail. Simply put, the ride is awe inspiring, and other rides pale in comparison after hitting this one on a good day. Plan a ride on this trail as a way to celebrate the existence of life and mountain biking.

To access the trail, drive 50 km north of Revelstoke on highway 23 passing the Revelstoke Dam, all the while skirting the edge of Lake Revelstoke. At the 50 km mark a large sign will direct you to go right, and up a logging road 15 km to the trail head. Each intersection on the logging road is marked to direct you to the correct parking spot. The Forest Service provides a registration box at the trail head to sign on and leave comments.

The ride is an out and back experience with a cabin at the main turn around point. The beginning of the trail is a technical climb that will have you

wondering if you can do this for 22 km. Don't despair, after about 2.5 km of climbing the trail flattens out and rolls through stunning alpine meadows,

(Continued on page 256)

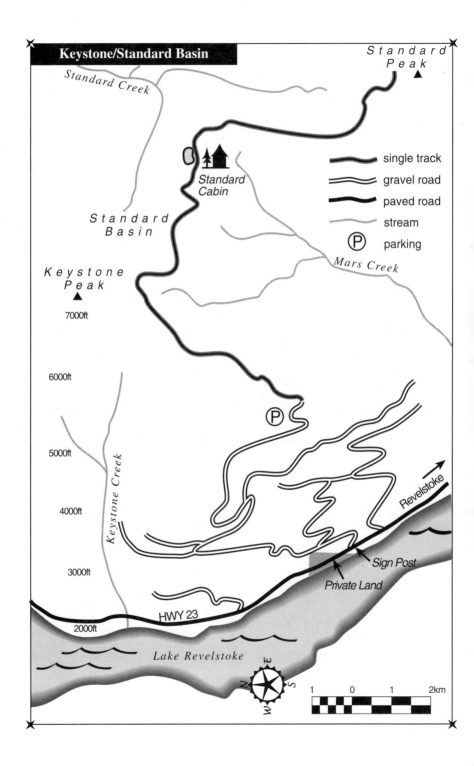

Keystone/Standard Basin

Standard Peak ▲

Standard Creek

Standard Cabin

Standard Basin

Keystone Peak ▲
7000ft

Mars Creek

single track
gravel road
paved road
stream
Ⓟ parking

6000ft

Ⓟ

5000ft

Keystone Creek

Revelstoke

4000ft

Sign Post

3000ft

Private Land

HWY 23

2000ft

Lake Revelstoke

N
W E
S

1   0   1   2km

MOUNTAIN BIKING
BRITISH COLUMBIA
The Trail Guide

(Continued from page 254)

across rocky scree slopes, through cold creeks, and possibly over summer snow fields, all the while begging you to slow down and drink in the view. The trail itself is a narrow track, and I often skidded off the side because of the visual distractions. You learn to trust the trail after a while, but less confident riders may struggle with the limited sight lines, and con- tinuous exposure. At one point the trail dissipates into an open grassy meadow. By following the rock cairns you will pick up the trail down the meadow as it continues to skirt along the contours of Standard Basin.

> *"The trail itself is a narrow track, and I often skidded off the side because of the visual distractions."*

After 11 km of near perfect single track you're confronted with the welcoming sight of Standard Cabin, which is located at the foot of an idyllic, un-named lake. The true hard cores can continue past the cabin to Standard Peak. The cabin is always open and visitors can leave their impressions of the area in a guest book. For the majority of us mortals the cabin means rest, something to eat, and the beginning of the return voyage. The way back can be a little tiring, but all of the climbing you did on the way there means plenty of downhill on the way back. For those desiring still more downhill, you can draw straws; the loser has to drive the vehicle down and the winners are left with 15 km of screaming forest service road descent to complete a perfect day.

High alpine rides can be risky ventures for the unprepared; consequently, several common sense things must be kept in mind to ensure a safe outing. Firstly, this ride is only possible in August and September; any earlier and it will be a mud and snow fest, any later and the weather could turn your ride into a potential made for TV movie. Secondly, the trail averages about 6000 feet in elevation. This means that 22 km of single track could be a personal death march to an unfit, sea level creature. Thirdly, the trail is always exposed, and in some sections, very exposed. Please walk your bike when the going gets scary. Simply put, the ride is a bit long, in thin air, and in a few places a wee bit hairy. But if you choose a day when the trail is dry and the weather stable, there is no better!

> *"This means that 22 km of single track could be a personal death march to an unfit, sea level creature."*

Keystone Standard Basin Trail (Map p.255)

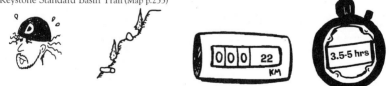

MOUNTAIN BIKING
BRITISH COLUMBIA
The Trail Guide

Revelstoke

Begbie Creek Trails

The Begbie Creek Trails are located South of Revelstoke on the western shores of Upper Arrow Lake. The trails are maintained by the Revelstoke Forest District, and are the result of an integrated resource plan which balances the needs of harvesting and recreation. The area has about *"The area has about 5 km of trails which were completed in 1994."* 5 km of trails which were completed in 1994. The trails are generally a moderate type of single track which are used by mountain bikers, as well as horses and climbers, hiking into the rock bluffs. Please keep this in mind when riding in this area.

To access the trails, ride or drive south on Highway 23 and turn left on Mt. Begbie Rd., or further down on Clough Rd. Both of these roads will bring you to the main Begbie Falls Rd. Another trailhead is located about 1km past the Mt. MacPherson XC Ski Trails.

The best way to explore these trails is to ride down the main Begbie Falls Rd. to the end. Be sure to walk down to the Falls for a look. Next, ride up the single track, which gradually climbs up a few meters from the falls parking area. Be sure not to take the old road but the single track. *"a perfect, bomb-proof, single track downhill that has plenty of fast switchbacks to test your bike handling skills."* This trail will bring you to an intersection in about 1 km. To bail out here go left to highway 23, or for a great twisty downhill, go right past some climbing areas and down a perfect, bomb-proof, single track downhill that has plenty of fast switchbacks to test your bike handling skills. For those who drive to the area, park on Begbie Falls Rd where the road starts to narrow, and if you follow the trail it will come out near your car.

Begbie Creek Trails (Map p.258)

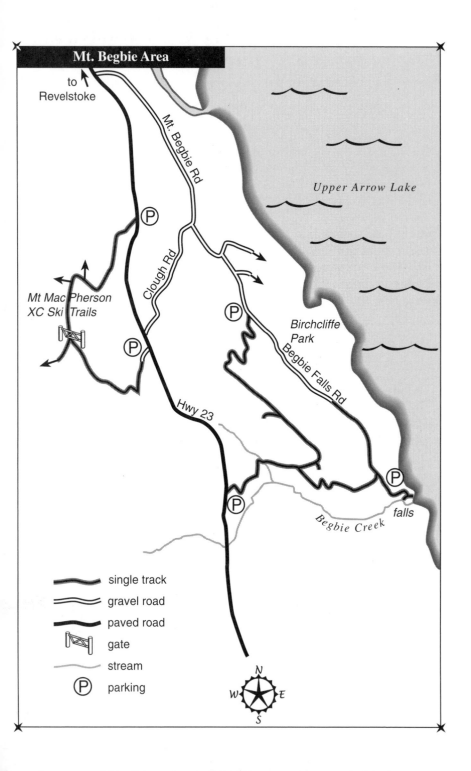

MOUNTAIN BIKING
BRITISH COLUMBIA
The Trail Guide

Nakusp

Kuskanax Hot Springs Trails

Nakusp is located in the Arrow Lakes Valley, one valley east of the Okanagan. The town of Nakusp sits on the eastern shore of Upper Arrow Lake, nestled between the Monashees and the Selkirks. The views of the mountains and glaciers are outstanding, and reason enough to visit this area and do some excellent _____ mountain biking. However, *"The views of the mountains and glaciers are* another rea- son people *outstanding, and reason enough to visit this* come to Nakusp is for *area and do some excellent mountain biking."* the natural hot springs. The _____ pools are nu- merous, and are either fully developed, or primitive. Either way, a 101° -106° degree pool is a welcome site after a hard day of riding, and a unique way to enjoy this uncrowded valley. Drop into the travel info center in Nakusp for details and directions to these pools that refresh your soul as much as your legs. Try out a few different pools, they all have unique charms. Now for the riding...

The Kuskanax Hot Springs Trail is a point to point single track that hugs the steep valley leading to the developed hot springs. The trail bed was built in the early 1900's as a horse route to the pools. Today, there is a sweet single track that gradually climbs up the valley taking the path of least resistance. The trail is quite exposed in some sections, but despite this potential danger the route is not too technical. One tight set of switchbacks provide the technically inspired with an outlet to vent.

To access the trail, ride east on Highway 6 for 1.5 km to Carsons Corner Store. Turn left onto Alexander Rd. Proceed north 1.5 km past the Glenbank graveyard, then look for the old road uphill and on your right. You now should be off-road and will _____ see the trail head sign. Ride 2 km up *"Today, there is a sweet single track* this old road thru a large logged area *that gradually climbs up the valley* keeping to the well worn path. This *taking the path of least resistance."* road terminates in an open area where _____ you can see the trail entering the forest about 300 meters ahead. The occasional orange trail marker on the trees will assist you at this point.

Upon entering the forest the single track will gradually climb taking you past the switchbacks and an A-frame cabin. The trail splits at one point but rejoins shortly after. A footbridge crosses a river and deposits you at the Nakusp Hot Springs.

MOUNTAIN BIKING
BRITISH COLUMBIA
The Trail Guide

Ride options include:

1) Ride a loop from town up the trail and down the paved road that leads to the hot springs. 2-3 hours

2) Ride the same loop but in reverse; up the paved road and down the trail. 2-3 hours

3) Leave your car at the hot springs and do a loop, or an out and back, finishing with a soak. 2-4 hours

Special thanks to Peter Roulston at the Bicycle Hospital for help with the trail details. I rode the trail in the spring of 1993 and, snowshoed the trail in the winter, and recommended it to all who are willing. The trail should be clear of snow by May. This trail would make a very cool riding destination for those who like to travel to discover unique riding opportunities. be sure and ride the old rail grade that heads southeast out of town toward summit Lake. This out and back ride is an easy outing for novice riders to the area.

The central location of Nakusp makes it easy to discover riding in the Okanagan, Revelstoke, or the Kootenays, during the same trip. Have fun and remember to bring your bathing suit which is an option at the numerous primitive hot springs.

Photograph by Blair Polischuk

South Central British Columbia

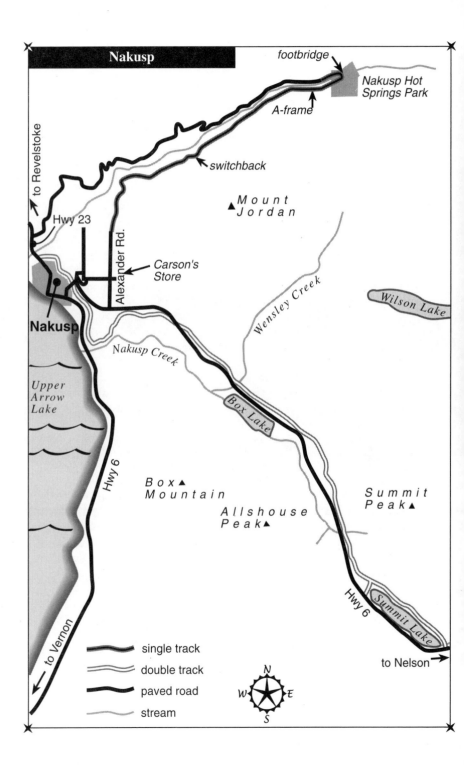

MOUNTAIN BIKING
BRITISH COLUMBIA
The Trail Guide

Grand Forks / Christina Lakes

Grand Forks / Christina Lakes

Thimble Mountain

The Thimble Mountain Trail is considered one of the best in the Grand Forks area because it gives riders outstanding single track, as well as nice views of the Granby River Valley. To access the trail drive 21 km west on Highway #3 from downtown Grand Forks and park at the pullout. Go through the gate and ride about 150 meters to where a road comes out on your left. Go left for about 500 meters and you will see the trail head sign in a box. A total of about 2000 feet of climbing begins as you pop out on the top of an old clear cut where the trail traverses, then _____ hooks onto an old road. Follow this road for about 500 meters on the right to a single track marked with diamond-shaped orange things. This single track rolls till a right

". . .considered one of the best in the Grand Forks area because it gives riders outstanding single track, as well as nice views of the Granby River Valley."

on the road, and then a left 300 meters later at the next intersection. This old road turns into a single track. Follow for about 3 km until a crows-foot type opening. Go through the gate and follow the trail until you hit a road. Go right and look for a trail immediately on your left. You're nearing the top of Thimble Mountain. Stay left at the next intersection and soon you will be in a bluff overlooking the Granby River Valley. After the necessary refueling pit stop, return back the same way or turn left on the road that gradually turned into a single track. The trail is faint in some places, so keep your eyes open until you eventually get to the fenceline again, turn left and ride the sweet downhill.

Another option from the start is to ignore the trail head and follow the road 1.2 km to a T intersection. Then turn right and go 3 km on B.C. Mines Road until you see an old mine and a road on your right. Follow this road up and turn left when you see the orange markers. This is a nice option to ride the single track back to the start. Rumor has it that a nasty little gnome lives in the Cedar trees near the bottom of the trail who punishes all riders who disregard the rules of the trail. Don't believe me? Ask the locals who have lived to tell the story!

(Continued on page 264)

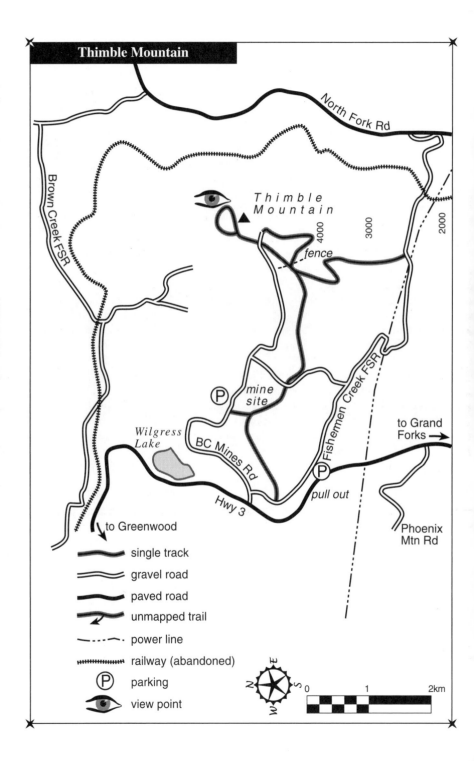

Thimble Mountain

North Fork Rd

Brown Creek FSR

Thimble Mountain

fence

4000   3000   2000

Fishermen Creek FSR

P

mine site

P

pull out

to Grand Forks →

Wilgress Lake

BC Mines Rd

Hwy 3

Phoenix Mtn Rd

to Greenwood

single track
gravel road
paved road
unmapped trail
power line
railway (abandoned)
parking
view point

0   1   2km

MOUNTAIN BIKING
BRITISH COLUMBIA
The Trail Guide

Thimble Mountain (Map p.263)

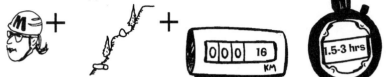

Grand Forks / Christina Lakes

Deer Point Trail / Sandner Creek Trail

These combinations offer a rider the best trails in the Christina Lake area. This is the most popular hiking trail in the summer, so be aware of others on your ride. The lower portions of the trail can have long seasons. To access the Deer Point Trail turn left off the highway onto East Lake Rd. Follow this road until you reach the boat _____ launch on your left. A sign at the end of the *"This is a great ripping finish* parking lot reads 'Deer Point Trail'. The best *that can't be missed."* way to get to the good stuff is to follow the _____ single track to a road, and go right and up the climb, and left at the T intersection. Follow this road about 1 km until it switches back, then go left onto the trail. This is Deer Point Trail. While riding out, notice a trail to your left about 100 meters from the start. This is a great ripping finish that can't be missed. If you choose to start from the boat launch parking lot it's a bit of a rude warm up.

The first climb is about 2 km, and just before the top there is a comfy bench to rest on overlooking the south end of the lake. From the rest stop the terrain is rolling with downhills and climbs of 1 - 2 km in length. Some tricky bridge crossings and exposure to the lake add technical difficulty to a trail that is mostly fast cruising with plenty of quick corners and rolling terrain. At the 6 km mark you can go right and on to Deer Point Lookout and return, or go left toward the head of the Lake.

From this point on, the ride and the technical difficulty goes up a few notches. Around the 9.5 km mark you are treated to a nice downhill to the head of the lake. This area is _____ private property and the owners *"...you are treated to a nice downhill* have generously allowed the trail *to the head of the lake."* through their land. The first road you _____ cross is the Sandner Creek Trail. Here you have the option to go right and ride further into a lush, green valley that is best experienced in summer due to wet conditions in

(Continued on page 267)

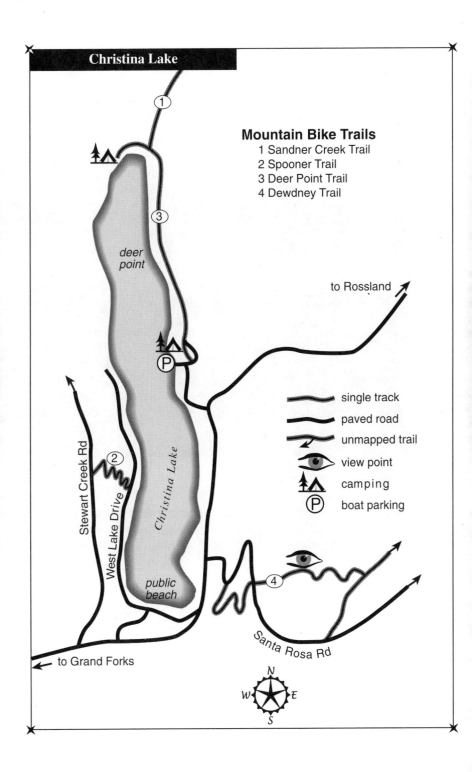

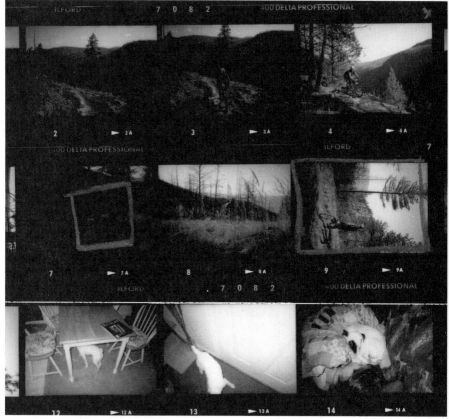

Photograph? by Darrin Polischuk

MOUNTAIN BIKING
BRITISH COLUMBIA
The Trail Guide

(Continued from page 264)

the spring. Your other option is to go straight, following orange markers through an old growth cedar forest which was selectively logged some time ago. But some old grandfathers still remain. Kokanee salmon can be spotted here in the fall, as can the bear's who dig nature's sushi. So be aware! Cross the creek, to go onto Troy Creek Campsite and home, or turn around and return the same way. This is by far the best out and back ride at Christina Lake!

Deer Point Trail / Sandner Creek Trail (Map p.265)

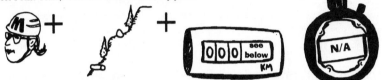

6 km to Deer Point, 10 km to head of lake, 12.5 plus km to Sandner Creek

Grand Forks / Christina Lakes

Spooner Creek Trail

This is a great ride for the summer because the creek can cool you off when the going gets too hot. On this superb downhill you go from loamy cedar forest to more open and fast single track. This fun, twisty, downhill single track is sandwiched between Stewart Creek Forest Service Road and West Lake Drive. While you can orga- nize a shuttle to do the downhill, the *"On this superb downhill you go* short paved sections should be ridden by *from loamy cedar forest to more* all except those with honest excuses for *open and fast single track."* not enjoying a brief warm up and cool down, before or after the trail. To access the ride, turn right off Highway #3 onto Stewart Creek Rd. Follow this road to the 9 km sign and look for the trail just up on the right. It should be marked with flagging tape. The trail drops you down to West Lake Road and a short 4 km spin brings you back to the public beach. About a third of the way down there is a trail going off to your right that leads to a nice rest stop overlooking the lake. From here you can double back to the main trail, and the view is well worth it. If you ride from the beach from West Lake Drive to the highway, be sure and turn right on Wolverton and right again on Thompson to the highway. This cuts off a heinous blacktop climb among the RV's.

Spooner Creek Trail (Map p.265)

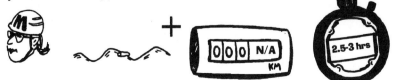

MOUNTAIN BIKING
BRITISH COLUMBIA
The Trail Guide

Grand Forks / Christina Lakes

Dewdney Trail

Starting from the town of Christina Lake drive east on Highway #3, cross the bridge, and turn right on Santa Rosa Rd. This long steady climb gradually turns into a gravel road. After climbing for about 7 km you go around a corner and turn left on a road. Next, you cross under powerlines and climb for about 2 km where you'll see the Dewdney Trail come in on your right and descend to the left. Go left and soak up some great views of Christina Lake to the west overlooking the Kettle Valley, and the south into the States. The ride down is major, screaming fast, downhill fun. You will cross over the road you climbed at one point, but just drop over the other side and keep ripping down. You come out at the first switchback, and from here it's a race to the lake for a swim. This is a very hot ride in the summer, so plan on an early morning or sunset ride to make the best of this route.

Dewdney Trail (Map p.265)

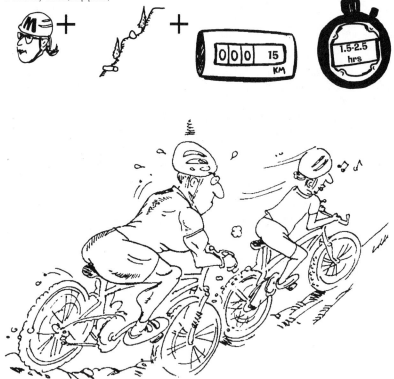

MOUNTAIN BIKING
BRITISH COLUMBIA
The Trail Guide

South East British Columbia

Photograph by Blair Polischuk

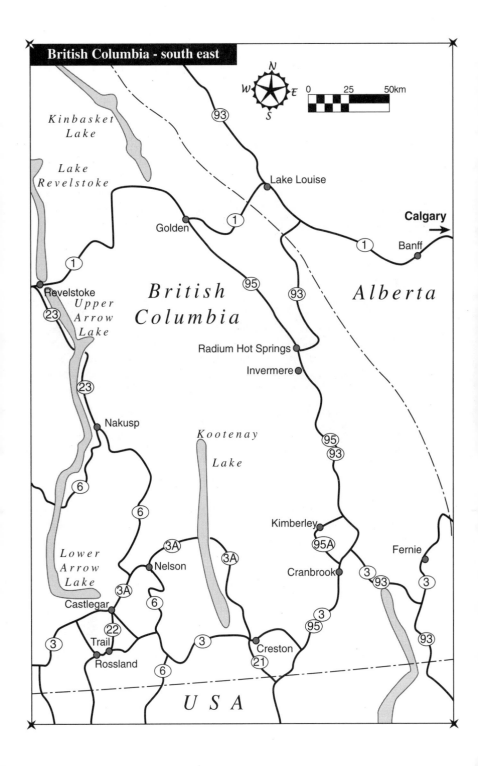

MOUNTAIN BIKING
BRITISH COLUMBIA
The Trail Guide

Field

Ottertail Fire Road Trail

The trail head for the Ottertail Fire Road Trail is located about 35 minutes east of Golden B.C., or approximately 8 km west of Field. If you are driving from Golden, the trail head will be on your right shortly after the bridge over Ottertail River. The trail is located in Yoho National Park, with the start located at the old site of the District Warden's Headquarters. At the trail head there is a sign board with information updating recent trail conditions, bear sightings, etc.

"The ride is generally smooth and not too technical, with the steeper grades developing within the first few km of the start."

The trail is an old fire road out and back to the McArthur Creek Warden Cabin, which unfortunately is closed to the public. Enroute you'll cross Float Creek, where the trail switchbacks, but eventually levels out as you go through an old burn sight that has naturally regenerated itself. Further up the trail you will ride past the McArthur Creek Trail which is a closed grizzly bear habitat. All of the trails that shoot off the the Ottertail Fire Road Trail are closed to mountain bikers.

"A spectacular view of the north faces of Goodsir Towers is your reward for a long day in the saddle."

Expect the trail to be accessible from June to October, with the best riding conditions in late summer and autumn. The ride is generally smooth and not too technical, with the steeper grades developing within the first few km of the start. A spectacular view of the north faces of Goodsir Towers is your reward for a long day in the saddle. A nice hiking trail extends beyond the cabin, but it's closed to mountaim biking. Please respect Yoho National Park and stay on the main trail.

Ottertail Fire Road Trail (Map p.273)

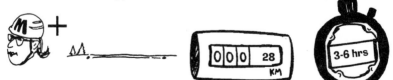

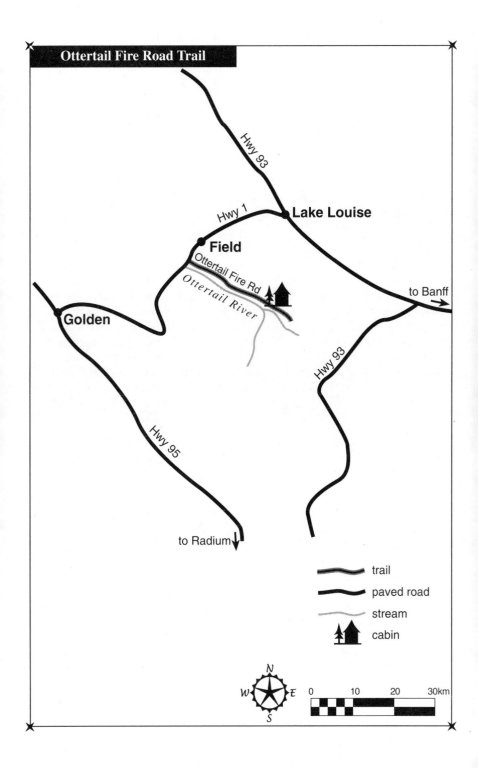

Golden's West Bench Trails

Introduction

Golden is an awesome little alpine town sandwiched between the Rocky and Purcell Mountains. The town has outstanding recreational pursuits, possible in any direction, in any season. A good crew of mountain bikers and alpinist-folk take full advantage of the area's potential. To catch a bit of the local milieu, drop by Summit Cycle and talk to Ian Millroy. Ian definitely gets the happy-shop-owner-living-in-paradise award. If you do any riding in Golden, drop by his shop to hook up with some locals, or to discuss rides that are not mentioned in this book. The riding mapped is all on the east facing slope of the Dogtooth range, the same slope as the local ski area. Access for all of these rides is found by going out of town and over the single lane blue bridge, and then following the signs toward the Whitetooth Ski Area. Be sure to ask at Summit Cycle about the riding on Mt. Seven and other secrets in the Golden area.

Golden's West Bench Trails

Canyon Creek Loop

If you can only do one ride while visiting Golden make it the Canyon Creek Loop. To access the ride, follow the signs to the ski hill, taking a left at the first T intersection about 7 km from town. Continue another 2 km to a three way intersection, and take the right fork. Climb about 2 km to the first clear cut and take the center road across the cut block. You go back into the forest and pop out in a second cut block. Go left, and down into the cleared area, and take the last climb out of the cut block on the more travelled path. You should pass a swampy area, and nearby, the trail head should be signed (although a segment of the population enjoys shooting down things like trail signs, especially after many beers).

> *"A good crew of mountain bikers and alpinist-folk take full advantage of the area's potential."*

MOUNTAIN BIKING
BRITISH COLUMBIA
The Trail Guide

Soon you'll spot the canyon. Stop, drink in the view, and get psyched for about a 3 km descent. At the bottom of the canyon you will hit a logged area, back up and take the single track on your right to milk the most of the downhill. Once at the bottom of the gravel pit go left on the gravel road. Be sure NOT to take the skidder trail but stay on the main gravel road that climbs gently. The steady climb will bring you past a wire gate and eventually up to the Cedar Lake Forest Service Rustic Campsite. You can start this ride from town or from Cedar Lake.

Canyon Creek Loop (Map p.276-7)

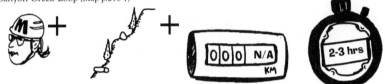

Golden's West Bench Trails

Moonraker Trails

On the descent portion of the Canyon Creek Trail there is a half-pipe type of thing. Once you are near this, look for a trail entrance on the left. This is the trail leading into the Moonraker trail system. These trails are slow and technical, but generally rideable in both directions. Use the radio tower as your main point of reference, because this area is quite confusing, and getting lost is a possibility. About a 1 km service road leads you from the radio tower back to the main road just before a gate.

Moonraker Trails (Map p.276-7)

Golden's West Bench Trails

West Bench Lower Road

From town, take the left fork just after the bridge over the Columbia River. The left turn is about 50 meters past the right turn to the golf course. This gentle ride rolls up and down offering continuous views of the Columbia River. It also passes by a great example of the Columbia Valley wetlands and should provide great wildlife viewing opportunities. The trail surface is a novice-friendly gravel road. The ride ends up in the Nicholson Subdivision where you can either

(Continued on page 278)

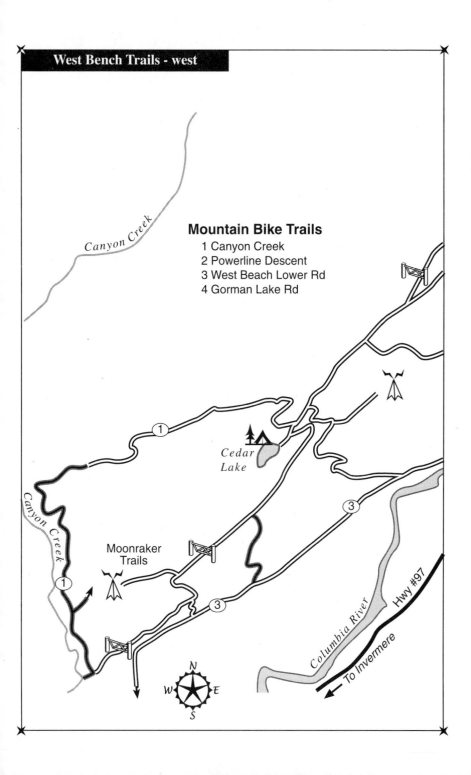

Mountain Bike Trails
1 Canyon Creek
2 Powerline Descent
3 West Beach Lower Rd
4 Gorman Lake Rd

Canyon Creek

Canyon Creek

Cedar Lake

Moonraker Trails

Columbia River

Hwy #97

To Invermere

N
W   E
S

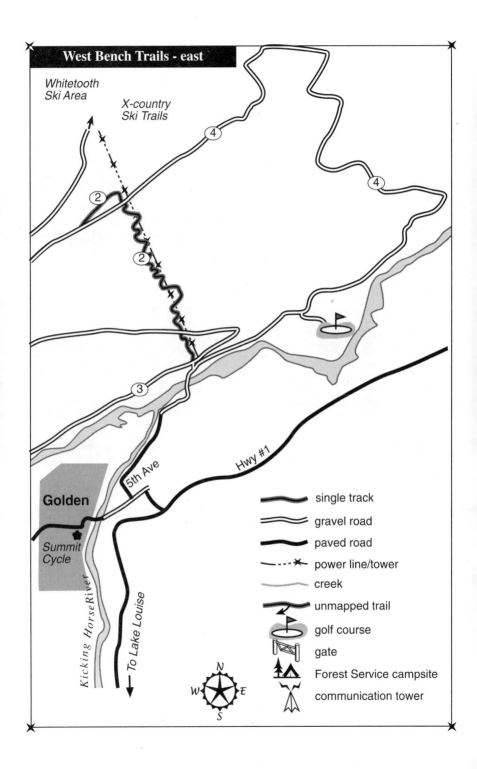

MOUNTAIN BIKING
BRITISH COLUMBIA
The Trail Guide

(Continued from page 275)

retrace your steps, ride home on the road, or continue up the five switchbacks to Cedar Lake. This trail passes through private property, but the land owner supports cyclists using the road.

West Bench Lower Road (Map p.276-7)

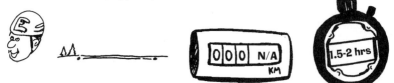

depending on option

Golden's West Bench Trails

Powerline Descent

Not exactly a winner in the original name category, but a good, screaming, bone-shaker nonetheless. To access the trail, turn right at the T intersection 7 km from town on the way to Whitetooth. Be sure to turn right and not take the road to the ski hill. The double track you are now on will cross 3 creeks before offering you a single track on the left. This trail meets up with the powerline and begins to shake, rattle and roll down. Be sure to go left at the swamp, and when you intersect the road the trail continues. This ride is a bit extreme in some sections and should be contemplated by skilled riders only.

Powerline Descent (Map p.276-7)

from town

Golden's West Bench Trails

Gorman Lake Connector

The connector continues past the turn off for the powerline descent. This ride is on old double track and is a long, moderate tour of the West Bench area. Be sure to miss the XC ski area because it is a bog in the summer, and if the mud doesn't get you the mosquitos will.

Gorman Lake Connector (Map p.276-7)

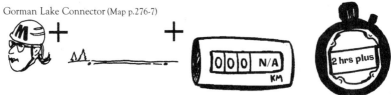

2 hrs plus

MOUNTAIN BIKING
BRITISH COLUMBIA
The Trail Guide

Invermere / Panorama Trails

Introduction

The Columbia River Valley is littered with old roads and trails. While this generally means it's a mecca for mountain bikers, the reality of private property ownership makes adventuring on these trails a potential problem. The valley bottom rides in Invermere criss-cross private land. Those wanting to ride in the valley bottom should try to hook up with local riders or check at the Forest Service for information on Mt. Swansea and Blue Mt. trails.

The riding in the valley pales in comparison to the rides in the high country around the resort of Panorama. To access the trails near Panorama, follow the signs toward the ski hill, on the road which follows Toby Creek. Novice riders can have a great time exploring the well marked Panorama XC ski area trails. Check at the Panorama Activity Center before venturing out onto these trails. Also, for some reason, the Toby Creek Rd. is signed in miles, and the Jumbo Creek Rd. in kilometers.

Invermere / Panorama Trails

Paradise Mine Trail

This is the classic mountain bike ride with plenty of climbing and a unique old mine site to visit that should keep you motivated while grunting up the 4000 ft. to the top. To do this ride it is recommended that a shuttle be dropped off in the village of ——————————————————— Wilmer and that another *". . . the classic mountain bike ride"* vehicle bring you to the base ——————————————————— of Panorama where the ride starts. You can take a 4 wd vehicle up to the mine site, but to truly call this a mountain bike ride, some climbing under your own power is required.

To access the trail head look for the main older gravel road on your right as you approach the ski hill turn off. 16 km later this road will bring you to the old

(Continued on page 282)

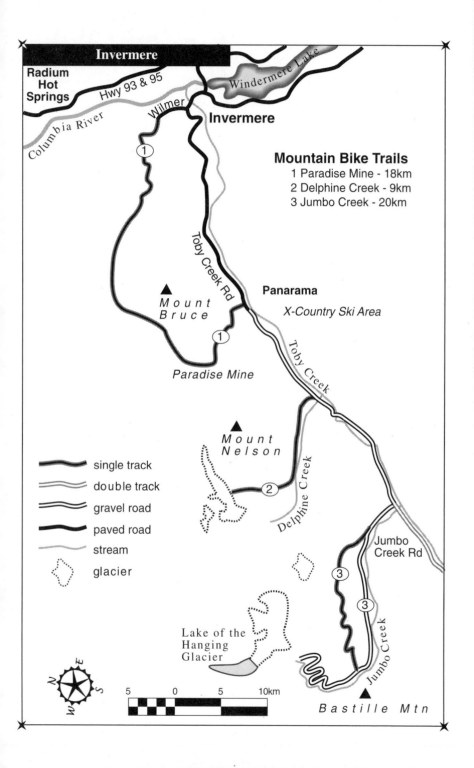

Invermere

Radium Hot Springs

Hwy 93 & 95

Columbia River

Wilmer

Windermere Lake

Invermere

Mountain Bike Trails
1 Paradise Mine - 18km
2 Delphine Creek - 9km
3 Jumbo Creek - 20km

Toby Creek Rd

①

▲ *M o u n t B r u c e*

Panarama

X-Country Ski Area

①

Paradise Mine

Toby Creek

▲ *M o u n t N e l s o n*

②

Delphine Creek

Jumbo Creek Rd

③

③

single track
double track
gravel road
paved road
stream
glacier

Lake of the Hanging Glacier

Jumbo Creek

N E S W

5   0   5   10km

B a s t i l l e   M t n

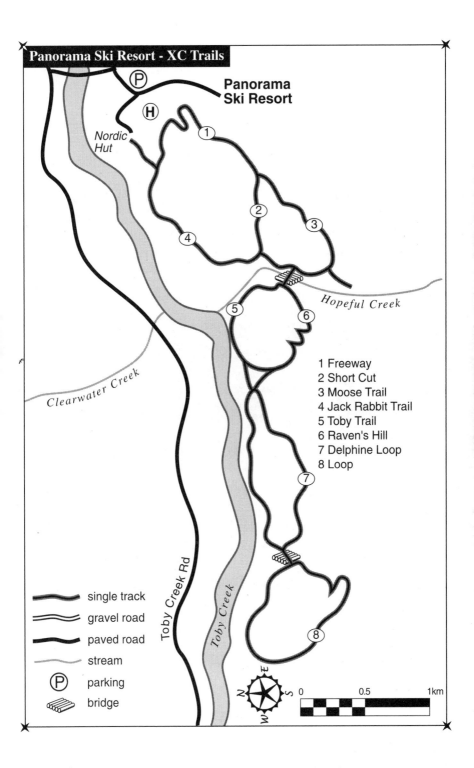

Panorama Ski Resort - XC Trails

Panorama
Ski Resort

Nordic Hut

Hopeful Creek

Clearwater Creek

1 Freeway
2 Short Cut
3 Moose Trail
4 Jack Rabbit Trail
5 Toby Trail
6 Raven's Hill
7 Delphine Loop
8 Loop

Toby Creek Rd

Toby Creek

single track
gravel road
paved road
stream
Ⓟ parking
bridge

0   0.5   1km

MOUNTAIN BIKING
BRITISH COLUMBIA
The Trail Guide

(Continued from page 279)

silver mine site which was open from the late 1800's to 1950. The old mining infrastructure is a close up look at an historical sight that few get the chance to visit. Be sure to bring your camera. From the mine site it is another 2 km to the ridge then a long 18 km descent to the town of Wilmer. The down hill is exciting and fast; a just reward for the long climb up.

Paradise Mine Trail (Map p.280)

from ski hill to Wilmer

Invermere / Panorama Trails

Delphine Creek / Glacier Lookout Trail

This is a technically challenging out and back trail. On a clear day, outstanding views of nearby Delphine Glacier can make it something to remember. The trail head is located 8.8 km from the main Panorama intersection. The old logging road from the beginning slowly deteriorates and becomes washed out. Riders must hike their bikes over a rocky scree slope section. The trail continues up to the right and eventually becomes unrideable. Return the same way.

Delphine Creek / Glacier Lookout Trail (Map p.280)

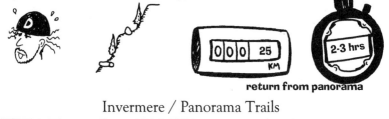

return from panorama

Invermere / Panorama Trails

Jumbo Creek Trail

The Jumbo Creek Trail is an overgrown single track found along side the Jumbo Creek Forest Service Road. The trail head is on your right just after the 6 km sign. Don't be confused by the fact that the Toby Creek Rd. is signed in miles and the Jumbo Creek Rd. signed in km. The single track has one gradual climb with a couple of creeks to cross. This trail has been known to be very overgrown in the fall so plan accordingly. Once you complete the single track you pop out on the main road. Continue climbing up to the glacier. At the 25 km marker the road starts to switchback giving you great views of Lake of The Hanging Glacier and Glacier Dome. This area is serious grizzly territory so resist the temptation to bring salmon sushi as your ride snack and feel free to talk loudly while riding to warn bears of your presence.

Jumbo Creek Trail (Map p.280)

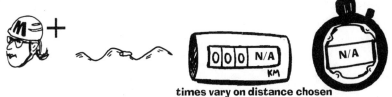

times vary on distance chosen

Radium Hot Springs

The Columbia River Valley provides the endless backdrop for this easy mountain bike ride. Get out of the car, jump on your bike, and take in the wonderful sights and sounds of this beautiful Rocky Mountain Valley. This ride is perfect for anyone who can ride a bike; and begs you to take a lunch and picnic atop one of the many viewpoints along this trail.

The trail itself is a gravel road, and descends slightly from the Mohawk gas station towards the Village of Radium, where it climbs up to the highway. You can also access the trail by descending on a gravel road between the go-cart track and playland. The trail has multiple spurs that veer toward the cliffs overlooking the river, and a few spurs drop down to the valley bottom. This ride is an easy way to get a close look at this unique river valley.

Radium Hot Springs (Map p.284)

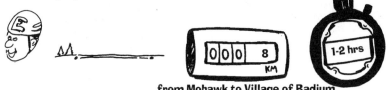

from Mohawk to Village of Radium

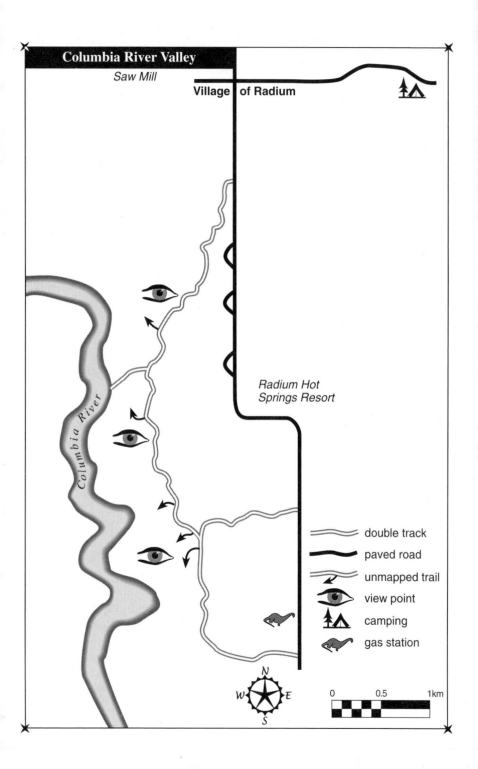

Columbia River Valley

Saw Mill

Village of Radium

Columbia River

Radium Hot Springs Resort

double track
paved road
unmapped trail
view point
camping
gas station

N
W   E
S

0   0.5   1km

MOUNTAIN BIKING
BRITISH COLUMBIA
The Trail Guide

Cranbrook

The Trails

Cranbrook

Forestry Hill Bypass Trail / Yellow Loop

The Forestry Hill Bypass Trail is an after work classic for those who need to do a little deep breathing ———————————— at the end of the day. This trail is conve- *"The highlight of this ride is* niently located just east of the city and *the final third which is a fast,* consists primarily of single track. The high- *downhill single track."* light of this ride is the final third which is a ———————————— fast, downhill single track. When bombing down this last portion of the loop be cautious of two-way traffic and hikers.

To access the trail head from the College Parking lot, ride back on College Way towards the city center, turn left on 24th ave., then left on 2nd. St. S. Follow this route uphill as it changes to a gravel road and leaves the residential areas of town. About 1.5 km past the last houses, at the start of an S bend, you will see a fence on the left and a small parking area. The trail begins just through the gate on the right. Look for the Yellow circles and Orange ribbons on the trees.

Forestry Hill Bypass Trail / Yellow Loop (Map p.287)

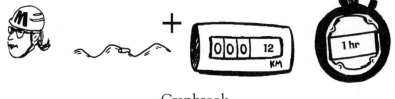

Cranbrook

Big Hill Trail

This trail shares the trail head with the Yellow Loop Bypass Trail. This long loop has two demanding climbs of about 200 meters each where excellent views of Cranbrook and the Rocky Mountain Trench reward your efforts. From the Big Hill Viewpoint the downhill is steep, loose, and rutted by the motorized folks. Once you are on the main road, follow it past the big puddle and down a long gradual hill for about 400 meters until you reach a small clearing on the

MOUNTAIN BIKING
BRITISH COLUMBIA
The Trail Guide

left. Look for white circles here, marking the start of a single track section. Once you finish this section at Kettle Lake you will join the Yellow loop for the remainder of the ride.

Big Hill Trail (Map p.287)

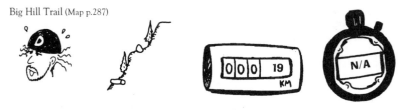

Cranbrook

Isidore Canyon Trail

This is a great out and back ride that is perfect for all levels of riders. The route is built upon an old rail bed that heads east from Cranbrook through a narrow canyon eventually opening up to views of the Rockies. The trail passes through ponds and marshes, offering good wildlife viewing opportunities. Bring a camera!

Trail head access is found at the north end of the Cranbrook strip. Follow Highway 3 / 95 through the underpass and immediately on the right you will see the trail head sign. Use care when accessing the trail near the highway. The route parallels the highway for about 3 km where it diverges to enter the tranquility of Isidore Canyon. Turn around and head back once the highway is in sight.

Isidore Canyon Trail (Map p.287)

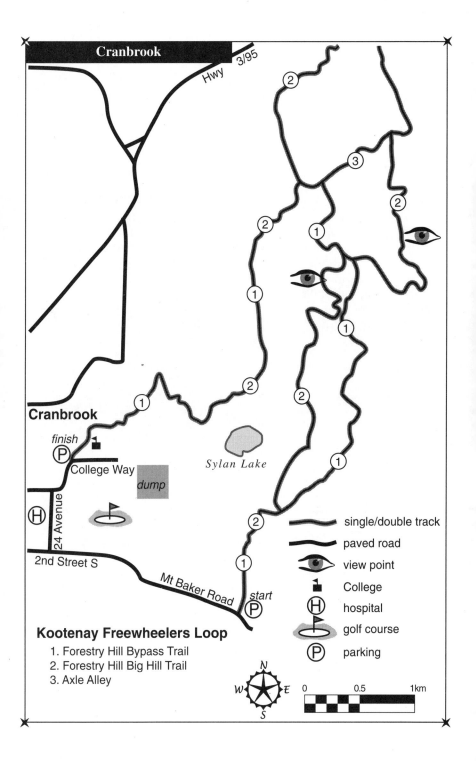

Cranbrook

Hwy 3/95

Cranbrook

finish

College Way

dump

Sylan Lake

24 Avenue

2nd Street S

Mt Baker Road

start

single/double track
paved road
view point
College
hospital
golf course
parking

Kootenay Freewheelers Loop

1. Forestry Hill Bypass Trail
2. Forestry Hill Big Hill Trail
3. Axle Alley

N
W · E
S

0   0.5   1km

MOUNTAIN BIKING
BRITISH COLUMBIA
The Trail Guide

Fernie

The Trails

Introduction

Fernie is the focal point of recreational activities in the East Kootenay. The famous powder stories from Snow Valley are now equalled by stories of stellar single track. The evidence of Fernie's history as a coal mining center is prominent on many of the rides. The old roads and railbeds leading into coal seams played a part in the trail infrastructure. The Coal Creek Trail and the Fernie Classic Trail are the two 'best of' rides detailed here, as well as some brief information and map containing most of Fernie's single track which emanates from the city center. Read on, and ride on, in the East Kootnay.

Fernie

Coal Creek Trail

This ride is not included on the map, but is user friendly and signed. Expect moderate grades, utilizing an overgrown road and railbed from downtown Fernie to the old Coal Creek Townsite. The trail begins on 2nd Ave., across from the SKI BASE. Signage and a trail map provide directions and historical information on the former town of Coal Creek. Intended as a lazy afternoon ride, the scented views of the forested valley should calm yet invigorate the most frantic, highway-frazzled urbanite.

If you feel adventurous, a strenuous ride or hike along a skidder trail will bring you to the closed mine tunnels that tell a story of this area's origin and purpose. You can coast all the way back as an alternative on Coal Creek Rd., although dust may deter you. If not, return the same way you came, back to the start.

Coal Creek Trail (Map p.289)

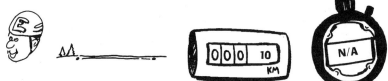

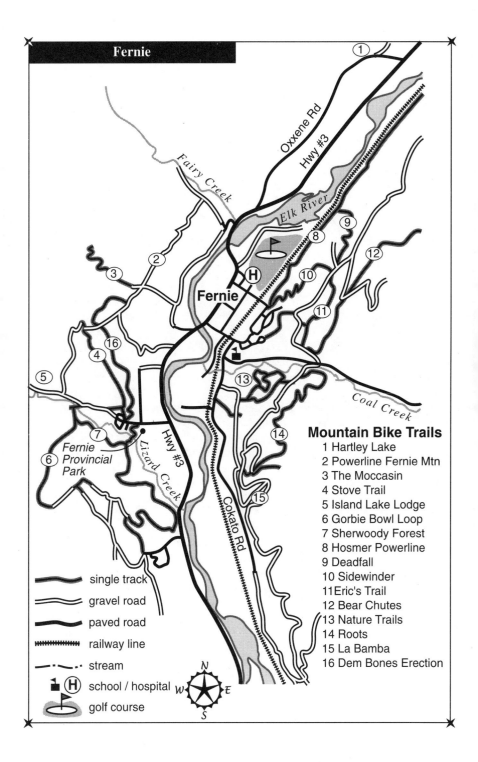

Fernie

Mountain Bike Trails
1 Hartley Lake
2 Powerline Fernie Mtn
3 The Moccasin
4 Stove Trail
5 Island Lake Lodge
6 Gorbie Bowl Loop
7 Sherwoody Forest
8 Hosmer Powerline
9 Deadfall
10 Sidewinder
11 Eric's Trail
12 Bear Chutes
13 Nature Trails
14 Roots
15 La Bamba
16 Dem Bones Erection

single track
gravel road
paved road
railway line
stream
school / hospital
golf course

MOUNTAIN BIKING
BRITISH COLUMBIA
The Trail Guide

Fernie

The Fernie Classic

The Fernie Classic is the mountain biking equivalent of a 'best of ' C.D. box set that you cherish. Several of the best trails in the valley are incorporated into this ride: Roots, Hyperextension, Eric's Trail, and Deadfall. Deadfall is a mean, masochistic challenge that will have you blowing lung chunks and counting your 'dabs'. The reward for those who 'clean' the ride is spiritual enlightenment in the sacred skeletal meadow.

Begin your journey at the nature trails off Coal Creek Road, which is 2 minutes by bike from town. The trails loop and twist drunkenly upon themselves, but if navigated properly, will deposit you at the powerline. The powerline direction is up. At the top, _____ River Road almost intersects. This is *"Several of the best trails in the valley* where Root's begins. A short up- *are incorporated into this ride."* hill climb to the window provides _____ an exceptional view south to Mt. Broadwood. The root, for which Roots is named, lies here. It's a sinister appendage of traction-stealing, bone-cracking evil. Ride over it clean and pat yourself on the back!

Next begins a twisting, single track downhill ripe with country charm. Be careful on the log bridge or you'll end up in the creek! Turn right and welcome yourself to Roots Extension, where some hard climbing on loose, mucky sidehill stuff will eventually bring you to Hyper Extension, which is marked by a rock cairn. This trail demands granny gear grinding up, and a slalom ride down. Retrace your original route, or pick a new one. Once at the bottom of Hyper Extension turn right, and continue on the single track until it exits onto River Road. Ride _____ down River Road, cross Coal Creek *"This trail demands granny gear grind-* and head up Ridgemont Rd. be- *ing up, and a slalom ride down."* hind the city dump. These are _____ logging roads so be careful. As you ride up Ridgemont Rd. watch on the uphill bank for a worn path, this is Eric's Trail. Eric's is a thunder-thighed, testosterone-fuelled, hill climbing feast. Eric has built this trail as a sado-masochistic grunt. Ignore the level areas, they're just teasers. About one third of the way up there is a bailout trail for those who wish to go home. If you continue on, however, you will pass the remnants of a cabin, and then a short downhill that will bring you to the clear cut, and onto Ridgemont Rd. Look up the road to where it forks at the treeline. At the crotch of the fork is a worn trail. Proceed along this trail but beware of moose.

You are now riding Deadfall, the original mountain bike trail in the valley. This is a wickedly fun, narrow, rooted and rutted, steep ride that will bring smiles and grimaces in equal measure. At the end of Deadfall is the powerline. Turn left and head back to town. Please close cattle gates, and don't chase the cows on this private property. Go feed your face as a reward for completing the Fernie Classic.

The Fernie Classic (Map p.289)

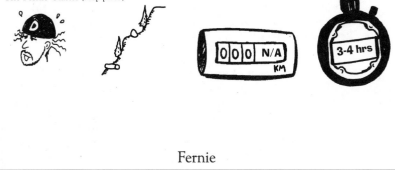

Fernie

Other Fernie trails to explore include the 10 km grind up to Hartly Lake on a smooth, generally easy road. The Moccasin trail is a brutal 4x4 road which leads to a hiking trail to the peak of Fernie Mountain. The Stowe Trail is a granny gear uphill and is very technical, return down the same route. The long, winding, dirt-packed road to Island Lake Lodge will surround riders with some of the B.C interior's largest cedar trees. The Gorby Bowl Loop uses old skidder trails and single track. This is a fun, strenuous loop that can be ridden in both directions. Stick with the climbing to get the reward of great views. Sherwoody Forest rips with plenty of technical challenges and logs to hop over. Cross the creek at the coral on Island Lake Lodge Road. The Hosmer Powerline will give you about 10 km of trail on a grassy hardpacked surface. Sidewinder is a tough one to find but has some fun, sweeping downhill turns. This trail can be ridden in reverse. The Bear Chutes are extreme technical challenges, rough and unforgiving. La Bamba is a short little trip up to River Road from Cokato Road. This trail is believed to be the resting place of Ritchie Valance. Dem Bones Erection is the home of the sacred skeletal meadow. It is a long, hard climb and part of the Fernie Classic mentioned above.

MOUNTAIN BIKING
BRITISH COLUMBIA
The Trail Guide

Nelson

The Trails
The Stanley Loop   292

The town of Nelson sits on the shore of the West Arm of Kootenay Lake. Surrounding Nelson, the Selkirk Mountains rise steeply, drawing your eye up into one of B.C.'s premier mountain playgrounds. The folks in Nelson play hard in all seasons and the steep rugged terrain dictates that recreation here is the real thing. The hard-core flavor of the town, coupled with the heritage look and feel of Nelson, make it a very cool mountain biking destination. If you like to climb and descend, the trails will surely please. There are no easy, flat rides in Nelson. It's climb and descend, climb and descend, granny gear to full brakes. Expect to average a hefty 9 km / hr on your rides.

I have mapped and described the Stanley Loop for your safe moderate mountain biking enjoyment It is really the only moderate ride the area has. If you are looking for the rippin' technical single track try any other trails. I recommend trying out Mountain Station where an access road located at the end of Cherry St. climbs up to a communication tower. Off of this road trails drop back to town in fine, West Kootenay style. *Experts only please*. The local West Kootenay Mountain Bike Guide, outlines all the rides in the Nelson area, and what to expect on the way up and down. It is a *must* purchase for any riders wanting to get beyond the Stanley Loop into the serious stuff. Enjoy!

Nelson

The Stanley Loop

The loop is fun to ride in either direction. To access the trail from town ride up Stanley St. to the top. Follow the trail until it dead ends. There is a trail to your left that follows a barbed wire fence up to abandoned rail tracks. Follow the tracks left, cross two main trestles, and find the trail on your left after the second trestle. Climb until you hit a logging road. Turn right and ride until you hit the active sand pit. Cross through the pit to the road on the far side. From Highway 6 go right for about 100 meters and left onto Giveout Creek Forest Service Road. At the 3 way road junction look for the trail down the Silver King Side Road to your right. After the glorious descent you pop out on Silver King Road. Follow this road back to town.

The Stanley Loop (Map p.293)

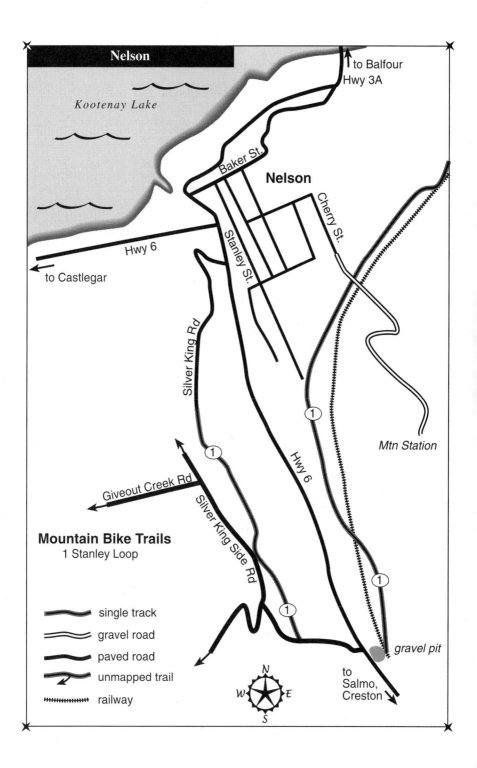

Nelson

Kootenay Lake

to Balfour
Hwy 3A

Baker St.

Nelson

Cherry St.

Hwy 6

Stanley St.

to Castlegar

Silver King Rd

①

Mtn Station

①

Giveout Creek Rd

Silver King Side Rd

Hwy 6

Mountain Bike Trails
1 Stanley Loop

①

①

gravel pit

single track
gravel road
paved road
unmapped trail
railway

N
W ✦ E
S

to Salmo,
Creston

MOUNTAIN BIKING
BRITISH COLUMBIA
The Trail Guide

Castlegar

The Trails

The Beaver Trails

Introduction

Castlegar sits at the confluence of the Columbia and Kootenay Rivers. It is also the junction of Highway 3, 22, and 3A. If you are touring around the Kootenays checking out the great rides you have to include a stop in Castlegar. Apart from The Beaver Trails, riders can go for an easy cruise around the campus of Selkirk College.

Castlegar

The Beaver Trails

The Beaver Trails are located on the lower east facing slopes of the Robson Range. The trails range in elevation from about 1600 ft. to a maximum of about 2300 ft. The generally low elevation of this ride makes it hot in the summer. To access the trails take Woodland Dr. up from Columbia Ave. and turn onto Chickadee Lane. When the pavement ends turn left on a loose sandy double track before the water tower. Once you ride under the powerline look for the single track on your left. This is a mostly rolling trail with a slight climb to an old cabin. Once past the cabin, a fast downhill cranks you quickly down to Merry Creek. This is a fun section but riders have to slow down for the creek crossing to avoid trouble. After the creek a 5 to 10 minute climb switches back and brings you to the top of a slick rock section. This slick rock is truly reminiscent of Moab Utah as riders experience the fast, pure-traction feel of the beloved slick rock. Follow the painted arrows and ride between the rock piles that indicate trail direction. The trail eventually turns into a fast single track downhill and shoots you onto a double track. Follow this trail left, back to the road you climbed earlier. Avoid the single track on your right. If you want to do it again simply go left and repeat the process. It is recommended that this loop be ridden until you are frazzled and start to hallucinate giant ice cream cones. On a hot summer day this should occur in about 3 laps.

The Beaver Trails (Map p.295)

0|0|0 5 KM
one lap

N/A

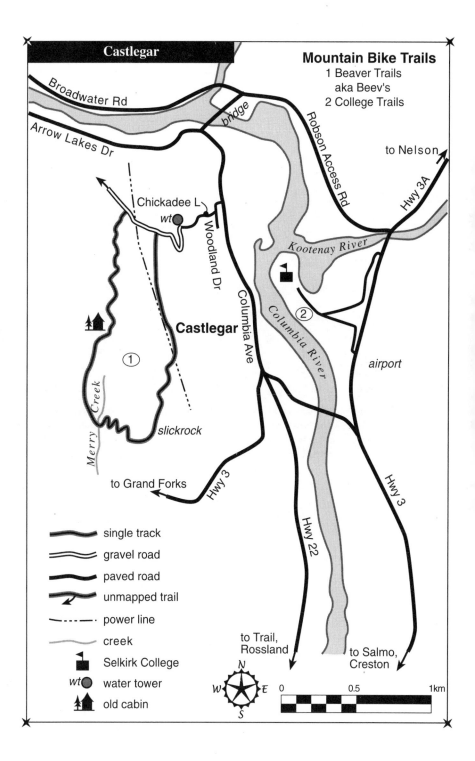

MOUNTAIN BIKING
BRITISH COLUMBIA
The Trail Guide

Rossland

The Trails

Rossland is a unique town located high above Trail B.C. The towns elevation of 3400 ft. gives it a shorter season then many areas. Rossland is called many things, among them " the Mountain Biking Capitol Of Canada", and " Canada's Alpine City". Both of these titles reflect the nature of riding in Rossland. There is an amazing network of trails that burst out of the city center to the surrounding hills, valleys, and mountains. As with many commonly used trails throughout B.C., those in Rossland often cross private prop- erty at least once on a ride. Please be doubly conscious of this when riding in Rossland and of course obey the rules of the trail. All riders who venture forth on Rossland trails must also realize that your are ultimately responsible for your own actions. The reputation of Rossland as the home to some serious single track is very true, but a surprising number of gentle rides on old road beds and rail grades can get the new mountain biker out of the city into the nearby terrain.

> *"There is an amazing network of trails that burst out of the city center to the surrounding hills, valleys, and mountains."*

As a visitor to Rossland you will get the feel that this is a real mountain biking town. It is a common sight to see a mud covered rubberhead white knuckled screaming down some crazy steep pitch, on a stout steed from the dark ages, with dare I say no suspension, and a crazy grin on their face! Riders drift

MOUNTAIN BIKING
BRITISH COLUMBIA
The Trail Guide

through town in search of the perfect post ride snack, gather in the morning to choose the perfect ride that will match the days mood, and the best trail conditions. The locals in Rossland are authentic people who ski hard, ride hard, and truly live for and with the mountains. The annual mountain bike festival called 'The Rubberhead' is the best time to dial into the Rossland experience and go play with your fellow rubberheads, always in September, the second weekend after Labor Day.

"The locals in Rossland are authentic people who ski hard, ride hard, and truly live for and with the mountains."

To find the rides check out this map, buy the local guide book, or best yet, hook up with someone who knows where the secret trails are hidden. The best place to start your mountain biking adventure is at Chico's Bike Shack and Tours [604] 362-5788. Chico's will also do private tours and technique workshops to help draw out the aspiring hard-core in you. If you can afford the dough there is no better way to get a great ride in then with a guide. What follows is a summary of the trails and what riders can expect when the go and explore in Rossland.

"hook up with someone who knows where the secret trails are hidden."

Rossland

Old Cascade Highway & Dewdney Trail

One of the longer rides that a visitor to Rossland ought to experience is the Dewdney Trail, part of the original Trans Canada Highway. To access the trail, head out of town to the west on Columbia Ave. until you get to the Mining Museum, then turn left and pedal down the highway for about 300 meters and turn right onto the Old Cascade Highway. You should see a sign about 60 meters down the road on the right that says "There is no dump along this road." If you miss this, double back. 13 km and 100 vertical feet later you reach a distinct plateau where above you are the powerlines. At this point there is a dirt road on your left where you turn into, and about 10 meters later on your left is the 2300 ft. downhill. Let em' rip baby and don't be too shy about letting out a big WHOOP!!

This trail is well marked except at two points but the best description is never as good as the simple local advice to follow tire tracks and chain ring marks over logs. Riders pop out on Highway 22 a good grunt away from town. Turn left and about 8 km later Rossland awaits. The Bryden sawmill marks about the halfway point on the journey home, or you could do it American style and use a shuttle.

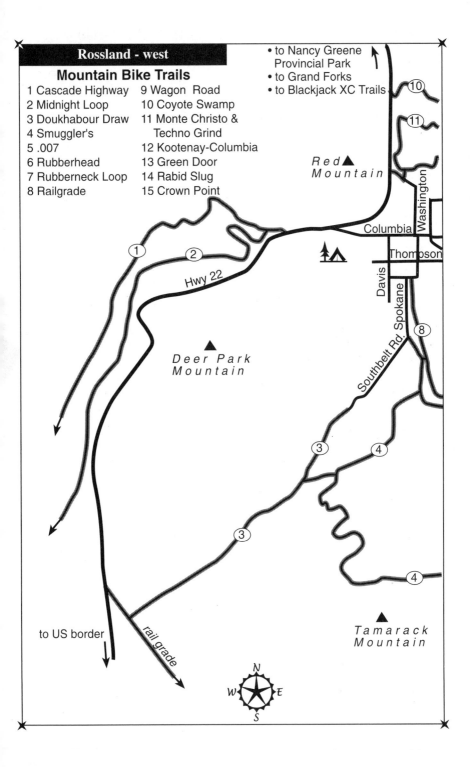

Rossland - west

Mountain Bike Trails

1 Cascade Highway
2 Midnight Loop
3 Doukhabour Draw
4 Smuggler's
5 .007
6 Rubberhead
7 Rubberneck Loop
8 Railgrade

9 Wagon Road
10 Coyote Swamp
11 Monte Christo &
   Techno Grind
12 Kootenay-Columbia
13 Green Door
14 Rabid Slug
15 Crown Point

• to Nancy Greene
  Provincial Park
• to Grand Forks
• to Blackjack XC Trails

Red ▲
Mountain

Columbia

Washington

Thompson

Davis

Spokane

Southbelt Rd.

Hwy 22

Deer Park
Mountain

to US border

rail grade

Tamarack
Mountain

N
W   E
S

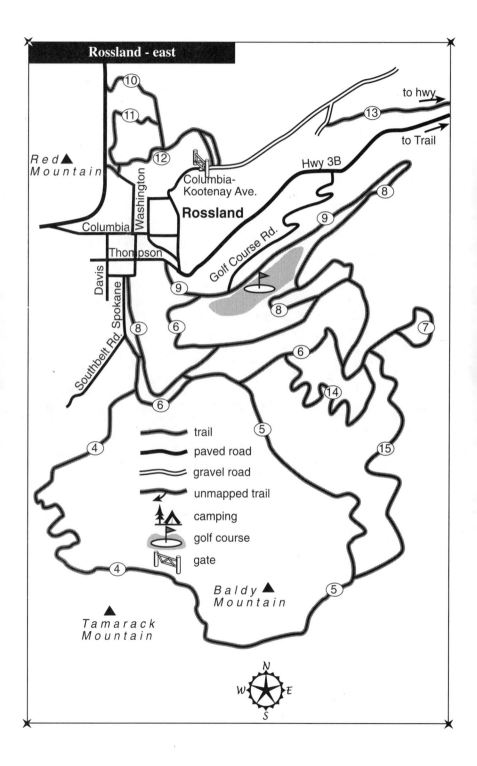

Rossland - east

Red Mountain

to hwy
to Trail

Columbia-Kootenay Ave.

Rossland

Hwy 3B

Washington

Columbia

Thompson

Davis

Spokane

Golf Course Rd.

Southbelt Rd.

trail
paved road
gravel road
unmapped trail
camping
golf course
gate

Baldy Mountain

Tamarack Mountain

N
W E
S

MOUNTAIN BIKING
BRITISH COLUMBIA
The Trail Guide

Old Cascade Highway & Dewdney Trail (Map p.298-9)

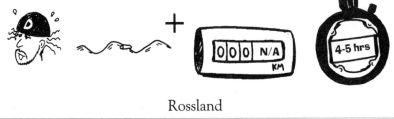

Rossland

Railgrade

The railgrade was used to transport people from the towns of Trail and Warfield. To access this easy smooth descending old rail grade from Main Street, head into lower Rossland via Spokane St. This road turns to the left and becomes Le Roi Ave. You go down this road about 150 meters and turn left on Davis St. Ride along Davis until you see Victoria St. at the bottom of a big hill. Turn left and then right up a short street, and then left on Union Ave. Travel along Union until you see the Railgrade Trail on the left about 60 meters from the top of a little hill.

Railgrade (Map p.298-9)

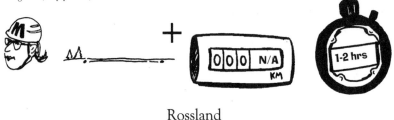

Rossland

Midnight Loop

This is a nice trail for those who want a steady workout without the hazards of a full on trail. To access this trail ride out the old cascade Highway about 200 meters until you see a road on the left. Follow this road until you see a yellow bridge, but don't go over the bridge. Turn left, and follow the road until you see the Bryden Mill. You can retrace your steps or ride back along the highway.

Midnight Loop (Map p.298-9)

300

MOUNTAIN BIKING
BRITISH COLUMBIA
The Trail Guide

Rossland

Doukhabour Draw

To access the trail use the same route as the Railgrade except you turn right on Spokane St. from Union Ave. Spokane turns into Southbelt Rd. where you ride out until you get to the end and look for the trailhead.

Doukhabour Draw (Map p.298-9)

Rossland

Smugglers Loop

To access this trail use the same route as Doukhabour Draw except you turn left at Gelesz St. onto a gravel road. Ride down for about 1 km and you will pass a road on the left called Maldy Creek Forest Service Road. The next road on the left is the Smugglers Loop. This is a demanding climb for about 30 to 45 minutes then rolls around and takes you to the Rubberhead or 007.

Smugglers Loop (Map p.298-9)

Rossland

007

Access this trail from the railgrade. Ride down the Railgrade for about 2 km and take the first road up to the right. You will see a carved sign about 20 feet up the road on a tree that says 007 / Rubberhead. You will come to a fork in the road, stay right for 007 stay left for Rubberhead and Rabid Slug.

007 (Map p.298-9)

MOUNTAIN BIKING
BRITISH COLUMBIA
The Trail Guide

Rossland

Rabid Slug

To access this sick and twisted beauty of a trail follow the instructions for 007. St the fork in the road go left and follow the **Rubberhead** until you come under the powerlines and then go back into the forest about 30 ft. the trail is on your right. This switchbacky test of balance and balls will shoot you out onto the **Rubberneck Loop**, go left back to town.

Rabid Slug (Map p.298-9)

Rossland

Crown Point

You access this trail from 007. After climbing the road starts to gently descend and then there is a big sweeping left with a stream crossing down the bank on the right. At this point there is a road to the left, this is the trailhead. This trail has plenty of logs, wet rocky sections, and some steep short sections.

Crown Point (Map p.298-9)

Rossland

Green Door

To access the **Green Door** ride up Main Street to the east until you get to park St., which is the ;last street on the left. here you turn left and follow this road staying to the left as it will turn into Crescent Ave, then onto Georgia St. Next turn off Georgia onto Columbia Kootenay Ave. Ride down, p[ass through a gate and be very cool because you are on Private land. Continue along until you see a road going sharply off to the right. Follow this road about 80 meters until you see a trail that goes over a little bank on the left. This trail has a couple of creek crossings some steep descents and a steep little climb.

This trail will take you to the sand pit corner of the highway where you cross the highway at its apex. Ride uphill and watch for a trail on the left down into a field. This will take you to the **Wagon Road** into Rossland. If you are a little

MOUNTAIN BIKING
BRITISH COLUMBIA
The Trail Guide

hungry or thirsty stop by the golf course and stock up, how many towns do you know that welcome mountain bikers after a ride? If you just want to get back to town peddle over the golf course road to the old grave yard and onto Thompson Ave. Turn left and head up to the 4 way stop and turn right onto Davis St. then left on Le Roi Ave, follow this road up to Main Street.

Green Door (Map p.298-9)

Rossland

Techno Grind & Kootenay Columbia

To access this trail ride up Washington St. to the top of town. At the junction of Kirkup Ave. and McLeod Ave. there is a road that goes up to the top of Monte Christo Mountain, take this road up. The fist fork on the right will take you to the top of Kootenay- Columbia Mountain, just follow the orange markers marked KC. To access Techno Grind keep going to the top of the road until almost near the top you turn left and in about 20 meters you will see a trail on the left. This is the one you want. Techno Grind does its name proud with a combination of gnarly Rossland trail fun.

Techno Grind & Kootenay Columbia (Map p.298-9)

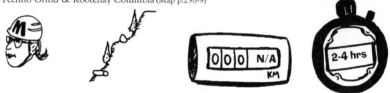

Rossland

Wagon Road

To access this easy trail go down Spokane St. which turns to the right onto Le Roi Ave. Go down to Davis St. and turn left. At the 4 way stop, Thompson Ave., turn left again and ride down and along the flats and as the road climbs Esling Drive is on the right, this road takes you to the trail.

Wagon Road (Map p.298-9)

MOUNTAIN BIKING
BRITISH COLUMBIA
The Trail Guide

For more on cycling in Rossland check out:

Chico's Bike Shak
&
Gavitational Pull Mountain Bike Clinics
P.O. Box 1682
Rossland B.C.
V0G 1Y0
(604) 362-5788
(604) 364-8302
email: ue517@ciao.trail.bc.ca

South East British Columbia

MOUNTAIN BIKING
BRITISH COLUMBIA
The Trail Guide

Northern British Columbia

MOUNTAIN BIKING
BRITISH COLUMBIA
The Trail Guide

Williams Lake

Introduction

Word has been trickling down from the north about some serious riding to be had in Williams Lake. The fact that a smaller town can have great riding is a testament to just how cool mountain biking is. No quad chairs or multi-million dollar infrastructure needed here, just some good natural terrain and caring mountain bikers who are willing to buff up what nature has bestowed them. According to the boys at RED SHREDS, Williams Lake has enough riding to satisfy the appetite of anyone, so read on about the Fox Loop, and plan your trip to a new mounting biking destination.

Williams Lake

Fox Loop

This loop starts just up the hill, north of the lights on Highway 97. Turn uphill past the car wash to the end of the road. Turn uphill and left on the power line access road and stay on this road until it goes through a gully. At the top of this gully look for the single track climbing off on your right. The constant climb has a number of switchbacks, some tight turns, and a reasonable grade to the top of Fox Mountain.

At the top, when the trail levels off, you'll come to another wide trail. Turn left onto a road, another left to paved Mt. Fox Rd., or stay on a short parallel double track to a gravel road. If you stay on the double track the trail opening is straight across up the bank. Look for Grundig tape. The trail now twists beside the gravel road for a short section till you hit a wider trail. Ignore the left and right trails at this intersection. The downhill now skirts along the cliffs edge. Note the two trails on your right, they are the entrance and exit to a short technical section you can add on if you wish.

At the cliff stay left, and note the view from high above Williams Lake. The ridge across the valley has another stellar ride to check out. The trail basically follows the ridge, with two short detours into the forest. The trail to the left is a bailout to Fox Mountain Rd. After you have left the cliffside and climbed slightly, the trail will turn to the right and start down. If you end up at the second fence, double back to the main trail.

(Continued on page 308)

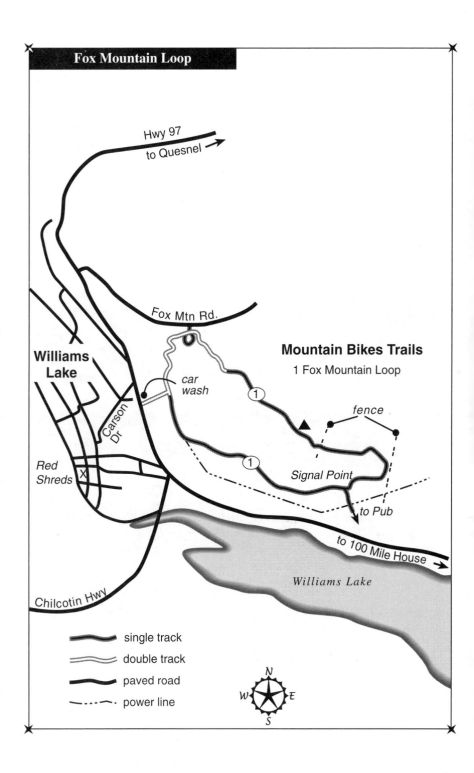

Fox Mountain Loop

Hwy 97
to Quesnel →

Fox Mtn Rd.

**Williams
Lake**

Carson Dr

car
wash

Mountain Bikes Trails

1 Fox Mountain Loop

① ①

fence

*Red
Shreds*

X

Signal Point

to Pub

to 100 Mile House →

Chilcotin Hwy

Williams Lake

〰〰 single track
〰〰 double track
━━ paved road
·—··—· power line

N
W E
S

MOUNTAIN BIKING
BRITISH COLUMBIA
The Trail Guide

(Continued from page 306)

The descent down Fox has a split where you can go straight down. This involves a log drop to a steep side hill, or turn to the right for a half pipe through a gully with a steep drop at the end. Take the sweeper right turn after the steep gully. Watch for the tape. The downhill now takes you through tight trees and sidehills. Ignore old skidder roads and stay on the single track until you T-bone another trail, turn right and up the other side.

When you come out of the trees at the ridge / power line, the single track goes straight across sidehill and to the right of the power poles. The trail then goes through some more tight trees, drops, and turns, till the cul-de-sac. From here you can ride back to the start.

Fox Loop (Map p.307)

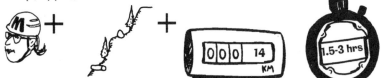

Photograph by Doug Herchmer

MOUNTAIN BIKING
BRITISH COLUMBIA
The Trail Guide

Prince George

Introduction

Prince George is a fairly large city located near the geographic center of B.C.
Those who live closer to the 49th parallel may consider Prince George so far up
north that mountain biking wouldn't be as popular as more typical outdoor
pursuits that involve motors and marksmanship. If the Prince George Cycling
Club is any indication, then this area is a hotbed for all types of cycling and club
activities. The P.G.C.C has a complete schedule of off road events including
sanctioned and nonsanctioned races. The spring of 1996 will see work on the
Cranbrook Hill Greenway, a trail which will link the Otway Nordic Center,
Forests For The World, UNBC, and the Partridge Creek area.

Prince George

The Otway Nordic Center

A nice warm up ride from town will bring you to the Nordic center. This area
offers a wide variety of terrain from wide, flat paths to steep descents like the
"descent of doom". This area is used extensively by the P.G.C.C. and new trails
are in the works. To access the Otway Nordic Center, take 5th ave west to
Ospika Blvd. north, and continue until you pass over two railway crossings.
The cabin and parking area are on the left. BRING YOUR BEAR BELL!!

Northern British Columbia

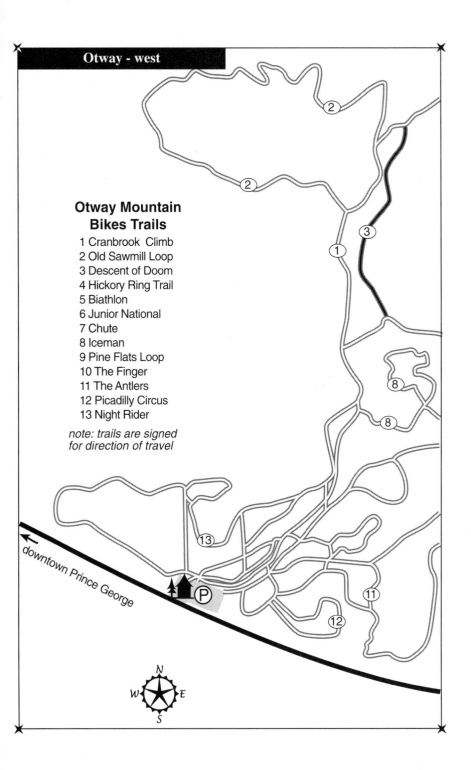

Otway Mountain Bikes Trails

1 Cranbrook Climb
2 Old Sawmill Loop
3 Descent of Doom
4 Hickory Ring Trail
5 Biathlon
6 Junior National
7 Chute
8 Iceman
9 Pine Flats Loop
10 The Finger
11 The Antlers
12 Picadilly Circus
13 Night Rider

note: trails are signed for direction of travel

downtown Prince George

N
W   E
S

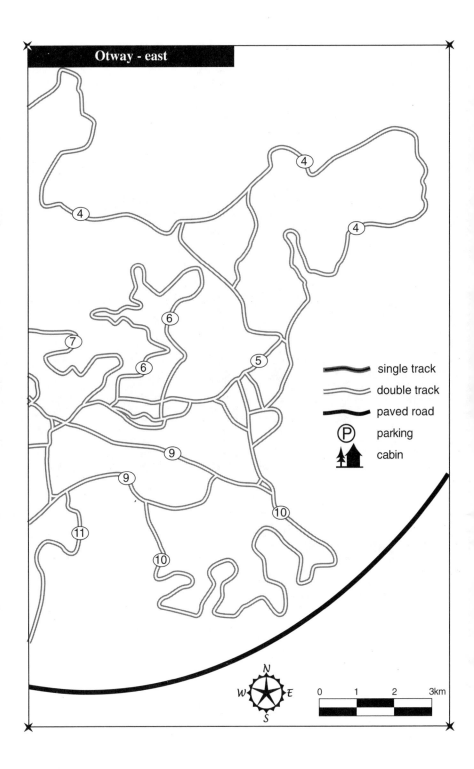

Otway - east

single track
double track
paved road
P parking
cabin

0 1 2 3km

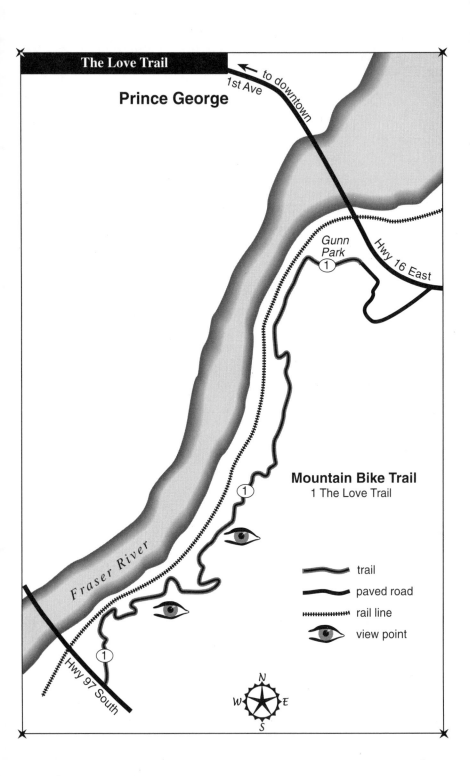

MOUNTAIN BIKING
BRITISH COLUMBIA
The Trail Guide

Prince George

The Love Trail

This trail was built in 1993 by the P.G.C.C. and has recently been included in the "Heritage River Trails" system, which will eventually include 85 km of trails encircling all of Prince George. The trail follows the eastern top edge of the Fraser River cut banks and includes some of the finest viewpoints of the city. The Love Trail can be ridden in either direction, but is best enjoyed from north to south. The trail head is a 10 minute ride from downtown along 1st Ave. East. Climb across the Highway 16 bridge, and look for the trail entrance 50 meters past the east end of the bridge. Follow the trail along the cut bank to the completion. Exit on Highway 97, and cross the bridge following the signs to town (about a 15 minute ride back).

The Love Trail (Map p.312)

plus return trip to town

Smithers-Bulkly Valley Area

Introduction

Rumor has it the Smithers B.C. has more Phd's per capita than any other area in BC. What does this unsubstantiated demographic have to do with mountain biking? If you are looking for good conversation while riding this may be the perfect destination. Hook up with a group of locals and check out some of the epic trails in this beautiful valley. Without the help of Doug Herchmer (Recreational Forester for the Prince Rupert Forest District), and Glenn Farenholtz, the maps and ride descriptions would not be available.

MOUNTAIN BIKING
BRITISH COLUMBIA
The Trail Guide

Smithers-Bulkly Valley Area

The Perimeter Trail

The Perimeter Trail is an excellent family ride which circumnavigates the town of Smithers. It was built as a multi-purpose trail to serve the needs of local bikers, horses, and pedestrians. The trail provides a connection with residential areas, neighborhood parks, and the downtown core.

There are many access points to the trail, which is approximately 9.4 km long. A good starting point is the municipal campground at Riverside Park, on the east side of town, along the Bulkly River. Take the first left, after 200 meters, and climb the short steep trail. Follow signs along the trail which parallels the Bulkly River until it crosses the main dirt road near Chicken Creek, and the trail meets highway 16. The trail continues along the west side of town behind a new subdivision. Riders can then select several options that combine dirt and gravel back roads, and paved roads. A popular variation is to ride to the west end of Toronto St. turning onto Railway Ave.

"A good starting point is the municipal campground at Riverside Park"

Signs will then lead you off to a single track on the left near Rupert St. A good short trail travels through a wooded area before meeting Highway 16, south of town 7.3 km from the start. Cross the highway, keep right on Frontage Ave. until the sign appears on the left. Follow this trail until Carnaby. From Carnaby turn left on Victoria where it meets Main St. and crosses over to Riverside Dr. You can ride to the campground or onto a single track where the trail turns off left. To return to the campground take any of the trails leading off to the right, or do another loop.

The Perimeter Trail (Map p.316-17)

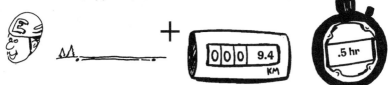

Smithers-Bulkly Valley Area

The Call Mountain Race Course

The Call Mountain Race Course is a fun, short loop engineered by our bovine friends. The trail goes out along the fenceline for the length of the lake, climbs to the ridge, and turns back with rolling fast single track to the start.

MOUNTAIN BIKING
BRITISH COLUMBIA
The Trail Guide

The trail is accessed 2km south of Smithers. On the east side of the highway is Viewmount Rd, turn off Highway 16 and immediately behind the church on the corner, turn right on Van Gaalen Rd. Follow this road through the turns and up a straight ————————————————— stretch to the very top (about *"Be sure to close the gate to keep Ed Wal-* 1.5 km) where the road turns *ton's cattle where they belong."* left into Moun- tainview Rd. ————————————————— Follow Moun- tainview to the end and park near the signs to Call Lake. The trail head is under the sign. Be sure to close the gate to keep Ed Walton's cattle where they belong.

The short, steep, beginning shouldn't discourage you (it's the hardest climb on the loop), or turn left, and begin your loop with a downhill. The trail follows the fenceline with two deviations, and there is a new section built to avoid a mud bog. Generally, if you follow the green painted arrows you won't get lost. Halfway along the bottom section go straight through the 4 way junction. Continue along the fenceline and past some houses on your left and up a short, steep, climb on your right. Watch for downed barbed wire.

The downhill section is fast and begs a rider to hang it out, or 'color outside the lines'. At the halfway point on the loop (about 3 km), an intersection confronts you. Go right, and you'll end up at the marshy end of the lake, which allows you to go right and repeat the loop. Don't go left. Continuing straight, you will meander along and eventually come across a black satellite dish and a fenceline at the end of the trail. Turn right, and down the steep hill to complete the course.

The Call Mountain Race Course (Map p.316-17)

Smithers-Bulkly Valley Area

Malkow Lookout Trail

This is a nice, moderate ride that leads to one of the best views of Smithers and the Bulkly Valley. On a clear day, the views of the Babine Mountains Recreation Area and Hudson Bay Mountain are superb. The effort needed to climb the steep, loose switchbacks is rewarded with great views about 300 meters above Smithers.

(Continued on page 318)

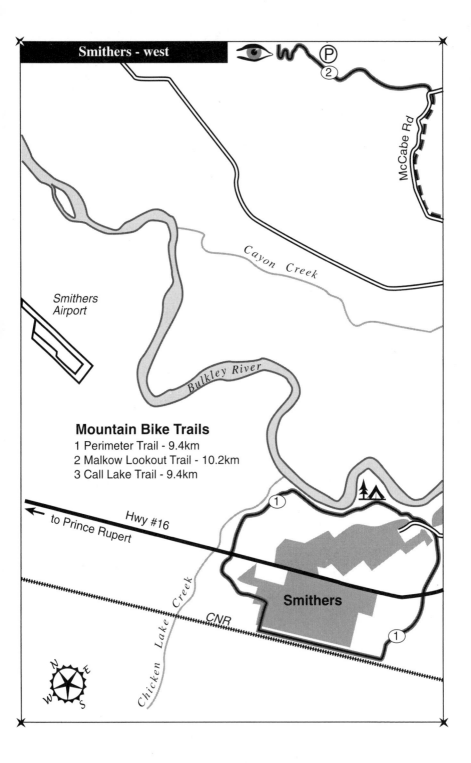

Smithers - west

McCabe Rd

Cayon Creek

Smithers
Airport

Bulkley River

Mountain Bike Trails
1 Perimeter Trail - 9.4km
2 Malkow Lookout Trail - 10.2km
3 Call Lake Trail - 9.4km

Hwy #16
to Prince Rupert

Chicken Lake Creek

CNR

Smithers

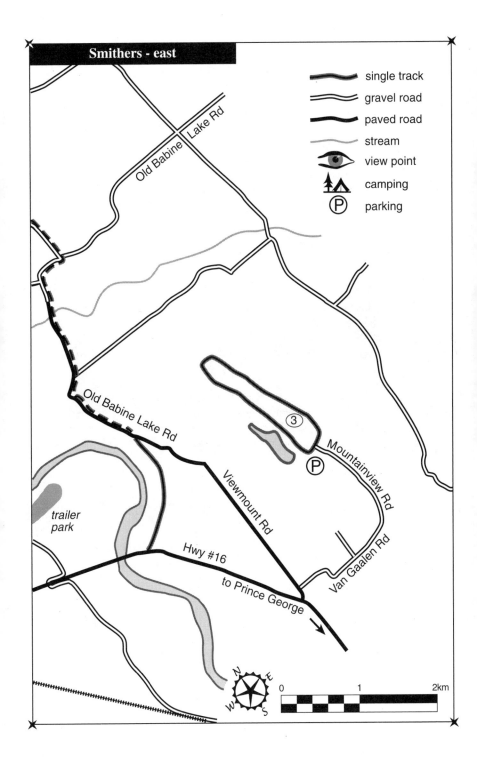

Smithers - east

single track
gravel road
paved road
stream
view point
camping
Ⓟ parking

Old Babine Lake Rd

Old Babine Lake Rd

③

Ⓟ

Mountainview Rd

Viewmount Rd

trailer park

Hwy #16

to Prince George

Van Gaalen Rd

N W E S

0   1   2km

MOUNTAIN BIKING
BRITISH COLUMBIA
The Trail Guide

(Continued from page 315)

You can easily ride from town, or drive to the base of the lookout road. Turn right off Highway 16 at Old Babine Road on the southeast side of the Bulkly River Bridge. Follow along for about 4.7 km and turn left onto McCabe Road. Follow for another 2.5 km and turn left onto an unmarked dirt road. Follow this dirt road, and park at the fork. Or if you're riding, take the right fork on the double track which leads through a wooded area, into an open grassy area, and finally up a series of steep switchbacks to the top of the former fire lookout.

Smithers-Bulkly Valley Area

Silver King Basin Trail

Silver King Basin Trail is a high alpine ride featuring slippery technical climbing, creek crossings, and a fast, gnarly descent on the ride out. The trail starts as a gradual climb, getting progressively steeper and wetter as you get higher and closer to the Basin. The last part of the ride is all downhill and very exhilarating.

To access the trailhead, drive on Highway 16 toward Telkwa, and turn left on Old Babine Lake Road. Next, turn left on Telkwa High Road, and right on Driftwood Road 1.5 km later. Driftwood Rd will slowly deteriorate into a beat up jeep road, and _____ cross a creek several times. Ignore the *"Enjoy the ripping descent and* signs for Lyon Creek, Harvy Creek, and *be aware of the sharp rocks, slick* McCabe Trails, and stay on the main *logs, and other trail nasties."* road. Once you reach Sunny Point there is _____ a foot bridge, turn right here and follow along the creek. This is the start of the technical riding. You have reached the basin when you see remnants of the old Silver King / Cronin gold mine. The bunk house is fixed up making for a great rest stop. Enjoy the ripping descent and be aware of the sharp rocks, slick logs, and other trail nasties.

Silver King Basin Trail (Map p.319)

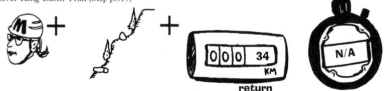

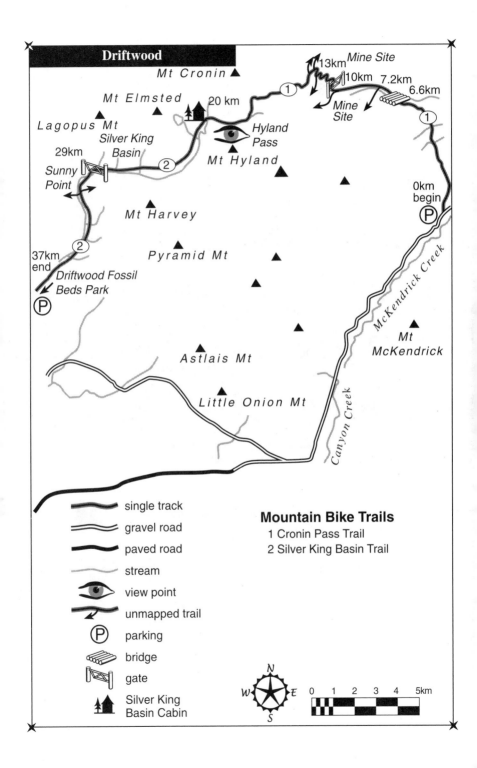

MOUNTAIN BIKING
BRITISH COLUMBIA
The Trail Guide

Smithers-Bulkly Valley Area

Cronin Pass Trail

The Cronin Pass Trail is a very scenic ride into the alpine meadows of the Babine Mountains. This ride combines the full spectrum of mountain biking trail types and will include a minimum of 1 to 2 hours of climbing. Summer and fall are the best seasons to ride in the alpine. Expect good wildlife viewing possibilities.

To access the trail on Cronin Creek Road drive east out of Smithers towards Prince George. Turn left on Eckman Rd and follow it about 33 km from Highway 16. Park just before the 34 km sign and Cronin Creek Rd.

The first 10 km of the ride is an old mine road with multiple creek crossings and gentle hills. Upon reaching the mine site the real climbing starts, and you'll be granny-gearing it or walking for about 3 km. Be sure not to take the fire lookout road which turns off to the left. About 13km into the journey you will reach another mine sight with many old cabins and shacks. Following the mine road through the _____ alpine you will reach the peak. At the peak, two green lakes are visible. Follow the trail through the alpine meadows over Hyland Pass. Upon reaching the peak, a very technical single track takes you to Silver King Basin and good camping. From the basin a fast, wet, slick, trail awaits. Once you reach the first bridge at Sunny Point, turn left over the creek. The remaining 8 km are easy cruising to the Driftwood Fossil Beds. To do a shorter version of this ride, shuttle a car from the parking area at Cronin Creek Road to The Driftwood Fossil Beds parking Area.

> *"This ride combines the full spectrum of mountain biking trail types and will include a minimum of 1 to 2 hours of climbing."*

Cronin Pass Trail (Map p.319)

Cronin Creek to Silver King Basin to Driftwood fossil Beds 37 km, round trip 100 km.

Smithers-Bulkly Valley Area

Telkwa - Terrace Route

This is a long, classic back country route that can be ridden in one long day or as an overnight trip. Much of the route is on logging roads and power line right of ways. The route crosses over Telkwa Pass (945m) within the Hazelton

(Continued on page 322)

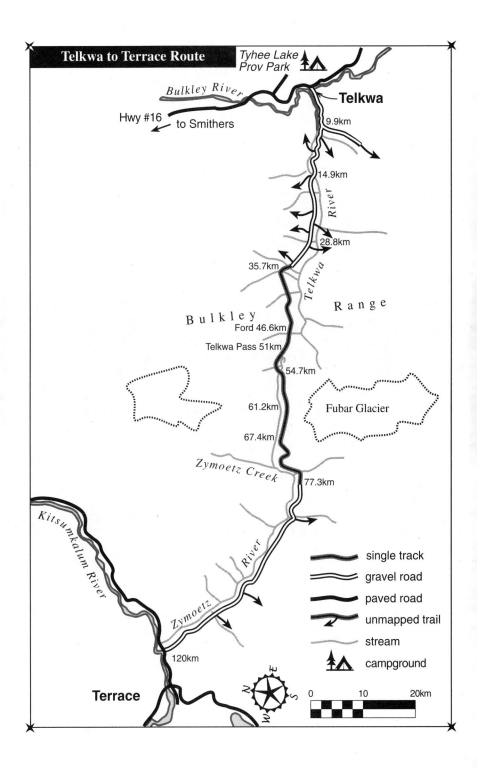

MOUNTAIN BIKING
BRITISH COLUMBIA
The Trail Guide

(Continued from page 320)

Mountains, and offers spectacular alpine views of the Howson Range. The ride is best planned for late summer or fall. Be on your best bear behavior to minimize your chances of becoming a snack for a hungry scared grizzly.

To access the route, turn off Highway 16 at the flashing light in Telkwa (bottom of big hill), and cross over the bridge onto Coalmine Rd. After 6.3 km take the right fork, follow along until a left fork onto the *"The route crosses over Telkwa Pass* Telkwa River Forest Road at 9.9 *(945m) within the Hazelton Mountains,* km. Cross over the bridge at 14.9 *and offers spectacular alpine views of* km, passing a B.C. Forest Ser- *the Howson Range."* vice Recreation Site, the Jonas Creek Recreation Site and finally over the bridge at 28.8 km. The next 20 km follows a logging road, with some power line and gas pipeline sections being rideable. Stay left at the junction at 36.1 km and climb the steep right fork when you reach the junction at 41.1 km, for another 1.5 km. Descend the steep grade and take the left road after the bridge at 44.4 km's, follow along to the top of the hill above Mill Creek. Descend down to Mill Creek (46.6 km), and begin to climb up to the Telkwa Pass (945m) at about 51 km. Top Lake is reached soon and has good camping with no facilities, while Blue Lake a bit further along has primitive campsite facilities.

The road through Telkwa Pass has many short steep sections as it passes along the north edge of Top Lake. The road crosses under the hydro line at the far end of Top Lake, then swings over to the south side of above Tauw Lakes at 54 km. This section crosses a number of scree slopes coming off the peaks on the north side of the Howson Range. Follow the pipeline road for about 12 km as it slowly descends the valley beside Limonite Creek. This main gravel road is in very good condition and can be followed for the next 52 km until it meets Highway 16 northeast of Terrace. An interesting side trip is to explore the fossil beds along the Copper River at 77 km. There is also a small undeveloped campsite about 1 km before the fossil beds.

This route is best travelled east to west, as there is far less elevation gain in this direction (415 meters compared to 825 meters). This is obviously a major tour, and riders should plan a trip like this with the worst case scenario in mind to keep the ride from turning into a fiasco. Simply plan ahead and be prepared. The views and experience on an epic such as this are always worth the effort.

Telkwa - Terrace Route (Map p.321)

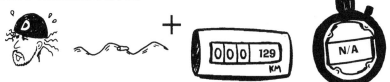

MOUNTAIN BIKING
BRITISH COLUMBIA
The Trail Guide

MOUNTAIN BIKING
BRITISH COLUMBIA
The Trail Guide

Index of Maps

Photograph by Blair Polischuk

Photograph by Matt Pinto

About The Author / Publisher

Darrin Polischuk is a self-confessed, recreational addict and teacher. He loves to share his passion for trail information, tips, and riding techniques, with others. Whether he is instructing a high school Social Studies or English class, coaching a mountain biking learn to race clinic, or teaching snowboarding, his primary motivation is fun. "Putting smiles on mountain biker's faces is what this book is all about".

Darrin has a B.A from S.F.U., a B.Ed. from U.B.C., is a level 1 off-road coach, a slow veteran expert mountain bike racer, a Can-Bike II instructor for traffic safety skills, and a caffeine addict.